CAMBR
HISTORY OF POLITICAL THOUGHT

—

BOTERO
The Reason of State

Niccolò Machiavelli's seminal work, *The Prince*, argued that a ruler could not govern morally and be successful. Giovanni Botero disputed this argument and proposed a system for the maintenance and expansion of a state that remained moral in character. Founding an Antimachiavellian tradition that aimed to refute Machiavelli in practice, Botero is an important figure in early modern political thought, though he remains relatively unknown. His most notable work, *Della ragion di Stato*, first popularized the term "reason of state" and made a significant contribution to a major political debate of the time – the perennial issue of the relationship between politics and morality – and the book became a political "bestseller" in the late sixteenth and the seventeenth centuries. This translation of the 1589 volume introduces Botero to a wider Anglophone readership and extends this influential text to a modern audience of students and scholars of political thought.

Robert Bireley, SJ, has frequently lectured on Machiavelli and the reaction to him, and his *The Counter-Reformation Prince: Anti-Machiavellianism or Catholic Statecraft in Early Modern Europe* (1990) identified a particular school of Antimachiavellian writers. Other books have dealt with early modern Catholicism and the relationship between religion and politics in the Thirty Years' War. His biography, *Ferdinand II, Counter-Reformation Emperor, 1578–1637*, appeared in 2014. He has been a fellow at the Institute for Advanced Study in Princeton and the National Humanities Center in North Carolina, and has served as president of the American Catholic Historical Association. He taught history at Loyola University Chicago for forty-three years and is now retired.

CAMBRIDGE TEXTS IN THE
HISTORY OF POLITICAL THOUGHT

General Editor

QUENTIN SKINNER

Barber Beaumont Professor of the Humanities, School of History,
Queen Mary University of London

Editorial Board

MICHAEL COOK

Professor of Near Eastern Studies, Princeton University

GABRIEL PAQUETTE

Professor of History, The Johns Hopkins University

ANDREW SARTORI

Professor of History, New York University

HILDE DE WEERDT

Professor of Chinese History, Leiden University

Cambridge Texts in the History of Political Thought is firmly established as the major student series of texts in political theory. It aims to make available all the most important texts in the history of political thought, from ancient Greece to the twentieth century, from throughout the world and from every political tradition. All the familiar classic texts are included, but the series seeks at the same time to enlarge the conventional canon through a global scope and by incorporating an extensive range of less well-known works, many of them never before available in a modern English edition, and to present the history of political thought in a comparative, international context. Where possible, the texts are published in complete and unabridged form, and translations are specially commissioned for the series. However, where appropriate, especially for non-Western texts, abridged or tightly focused and thematic collections are offered instead. Each volume contains a critical introduction together with chronologies, biographical sketches, a guide to further reading and any necessary glossaries and textual apparatus. Overall, the series aims to provide the reader with an outline of the entire evolution of international political thought.

For a list of titles published in the series, please see end of book

BOTERO

The Reason of State

ROBERT BIRELEY
Loyola University Chicago

CAMBRIDGE
UNIVERSITY PRESS

CAMBRIDGE
UNIVERSITY PRESS

University Printing House, Cambridge CB2 8BS, United Kingdom

One Liberty Plaza, 20th Floor, New York, NY 10006, USA

477 Williamstown Road, Port Melbourne, VIC 3207, Australia

4843/24, 2nd Floor, Ansari Road, Daryaganj, Delhi – 110002, India

79 Anson Road, #06–04/06, Singapore 079906

Cambridge University Press is part of the University of Cambridge.

It furthers the University's mission by disseminating knowledge in the pursuit of education, learning, and research at the highest international levels of excellence.

www.cambridge.org
Information on this title: www.cambridge.org/9781107141827

DOI: 10.1017/9781316493953

First published 2017

Printed in the United States of America by Sheridan Books, Inc.

A catalogue record for this publication is available from the British Library

Library of Congress Cataloging-in-Publication Data
Names: Botero, Giovanni, 1540–1617. | Bireley, Robert, editor.
Title: The reason of state / Botero ; edited by Robert Bireley.
Other titles: Della ragion di stato. English. 2017
Description: Cambridge, United Kingdom ; New York, NY : Cambridge University Press, 2017. | Series: Cambridge texts in the history of political thought | Includes bibliographical references and index.
Identifiers: LCCN 2017020177 | ISBN 9781107141827 (hardback) | ISBN 9781316506721 (paperback)
Subjects: LCSH: Political science – Italy – Early works to 1800. | State, The – Early works to 1800. | Reason of state – Early works to 1800.
Classification: LCC JC158 .B812 2017 | DDC 320.1 – dc23
LC record available at https://lccn.loc.gov/2017020177

ISBN 978-1-107-14182-7 Hardback
ISBN 978-1-316-50672-1 Paperback

Contents

v

Contents

Contents

Acknowledgements

I want to thank Professor Quentin Skinner and the other editors for accepting my translation in the series Cambridge Texts in the History of Political Thought. I am also grateful to Professor Skinner, Elizabeth Friend-Smith, Katherine Law, and Damian Love for seeing this manuscript through the press.

Robert Bireley, SJ

Further Reading

Baldini, A. Enzo, "L'Antimachiavélisme en Italie au début de la littérature de la raison d'État," in Alain Dierkens (ed.), *L'Antimachiavélisme de la Renaissance aux Lumières* (Brussels, 1997).

"Aristotelismo e Platonismo nelle dispute romane," in Baldini (ed.), *Aristotelismo politico e ragion di stato: Atti del convegno internazionale di Torino 11–13 febbraio 1993* (Florence, 1995).

"Botero e la Francia," in Baldini (ed.), *Botero e la "ragion di stato"*, 335–59.

(ed.), *Botero e la "ragion di stato": Atti del convegno in memoria di Luigi Firpo, Torino 8–10 marzo 1990* (Florence, 1992).

Bireley, Robert, *The Counter-Reformation Prince: Anti-Machiavellianism or Catholic Statecraft in Early Modern Europe* (Chapel Hill, NC, 1990).

"Scholasticism and Reason of State," in A. Enzo Baldini (ed.), *Aristotelismo politico e ragion di stato: Atti del convegno internazionale di Torino 11–13 febbraio 1993* (Florence, 1995), 83–102.

Chabod, Federico, *Giovanni Botero* (Rome, 1934).

De Mattei, Rodolfo, *Il problema della ragion di stato nell'età della Controriforma* (Milan and Naples, 1997).

Descendre, Romain, *L'état du monde: Giovanni Botero entre raison d'État et géopolitique* (Geneva, 2009).

Firpo, Luigi, "Botero, Giovanni," in *Dizionario biografico degli Italiani*, vol. XIII (Rome, 1971), 352–62.

"Introduzione," in Giovanni Botero, *Della ragion di stato*, ed. Firpo (Turin, 1948).

Meinecke, Friedrich, *Machiavellism: The Doctrine of "raison d'État" and its Place in Modern History*, trans. Douglas Scott, introd. W. Stark (New York, 1965; orig. 1924).

Senellart, Michel, *Machiavélisme et raison d'État* (Paris, 1989).

Skinner, Quentin, *The Foundations of Modern Political Thought*, 2 vols. (Cambridge, 1978).

Viroli, Maurizio, *From Politics to Reason of State: The Acquisition and Transformation of the Language of Politics* (Cambridge, 1992).

Abbreviations

Introduction

"If a ruler who wants always to act honorably is surrounded by many unscrupulous men his downfall is inevitable. Therefore, a ruler who wishes to maintain his power must be prepared to act immorally when this becomes necessary." So Niccolò Machiavelli wrote in the fifteenth chapter of *The Prince* in 1513. Writing in 1924, Friedrich Meinecke, a historian of Machiavellianism, contended that "Machiavelli's theory was a sword which was plunged into the flank of the body politic of Western humanity, causing it to shriek and rear up. This was bound to happen; for not only had genuine moral feeling been seriously wounded, but death had also been threatened to the Christian views of all churches and sects."[1] If by success was meant the creation and maintenance of a powerful state, it was not possible for a prince or man of politics to be successful who adhered to Christian or moral principles. This position was not completely new; it had been asserted in the ancient world and often enough reduced to practice. But Machiavelli's *The Prince* and its companion volume, *Discourses on the First Ten Books of Livy*, now gradually circulated first in manuscript and then after the early 1530s in print. His blatant assertion of the incompatibility of political success with traditional Christian morality raised the issue of the relationship of religion and morality to politics to a new prominence in the sixteenth century, and it has retained its relevance up to the present day. One need only think of the negative connotation often attached, unfortunately, to the designation "politician" and to the widespread conception of politics as "dirty."

---

[1] Friedrich Meinecke, *Machiavellism: The Doctrine of "raison d'État" and its Place in Modern History*, trans. Douglas Scott, introd. W. Stark (New York, 1965; orig. 1924), 49.

Several writers criticized Machiavelli vigorously, including the Portuguese bishop Jeronymo Osorio in his *On Christian Nobility* first published at Lisbon in 1542, and both *The Prince* and the *Discourses* were placed on the Index of Pope Paul IV in 1559. But the Italian priest Giovanni Botero took a new approach in his *Reason of State*, first published in 1589. In his dedication of the volume to Wolfgang Theodore, the prince-bishop of Salzburg, he first noted that in the course of travels in Italy and France he had often heard people talking of "reason of state," a term that they associated with Machiavelli and with the Roman historian Tacitus. Both authors showed little respect for conscience, and Botero wondered at and disdained this "barbarous style of government that is so shamelessly opposed to the law of God to the point of saying that some things are licit by reason of state and others by conscience." Nothing could be "more impious or irrational." At first he was inclined to write another critique of Machiavelli. But then he was persuaded that much more effective would be a book that laid out a program counter to Machiavelli, that is, that showed how a prince could become great and successfully govern his people by using moral methods, indeed that he could do so more efficiently. Members of the Roman curia, including the powerful Cardinal Giovanni Antonio Facchinetti, who reigned briefly as Pope Innocent IX in 1591, may have encouraged him, as too may have Minuccio Minucci, former papal emissary in Bavaria and now a papal advisor on German affairs, who later recommended *The Reason of State* to Duke Maximilian of Bavaria. So Botero published his *Reason of State* in 1589. He co-opted the term "reason of state," and used it in a positive sense. The very first sentence in the original edition read "Reason of state is the knowledge of the means suitable to found, preserve, and expand a dominion." His was a Catholic reason of state that pointed the way to a moral politics.

The book became an immediate bestseller, the "book of the day" as one historian has written.[2] A contemporary writer explained its success: "Botero is marvelous. He has so accommodated morality, justice, and obligation with the advantage of the prince as to merit in this respect immortal praise."[3] Fifteen Italian editions appeared before 1700, six

[2] Rodolfo De Mattei, *Il problema della "ragion di stato" nell'età della Contrariforma* (Milan and Naples, 1979), 65; see also among many others, André Stegman, *L'héroisme cornélien: Genèse et signification* (Paris: 1968), vol. II, 173–74.
[3] Apollinare de' Calderini, *Discorsi sopra la ragion di stato del Signor Giovanni Botero* (Milan, 1597), 64.

Spanish editions by 1606, a French edition in 1599, three Latin editions between 1602 and 1666. The book was known at the court of the Wittelsbach Duke Maximilian of Bavaria probably by 1591, and at the Habsburg courts of Madrid and Graz in the early 1590s. Emperor Ferdinand II later had two copies in his private library. The book was also read in Protestant lands. The well-known German professor Hermann Conring praised Botero's christianization of Machiavelli in his introduction to his Latin translation in 1666. Meanwhile, also in 1589, the Dutch humanist Justus Lipsius published a similar treatise, *Six Books on Politics*, that also aimed to lay out a program for a Christian reason of state. So the two of them inaugurated an Antimachiavellian tradition that endured well into the seventeenth century.

Botero was a child of the Italian Counter-Reformation. The European world had undergone convulsive changes between the appearance of Machiavelli's *Prince* in 1513 and the publication of *The Reason of State* in 1589. The great European monarchies France, Spain, and England had consolidated to a degree, and most of the smaller Italian and German states had moved in the same direction. But France had erupted in a religious, civil war in 1562 that would last until the end of the century, and the Dutch rebellion against Spanish rule broke out in 1566. Spain and Portugal had established their colonial empires in America and in Asia, and this development was accompanied by commercial expansion both in Europe and beyond. Urban populations grew rapidly. Rome's population numbered 55,000 in mid-century; by the end of the century it had reached 100,000. The cultural ideals of the Renaissance, with its fascination with the ancient world of Greece and Rome, persisted and the arts flourished. Michelangelo died only in 1564. Above all, there was the Reformation which, starting with Martin Luther's *Ninety-Five Theses* of 1517, divided Europe into Catholic and Protestant areas, the latter divided further into various churches. The Calvinists had now become the more militant branch of Protestantism. The Counter-Reformation and Catholic Reform can best be understood as the attempt of the Catholic church to adapt to this changing world. The Council of Trent, which met on and off from 1545 to 1563, represented a milestone in this process. The Antimachiavellians belonged to this effort at adaptation inasmuch as they sought to outline a Catholic, moral politics that would result in the effective government of the evolving state.

Giovanni Botero was born at Bene Vagienna in Piedmont in 1544. When he reached fifteen his parents sent him to study at the Jesuit college in Palermo in Sicily, where his Jesuit uncle taught. The following year he transferred to the Roman College and soon entered the Jesuit novitiate in Rome. He continued his studies at the Roman College, where the future theologian and cardinal Robert Bellarmine was a classmate. He was then sent to teach rhetoric and philosophy at several small Jesuit colleges in Italy and France. For much of 1568 and 1569 he was assigned to Paris, and this opened his eyes to what he later considered the greatest city in Christendom. But the young Jesuit suffered from moodiness and poor health, and he had trouble settling down in the Society even after he was ordained to the priesthood in 1572. In 1580, quietly and honorably, he left the Society.

At this low point in his life, Carlo Borromeo, the saintly archbishop of Milan, picked him up. Borromeo assigned him to a parish and then brought him to Milan in 1582 as his secretary. The two years that he served in this capacity before Borromeo's death in 1584 left a strong impression on him, and he published an account of the saint's death and burial that circulated widely. Botero now became closely associated with the ruling dynasty of Savoy. In 1583 he had dedicated a small volume, *On Kingly Wisdom*, to Duke Charles Emmanuel. The duke now sent him on a mission to Paris, probably to make contact with the reconstituted Catholic League or possibly with Henry III. There he remained from February to December of 1585, during the height of the Religious Wars which he experienced at first hand. The duke of Anjou died shortly before his arrival, and so the Huguenot Henry of Navarre now stood next in line for the throne. The Huguenots, the Catholic League, and the party of Henry III faced off against one another. While in Paris Botero established a close bond with the Savoyard ambassador to the court of France, René de Lucinge, lord of Allymes, who had made a brilliant career in the service of the duke of Savoy. Lucinge exercised considerable influence on him, especially in the direction of political realism. Botero was to draw many examples from a volume that Lucinge was then writing, *Of the Birth, Extent, and Fall of States*,[4] that would be published in 1588. It was also at this time that Botero first read Jean Bodin's *Six Books of the Republic*, from which he would subsequently draw material, especially on the economy. When he returned to Italy, Botero had learned about the difficulties of politics in the real world.

---

[4] René de Lucinge, *De la naissance, durée et chute des estats*, ed. Michael J. Heath (Geneva, 1984).

Botero now accepted a position as tutor and councillor to the twenty-two-year-old Federico Borromeo, cousin of Charles, and accompanied him to Rome in 1586. Federico was made a cardinal in the following year, and this facilitated Botero's contact with high ecclesiastical circles. It was a flourishing period in the history of papal Rome. Sixtus V was about to initiate "a program of urban development without parallel in any other European city."[5] Intellectual life was lively and characterized by a "new humanism."[6] There Botero associated with the humanist Piero Maffei, the philosopher Francesco Patrizi, and the Florentine political writer Scipione Ammirato. On July 14, 1587 he was named a consultor to the Congregation of the Index, of which Robert Bellarmine was a leading member. As a councillor to Borromeo, Botero took part in four papal conclaves, three in the year of the three popes, 1590–91, and the fourth that elected Clement VIII in 1592.

Botero's years in Rome from 1586 to 1595 turned out to be the most productive of his life. He returned from France prepared to write his three main works: *On the Causes of the Greatness and Magnificence of Cities* which appeared in 1588, *The Reason of State* in 1589, and *The Universal Relations*, which appeared in four parts between 1591 and 1596. Subsequently, *On the Causes of the Greatness and Magnificence of Cities* was usually published with and was to a degree overshadowed by *The Reason of State*.[7] It is a small book of only sixty-six pages in the Firpo edition compared to the 289 pages of *The Reason of State*. The volume represented a pioneering look at the phenomenon of the European cities which had been expanding since the late fifteenth century. Botero's reputation as the founder of demographic studies derives largely from this book. For him the strength of a city or state was measured largely by the size of its population, a theme on which he elaborated in *The Reason of State*. He also speculated about the way that disease, famine, and war limit the growth of population and the manner in which productive capacity sets restrictions on the number of people in a region and forces them

---

[5] Torgil Magnuson, *Rome in the Age of Bernini*, vol. i: *From the Election of Sixtus V to the Death of Urban VIII* (Stockholm and Atlantic Highlands, NJ, 1982), 16.

[6] Alphonse Dupront, "D'un humanisme chrétien en Italie à la fin du XVIe siècle," (1935) in Dupront, *Genèses des temps modernes: Rome, les réformes et le nouveau monde: Textes réunis et présentés par Dominique Julia et Philippe Boutry* (Paris, 2001), cited in Romain Descendre, *L'état du monde: Giovanni Botero entre raison d'État et géopolitique* (Geneva, 2009), 35.

[7] A new translation of *Delle cause della grandezza e magnificenza delle città* has recently appeared: *On the Causes of the Greatness and Magnificence of Cities*, trans. and ed. Geoffrey Symcox (Toronto, 2014).

to relocate elsewhere. *On the Causes of the Greatness and Magnificence of Cities* also revealed Botero's interest in areas beyond Europe, especially China. He shared with many of his contemporaries the utopian view of the Chinese Empire, which provided order and prosperity for its population of 60 million which far outstripped the most populous European state, France with its roughly 15 million people.

The Universal Relations was a compendium of contemporary knowledge about the known world rather than a creative effort like *The Reason of State*.[8] It may have originated as a response to a request from Borromeo for a description of the state of Christianity worldwide. The volumes represented a vast mine of information about the known world, physical, geographical, anthropological, economic, political, and religious. Of particular importance was the attempt to accumulate positive data, and the interest in numbers contributed to the development of an early science of statistics. Botero surpassed Jean Bodin in his emphasis on the influence of climate and geography on history. Many travel accounts as well as reports from missionaries in the field available in Rome served as his sources. The first edition of all the parts of *The Universal Relations* was published at Bergamo in 1596, and the whole and various parts went through over sixty editions and translations into Latin (1596), German (1596), English (1601), Spanish (1603), and Polish (1609).

The *Relations* included many digressions on topics treated in *The Reason of State* and modifications of Botero's thought, generally in the direction of a greater unity of Christendom. He came explicitly to embrace positions close to Robert Bellarmine's on the *Respublica Christiana*, characterized by indirect papal authority in temporal affairs. He acknowledged a new preference for a great empire like the Spanish over the medium-sized state he had favored in *The Reason of State* largely because it better facilitated the conditions for the effective preaching of the Gospel. Now he praised the Spanish expulsion of the Jews and Moors in 1492, for which he saw God rewarding the Spaniards with the conquest of the New World. He had shown little enthusiasm for these measures in *The Reason of State*, where he considered them from an economic perspective.

The Reason of State derived from three related traditions: the medieval "mirror of princes" tradition, the Scholastic, and the Florentine. It

---

[8] The first modern edition of *The Universal Relations* has just appeared: *Le relazioni universali*, ed. Blythe Alice Raviola, 2 vols. (Turin, 2015).

represented a modernized, updated version of the "mirror of princes" inasmuch as it laid out a program of successful rule based loosely on Christian moral virtues. Botero focused on the means to effective princely rule. Only with the edition of 1596 was a definition of the state as "a firm rule over people" inserted at the start of the first chapter, this in response to criticism that he had not defined the state. He wrote primarily from the perspective of the contemporary, medium-sized Italian states, especially those that had initially grown out of an urban base like Tuscany, Venice, or the Papal States rather than those like his native Savoy which had been princely territorial states from the start. This was neither a juridical work à la Bodin nor was it a work of political philosophy. There was little attempt to define the state further, to discuss the origins of the state, or to evaluate the circumstances that might justify rebellion. Nor did Botero discuss the advantages and disadvantages of the different forms of government or the constitutional structure of the state.

Botero and other Antimachiavellian writers usually treated in a cursory fashion these issues of political philosophy and the theological and metaphysical arguments to the effect that Machiavelli was unchristian and immoral. One exception was the usual support of princely absolutism, which was a response to the civil conflicts of the time just as it was for Bodin; Botero had experienced them personally in France. The restraints he placed upon the ruler were moral not constitutional, though he warned the prince of his need for popular support and so introduced a democratic element. Yet Botero esteemed republics. Venice was frequently noted in *The Reason of State* for its love of liberty. For his political philosophy he generally assumed the position of contemporary Scholastic authors who on a more theoretical level were involved in adapting the church to the growth of the modern state. Among these, three of the most prominent were the Dominican Francisco de Vitoria who taught at Salamanca from 1526 until his death in 1546, the Spaniard Francisco Suarez who taught in Rome from 1580 until 1585 though he did not begin to publish until later, and Robert Bellarmine who taught in Rome from 1576 until 1588 when he became consultant to the Roman curia and then a cardinal. All three of them accepted the modern sovereign state along with the indirect power of the papacy in temporal affairs which could be invoked when a government took measures harmful to the salvation of souls. They discussed the origin of the state, the role of consent within the state, and the requirements for a just war. All in all, they attempted to adapt the church to the changing times but on a level different from Botero and the Antimachiavellians.

The Florentine political tradition served as another major source for Botero. First of all in this regard comes Machiavelli himself. Though writing against "the Florentine chancellor," he took over many of his ideas and much of his vocabulary. Botero argued from historical examples much as did Machiavelli and Bodin, and he frequently called to the bar the ancient writers, especially the Romans but also the Greeks, as Renaissance writers were wont to do. Despite his assignment of Tacitus to a place alongside Machiavelli – Botero was in fact the first writer to link the two – he cited Tacitus seventy-three times, while Livy, the next in line, has fifty-six citations.[9] No Scholastics were cited, nor were any other Renaissance historians except Polydore Vergil, who was cited once. But these figures are deceptive. Botero used many examples, historical and contemporary, as we have seen, drawing upon the many sources available to him in Rome, including Muslim and Byzantine ones, without naming them, and these were balanced more or less evenly between the ancient world and more recent history, that is, the Renaissance and the sixteenth century. He also frequently alluded to medieval events.

Botero's use of the term "reason of state" was much more positive and more general than the usage of most of his contemporaries. For many of them it meant, as he himself noted with a certain vagueness, "those things which cannot be reduced to an ordinary or common reason."[10] This was the case with Scipione Ammirato, for example, where reason of state indicated the necessity to bypass, for the sake of the common good, common practice or positive law but not natural or divine law.[11] Others, like the satirical republican Traiano Boccalini in his *Reports from Parnassus* (1612), considered it "a law useful to states but in everything contrary to the laws of God and of men."[12]

Botero was interested in the conservation, then the expansion of the state; he had scarcely anything to say about its foundation. Certainly in the *Discourses*, Machiavelli's chief concern had been the preservation of the state in a hostile environment and against the ravages of time. Botero

[9] This figure applies to *RS* 1598.
[10] *RS*, 1.1 (p. 4), see note 2. Botero added this in *RS* 1596 in response to criticism.
[11] *Discorso sopra C. Tacito* (Florence, 1594), book 12, chap. 1 (pp. 228–42).
[12] *Ragguagli di Parnaso*, book 2, ragguaglio (report) 87, p. 290.

nourished few illusions about the environment. In discussing prudence he introduced the concept of princely interest (*interesse*) or advantage, contrasting it with friendship, blood relationship, obligations to allies, or any other bond. To the ruler he made it clear that "in the deliberations of princes interest is that which overcomes every other consideration."[13] To preserve a state was a greater achievement than to found one, precisely because of the variability of things human. A ruler often gained power by accident or force, he wrote, sounding like Machiavelli, "but the retention of what has been acquired was the fruit of an excellent *virtù*," and called for great wisdom. The Spartan custom of punishing those who in the fight lost their shields not their swords showed their esteem for preservation.[14] His predilection for medium-sized states showed that for Botero it was not a question of conquest and glory or mediocrity and probable extinction, as Machiavelli seemed to argue in the *Discourses*. Botero distinguished, formally, between maintenance and expansion; he devoted the first six books of *The Reason of State* to maintenance and the last four to expansion. The purpose behind his distinction was to show that within a Christian, moral framework it was possible for a prince to enlarge his medium-sized state and so to gather the resultant glory. Botero forged a new concept of expansion that had much less to do with military conquest than Machiavelli's.

Botero's understanding of virtue or *virtù*, reputation, and power, and the relationship among them characterized his thought and that of other Antimachiavellians, and it provides a key to the political culture of the Counter-Reformation and the Baroque. The Spanish council of state reminded Philip III in 1616 when war threatened in Italy that "religion and reputation ... are the two great matters which sustain states," and there could be no compromise on them.[15] Reputation played a significant role in the policy-making of Olivares and Richelieu, and *réputation* and *puissance* turned up frequently in the cardinal's *Political Testament*, where *prudence* or *raison* frequently replaced the more general *vertu*.

Both Machiavelli and Botero featured the role of the ruler's *virtù*; for both, it constituted a congeries of qualities that enabled him to gain and retain the support of his people. But Botero reunited Christian moral virtue with the political skill of Machiavelli's *virtù*.[16] The ruler of *virtù*

---

[13] *RS*, 2.6 (p. 41); see also 8.14 (p. 149).   [14] *RS*, 1.5 (p. 7).
[15] Cited in Geoffrey Parker, *Europe in Crisis, 1598–1648* (Glasgow, 1979), 156.
[16] Machivelli also at times included moral virtue in his concept of *virtù*.

was both virtuous and virtuoso. *Virtù* produced reputation, understood as the support of the people, and reputation made up the basic element in the ruler's power, which then in turn augmented his reputation. Immoral conduct as well as political ineptitude – the two nearly overlapped for Botero – subverted his power by undermining his reputation. *Potenza* for power did not figure nearly as much in Botero's vocabulary as did *virtù* or *riputazione*, but the reality was as central to his thinking as they were.

Botero devoted most of Book One of *The Reason of State* to princely *virtù*, including justice and liberality, and Book Two to its vital components, prudence and valor, temperance and religion. Books Three to Six then developed further techniques of government for dealing with particular classes or groups of people, including heretics, infidels, and foreigners. With Book Seven he began his discussion of the state's expansion that filled the last four books. It revolved around "the instruments of prudence and valor," or *virtù*, the tools of expansion. These came to be the prince's resources (*forze*), which he reduced to "people (*gente*), many and of high quality, and money and food supplies and munitions and horses and offensive and defensive arms";[17] they too were basic features of his power and likewise a source of reputation.

A prince could not rule successfully for any length of time without the support of his people. It consisted in their love (*affezione*) for him and his reputation (*riputazione* or *stima*) among them. These were "the foundation of every government of a state."[18] So Botero introduced a nonjuridical form of consent into government; he incorporated the democratic element in princely rule found in Machiavelli, and the role of consent insisted on by Scholastic authors. Benefits and moderate *virtù* could elicit the love of the people but only outstanding *virtù* displayed in matters vital to the people could evoke reputation. These Botero summed up as "abundance, peace, and justice," terms which included much of the traditional concept of the common good. People could not but be content "who without fear of foreign or civil war, who without fear of being assassinated in their houses through violence or fraud, who have the necessary food at a good price are not concerned about anything else."[19] The

---

[17] *RS*, 7.1 (p. 121) Botero uses the term "*forze*" in two different ways: sometimes it designates military resources and sometimes resources more generally. The same is true of "*gente*": sometimes it designates soldiers and at other times people or population. The meaning has to be drawn from the context. Here it would seem to mean soldiers.
[18] *RS*, 3.1 (p. 71).   [19] Ibid.

prince who fulfilled his obligation to provide for the common good would enjoy his people's support. Good government was good politics because it helped secure reputation.

Botero elaborated on his concept of reputation in the *Additions to the Reason of State (Aggiunte alla ragion di stato)*, which was first published separately in 1598 and often with later editions of *The Reason of State*. He did not directly address its role in a ruler's foreign relations, yet the reputation or support that he enjoyed among his subjects clearly influenced his international standing. Reputation now amounted to a composite of love and fear that his subjects felt toward him; it was similar to the reverence that was engendered by a holy person. It designated awe and wonder elicited by the ruler's *virtù*, which "have the quality of the lofty and the admirable and elevate the prince above the earth and carry him beyond the number of common men."[20] An element of mystery enshrouded the prince which his subjects could not fathom.

Which was more important in reputation, Botero now asked, love or fear? Siding with Machiavelli and in opposition to the tradition of the "mirror of princes" tradition, with a certain sadness, he came down on the side of fear. Given the world as it was, no government was more unstable than one based on love. To satisfy all his subjects and unite thousands in love of himself was a nearly impossible task for a prince. Subjects murmured and longed for change. The subjection that followed from fear was necessary. Moreover, it lay within his power for a prince to create fear in his subjects, whereas to elicit love often exceeded his powers. But fear was a far cry from hatred, Botero warned, as had Machiavelli and Aristotle long before him. Hatred as well as contempt quickly undermined government and had to be avoided at all costs.

Reputation had to be based on genuine virtue. Here his response to Machiavelli led him into the favorite Baroque topic of the relationship between appearance and reality. Feigned virtue would not long convince. A prince simply could not counterfeit piety over a long period as Machiavelli recommended. Botero distinguished three types of reputation: natural, which actually corresponded to the *virtù* of the prince; artificial, which resulted from conscious exaggeration of his *virtù*; and adventitious, which exaggerated the prince's reputation but was not caused by a conscious attempt to do so. Neither of the second two would last, and they could lead to trouble. The Venetians had executed the condottiere

---

[20] *Additions*, Appendix D, 4 (pp. 223–24).

Carmagnola because he failed to win a battle that his reputation led them to think that he should have won.

But a prince could and should polish his image. It was a fault if his reputation fell short of what he deserved. A ruler might improve his standing by, for example, hiding his weaknesses or assigning unpopular duties to others. A prince's image was similar to a painting. Just as a painter might exceed the limits of truth so long as he remained within those of verisimilitude, so might the prince in fostering his image, wrote Botero, drawing on contemporary art theory. But a reputation that endured had to be rooted in reality; appearance was never enough.[21]

The prince gained the love of his subjects especially by justice and liberality, the virtues "which are totally aimed to benefit [others]."[22] Botero discussed two forms of justice distinguished by Aristotle and usually treated by the Scholastics: distributive, which dealt with the fair distribution of honors and burdens in the state, and commutative, which protected the subjects from violence and fraud at the hands of one another. They had to be present in those areas where the hand of government most touched the lives of subjects, in the collection of taxes and the administration of justice where the people desired above all fairness and speed. Botero criticized the sale of offices: "this is nothing other than to promote avarice rather than justice to tribunals," he wrote.[23] The prince should pay judges well and prohibit them from accepting any gifts. Botero praised the way the Chinese prepared their officials, and he lauded the system of spies used by Cosimo de' Medici, Grand Duke of Tuscany, to check on his judges.

Liberality aimed at two goals, relief for the poor and patronage of the arts. No work was more praised in Scripture than assistance of the unfortunate, nor was there "anything more suited to and effective to win over the minds of the populace and to bind them to their lord."[24] The good and the useful were in harmony. The prince should demonstrate his concern especially at times of natural disasters such as earthquakes. Here Botero added the Machiavellian advice that at the time of such calamities the ruler ought not permit any private person to become too prominent in the aid effort since this easily led to a popularity with the people that might prove threatening to the government. So the Gracchi brothers had created a party in ancient Rome. Secondly, the ruler should exercise

---

[21] Ibid., 4 (p. 223).   [22] *RS*, 1.11 (p. 17).
[23] *RS*, 1.16 (p. 23).   [24] *RS*, 1.20 (p. 30).

liberality by fostering the *virtù* of subjects, that is, their literary and artistic abilities. The ruler ought to patronize the arts and sciences, as many contemporary princes did, thus attaching prominent personalities to the state. Nor did Botero fail to add the admonition that the prince should not be so liberal with his gifts that he notably increased the tax burden on the population, and so provoked discontent, a point also made by Machiavelli.

Prudence and valor made up the leading components of *virtù*; they were the source of reputation, "the two pillars on which every government ought to rest,"[25] he wrote at the start of Book Two. Prudence was of the eye, corresponding to Machiavelli's fox, valor of the hand, corresponding to Machiavelli's lion. The overwhelming amount of space given to prudence in *The Reason of State* indicated that the eye was more important than the hand, and prudence soon became for the Antimachiavellians the cardinal virtue of the ruler or politician, combining moral virtue with political skill as it had long done in the Aristotelian and Thomistic traditions. Prudence was acquired above all by experience. A major part of a prince's or statesman's education was the study of history, for Botero as for Machiavelli. It was "the most vast theater that one can imagine."[26] Botero then turned to an idea that he took from Bodin which he elaborated much more fully in *The Universal Relations*. Peoples were different. Geography and climate greatly affected their character. Those who inhabited mountainous areas, for example, tended to be fierce and wild, those who dwelt in valleys tended to be soft and even effeminate. The ruler had to acquire an understanding of his own and other peoples. So Botero began to think in terms of an individualized reason of state or means to construct and maintain a state, adapted to the population and situation of particular states. Thus he helped to prepare the way for further thinking about reason of state in terms of the interests of particular states.

Under prudence Botero then listed a number of precepts or maxims, "headings of prudence (*capi di prudenza*)," that are impossible to summarize but were of great importance for his political outlook. Many have a Machiavellian ring and reveal a pessimistic vision of the world but they never recommend clearly immoral actions. Reference has already been made to the first of them, that interest always prevailed in the deliberations of princes. The prince should never trust anyone whom he had

---

[25] *RS*, 2.1 (p. 34). [26] *RS*, 2.3 (p. 37).

offended or who felt himself to have been offended by him. The desire for revenge remained latent and came to the surface when opportunity beckoned. Botero urged princes not to go to war with powerful republics unless victory was certain. "The love of liberty is so powerful and has such roots in those who have enjoyed it for a while that to conquer it and to extirpate it is nearly impossible, and the enterprises and counsels of princes die with them but the designs and deliberations of free cities are as it were immortal,"[27] he wrote, sounding much like the republican Machiavelli.

For Botero as for Machiavelli a sense of timing was fundamental in politics. Philip II of Spain exemplified the prudent ruler who refused to yield to the whim of chance or fortune. A prince had to know when to act. "Nothing is of greater importance than a certain period of time which is called opportunity (*opportunità*); it is nothing other than a combination of circumstances that facilitates an endeavour that before or after that point would be difficult."[28] As for Machiavelli, a ruler had to know when to take advantage of the occasion (*occasione*), a term used elsewhere by Botero in a similar context and divorced from any connection with fortune. Botero warned also about sudden change, "because such actions have something of the violent, and violence rarely succeeds and never produces a lasting effect."[29] Especially at the start of his reign, a prince ought to be slow to make changes. When they are necessary, they ought to be made after the example of nature, which does not move directly between summer and winter but passes through the intermediate phases of fall and spring. Charles Martel had demonstrated how to do this by the way he prepared his son to succeed to the Carolingian throne.

Fidelity to treaties and agreements belonged to prudence and was an essential element in a ruler's reputation. His outstanding example of this was Alexander Farnese, duke of Parma, governor of the Netherlands, and commander of Philip II's army there from 1578 to 1592, who successfully tamed the Dutch rebels and who seemed to serve, consciously or unconsciously, as Botero's counterpart to Cesare Borgia. A ruler ought not to make promises that he could not keep; this also undermined confidence. Elsewhere Botero insisted that a ruler had to remain faithful to the terms on which another people had submitted to him. Any other way of proceeding would stir fears and cause trouble. It was counterproductive to

[27] *RS*, 2.6 (p. 44).   [28] *RS*, 2.6 (p. 45).   [29] *RS*, 2.6 (p. 43).

build on any other basis than truth and fidelity to one's word. But Botero failed to supply any guidance regarding when newly perceived interests might allow a ruler to abandon an agreement. The Scholastics had shown flexibility in this regard.

Botero devoted much less space to valor or *valore*, the second source of reputation. He sometimes used the term *valore* nearly as a synonym for *virtù*, blurring the line between prudence and valor. More narrowly, valor meant boldness or *ardire*. Together with prudence it brought forth "marvelous deeds."[30] Their common achievement was that they won subjects' attention and harnessed their energies either by exciting their wonder and awe at the prince's undertakings or by keeping them occupied and so preventing them from causing trouble. A prince ought never to risk a venture that was not certain to result in success with honor nor undertake projects of little importance that were unlikely to magnify his reputation. Something "lofty and heroic" ought to characterize all his deeds.[31] Two types of deed were the military and the civil, with the former of greater importance. The civil comprised building projects of grand scale or marvelous utility, like the aqueducts, bridges, and roads of the Romans or the Propylaeum of Pericles in Athens. So Botero appeared to endorse the construction projects of Sixtus V in Rome. One was the completion of the aqueduct still called *Acque Felice* that channeled water to Rome from 20 kilometers east of the city, and another a new configuration of the city's streets.

Gradually, then, Botero's perspective shifted from the magnificence of the projects themselves to their ability to keep the people occupied; by people he now meant principally the growing urban population and especially the urban poor who were by nature unstable and eager for change. He envisaged the capital cities, first Rome, then Paris, Madrid, and others where a restive population had to be controlled. Pope Sixtus's building program provided work for many in Rome. In one passage Botero showed an uncharacteristic support for war. He seemed to endorse Machiavelli's traditional view that foreign war was useful to maintain peace at home, and he explained the domestic peace enjoyed by Spaniards and Turks partly by their engagement in foreign wars. For Christians there were always the Turks, the traditional enemy against whom they could always make war legitimately, as he was later to elaborate at the end of *The Reason of State*. Botero considered the popular entertainments provided by

---

[30] *RS*, 2.10 (p. 51).   [31] *RS*, 2.11 (p. 56).

the Medici in Florence suitable to distract the people. They should educate as well as entertain. Botero was highly critical of the contemporary theatre, but he praised the ecclesiastical pageants staged by Carlo Borromeo in Milan. "In short, it is necessary to do this in such a way that the people have some occupation, pleasurable or useful, at home or abroad, that engages them and so keeps them from impertinent actions and evil thoughts."[32]

Botero subsequently divided the population into three groups: the nobles or the wealthy (*grandi, opulenti*), the middling sort (*mezani*), and the poor (*poveri, miseri*). He quickly dismissed the middling sort as a peaceful lot who posed no threat and turned to the other two who did. We have already seen recommendations for handling the urban poor. At this point he anticipated his program for economic development by showing that the poor needed to be provided opportunities in agriculture and in the crafts so that they would have a stake in the state. Among the nobles three groups could be dangerous: princes of the blood, great feudal lords, and those who stood out by their valor. Botero was concerned about the threat to the prince from the overmighty subject, a threat that the wars in France had led him to realize. The prince ought not to create offices with excessive authority and should suppress existing ones like the Great Constable of France. Rulers should avoid granting offices in perpetuity like the governorships in France, so that incumbents could be removed. There should be a clear distinction between members of the king's council who possessed no jurisdiction and officers with jurisdiction such as governors, generals, and captains of major fortresses. Ferdinand the Catholic, Botero remarked, never appointed the general who conquered a province to be its governor.

The last pair of virtues that constituted *virtù* was temperance and religion, upholding the others and so preserving the state. They were needed in the people as well as in the prince. Religion was the mother of virtues, temperance the wet-nurse. For Botero religion was valuable because of the divine aid that it won for the state and for the virtues that it fostered in the subjects, especially obedience. Like Machiavelli, he played up the importance attached to religion by the Romans, who undertook no campaign without first consulting the augurs and seeking the favour of the gods. Like the Carolingians and the Capetians before them, the

---

[32] *RS*, 3.3. This citation does not appear in the 1589 edition; it was added in *RS* 1596; see the Firpo edition of 1948, p. 153.

Habsburgs owed their prominence to their piety. Botero recounted a tale already a part of Habsburg lore. Back in the thirteenth century, Count Rudolf of Habsburg assisted a priest bringing Viaticum to a peasant in the midst of a violent storm. The house's subsequent good fortune resulted from the blessing of the grateful priest. God rewarded princely piety.

"Religion is of such power for government that without it every other foundation of the state wobbles," Botero declared as he turned to the subjects.[33] The ruler must foster their piety. Religion was useful to the prince in many ways. It inspired courage in battle, civic responsibility, and a spirit of obedience. According to Christian teaching, all authority came from God. Christians were bound in conscience to obey even unworthy rulers except in the case when a command clearly contravened the law of God, and even then, Botero continued – coming as close to a discussion of the right of resistance as he ever did – a clear break with the ruler ought to be the last resort. Under the Roman persecutions Christians had demonstrated patience and long-suffering. At present, Botero contended, Catholics endured patiently their trials in France, the Netherlands, England, and Scotland, whereas the Protestants inclined to rebellion; he overlooked the role of the Catholic League in France. Christianity and specifically Catholicism served as a bulwark of the state despite Machiavelli's charges to the contrary.

His apparent opposition to the growing interference of rulers in ecclesiastical affairs did not keep Botero from conceding to the prince a major role in church matters. His assignment to the prince of responsibilities for religion opened the door for an expansion of the state's activity that was typical of the Counter-Reformation as well as the Reformation. Indeed, the growing role of government was as important to the development of the state as was a standing army or a nascent bureaucracy. Botero proposed a program of reform and Counter-Reformation. The prince should provide an example to his people by genuinely and intelligently practising his faith, avoiding pretence and superstition. He should make sure that the people were provided with qualified pastors and preachers, that suitable churches were available, and that the material needs of the clergy were cared for.

Botero was wary of excessive wealth, as the republican Machiavelli had been, who had seen it as weakening civic loyalty. In the name of temperance Botero advocated luxury taxes and sumptuary laws regulating

[33] *RS*, 2.16 (p. 64).

expenditures on food and clothing, not to encourage a Christian simplicity of life nor to express social distinctions as was frequently the case with contemporaries, but to ward off dangers to the state. Temperance prevented the people from falling into indulgence, luxury, and ostentation, all of which blinded the mind, undermined resolve, and led to public and private ruin. Such had been the case in ancient Rome where luxury and softness enabled the tyranny of a Tiberius and a Caligula. Overrun as it was with the delicacies of the East, Portugal was headed in the same direction. Botero placed much of the blame on women. "The ladies are much more apt to corrupt men than men are to restrain the ladies; few husbands are masters of their wives." All the great empires have been ruined because of two vices, luxury and avarice, "and avarice is born of luxury, and luxury of women."[34] Besides this, as a mercantilist Botero was aware of the loss of money to the state as a result of the purchase of imported jewels, perfumes, finery, and other luxury goods.

Books Three to Five discussed techniques of government and the way to deal with particular classes of people. Here he dealt with religious dissidents, who had become an acute problem following the Reformation. For Botero as well as for many of his contemporaries, religious differences were the principal cause of division within states, and religious unity was essential to a state's power. Botero treated policy toward dissidents not under religion but under the means to reconcile newly acquired subjects to the rule of a prince; it was less a religious than a political matter. The ideal was their conversion, and Botero recommended many ways to bring this about. The first requirement was good missionaries, men of solid doctrine and exemplary life. Education helped to win over the parents as well as the children, and Botero praised the Jesuit schools in Germany, India, and the New World. One could legitimately bring pressure to bear on unbelievers as well as heretics by the concession or denial of privileges like tax exemptions. Charity and almsgiving were also effective.

But what about the irreconcilables who resisted all efforts at conversion? These were for Botero the Muslims among the unbelievers and the Calvinists among the heretics. The Calvinists stirred up constant unrest and were responsible, according to a passage that he later deleted, for the war in France, the rebellion in the Netherlands, and the overthrow of Mary Stuart in Scotland. The prince had to resort to stern measures

---

[34] *RS*, 2.17 (p. 70).

when it became clear that they would not convert and intended to oppose the new arrangements. But it should be noted that the governmental measures that he proposed were not aimed directly at conversion but at the prevention of rebellion. Botero first suggested ways to undermine the spirit of recalcitrants, for example by denying them the use of the horse, as the Turks did the Christians, or by requiring them to wear distinctive dress. Secondly, the prince was to close off their sources of men and money. Then he should prohibit them from bearing arms and holding fortified places, and assess special taxes. The Turks seized Christian youths to serve in the Janissaries; Christian rulers might have to do the same. Lastly, one should sow dissension among dissidents, sever their contacts with foreigners, keep out preachers and subversive publications, and in extreme cases one might have to relocate populations as the Assyrians did with the Jews. Significantly, Botero did not cite as an example in this context the expulsions of the Jews and Moors from Spain.

But, inevitably, troubles would break out. Once he took up the topic of actual rebellion, Botero approached the position of Bodin and the French *politiques* and showed an aversion to civil war that he undoubtedly owed to his experience in France. If rebellion could be quickly suppressed by force, this should be done, the more quietly the better. The part of prudence was to know when to take a hard line and when to yield. Botero made several suggestions about how to manage a mob. One was simply to dissimulate, that is, to pretend not to notice a provocation; another was to let the mob exhaust its energy for lack of leadership. But if it appeared that this and other measures would not work, it was usually better to yield in part or in full before actual hostilities began. In this way the prince retained the affection of his subjects if not his reputation, and even his reputation if he could make it appear that he was freely making concessions. Once civil war broke out, it was unusually difficult to end it without compromises, he wrote, again with the French experience probably in mind. Better to make concessions at the start, Botero seemed to imply. He was not prepared to wage a war for the suppression of heresy. The sum of wisdom was to resist beginnings. Trouble could usually be foreseen well ahead of time; it rarely started with a full-scale rebellion.

The chief topics of Book Six were security and foreign policy. Here Botero argued that the methods for expanding the state were fundamentally the same as for preserving it. The distinction between preserving a state and expanding it was a nominal one. Botero made it, it seems, to show that the Christian ruler of a mid-sized state could enlarge his state without resorting to territorial conquest. He did this with economic development and military preparedness. The prince's resources were reduced basically to men and money. Men were more important than money, as they were for Machiavelli. But whereas for Machiavelli men were essentially soldiers, for Botero they extended to the whole population. This population was the most fundamental resource of a state because it produced the state's wealth, which in turn was the source of the prince's treasure. This treasure Botero understood to be ready funds in the form of precious metals. Reputation required treasure, Botero wrote, indicating his awareness of the change of thinking since the time of Machiavelli; "the power (*potenza*) of states is assessed today no less from the supply of money than from the size of the territory."[35] Botero cited the familiar dictum that Machiavelli had rejected, "money is the sinews of empire."[36]

How much treasure ought a prince to accumulate? This was a thorny question, and the answer varied from state to state. Obviously, the amount of treasure needed was greater in time of war than peace. One reason to avoid war was to prevent overtaxing the economic resources of a state. For peacetime a general rule was that the prince never draw into his treasury more than the amount by which the inflow of treasure into the country surpassed the outflow. A balance of payments was necessary. To draw in more than this was to hinder the availability of funds for the normal course and growth of agriculture, commerce, and industry. A limitation of Botero's economics was that he failed to take into account currency fluctuations as Bodin had done, and that he prohibited interest or usury, which he saw as taking money out of circulation just as the ruler's treasure did, and as against church directives.

How was the prince to raise revenue? There were patrimonial lands as well as levies on imports and exports and other, extraordinary sources of revenue. Botero was one of the first political writers to declare that regular taxes should provide an ordinary source of revenue. They should be levied on property, not persons, in order to avoid burdening the poor. And in light of the rebellion in the Netherlands fomented in part by Philip II's attempt to tax movable property, Botero proposed taxes only on land. Should it be necessary to tax movable goods, this should be

---

[35] *RS*, 7.3 (p. 124, note 10).
[36] *RS*, 7.3. This citation from Dio Cassius, *Roman History*, 66.2 was only added in later editions; see *Della ragion di stato*, ed. Luigi Firpo (Turin, 1948), 225.

carried out as it was in the German cities where the citizens assessed the value of their own property.

Even more important than treasure was a large population; it was both the cause and the result of the state's wealth. The ruler should actively encourage agriculture and industry. Agriculture was the basis for all demographic growth; first one had to feed the people. The prince should encourage the development of the "infrastructure," for example with irrigation and drainage projects as the Romans had done. But industry was still more vital than agriculture. It supported more people – according to Botero two-thirds of the Italian cities lived by the silk and wool industries – and produced more wealth. Botero marveled at the ability and ingenuity of human beings. Look what they did with the excrement of worms. Neither Italy, nor the Netherlands, nor France possessed extensive natural resources, yet they were the wealthiest areas of Europe. Foreign trade also enriched a state. In *The Reason of State* Botero said little about it, but in *On the Causes of the Greatness and Magnificence of Cities* in a lyrical passage he praised God who had created the various peoples dependent on one another for various goods in order to lead them to mutual love and union.

In his discussion of military power Botero took up many of the topics raised by Machiavelli. When writing of discipline, he stressed the need for rewards and punishments. His vision of human nature led him to see punishments as more important than rewards. In war if the prince did not reward, he would not be loved; if he did not punish, he would not be obeyed, and nothing was worse than that. Like Machiavelli, he contended that soldiers fought best under necessity (*necessità*) which heightened valor and *virtù*. Botero agreed with Machiavelli that a ruler ought to draw his soldiers from his own subjects because this promoted his independence, but he had nothing against the use of foreigners in a secondary capacity. Subsequently, and somewhat inconsistently, he noted that recent experience had shown that the most effective armies of the day were multinational ones because the different nations strove to have the honor of the victory. So he set aside Machiavelli's view that similarity of language and culture was necessary for the unity and esprit of any army and recognized what one observer had called the Noah's ark of contemporary armies, perhaps with a view to Parma's army in the Netherlands. A general had to convince his troops that they were fighting in a just cause; this greatly added to their effectiveness. Botero did not address directly Machiavelli's criticism of Christian soldiers, but he certainly had it in mind when he stated that hope in eternal life undoubtedly stimulated their courage.

The final chapter of *The Reason of State*, entitled "Against Whom the Prince Ought to Deploy his Military Forces," was added to the edition of 1590.[37] Here just war theory shone through. "If a defensive war is just and an offensive [that is, aggressive] war is just only insofar as it is defensive in nature, then there is no case in which it is licit to take the offensive except to defend [the state]. How therefore will I – someone might say – expand my state?" Botero had already shown how a prince might enlarge his state by promotion of the economy. Now he wanted to point out that an opportunity was always at hand to make war for the public good if a ruler was intent on securing military glory. This was to make war on the Turks, who had long occupied Christian lands in southeastern Europe. Here Botero's sense of Christendom came to the fore; it anticipated the more universal outlook of *The Universal Relations*. War with the heretics was still a civil war within Christendom. He shared the concern about the real Turkish threat and the enthusiasm for a crusade that had not died out at Lepanto. The empire's forces would accept the challenge in 1593 and continue in the field until 1606. Botero accordingly concluded *The Reason of State* with a summons to a campaign against the Turks; it paralleled Machiavelli's call in the last chapter of *The Prince* to a war to drive the foreigners out of Italy. Machiavelli was an Italian patriot, Botero a European one. Surely divine support and assistance for such a magnificent venture would be forthcoming.[38]

The Text

The basis for this translation is the edition of the original version of *The Reason of State*, *Della ragion di stato*, published in Venice in 1589, edited with an introduction by Chiara Continisio (Rome, 1997; repr. 2009). There were three further editions overseen by Botero himself, in 1590, 1596, and 1598. Most of the additions were further examples or Latin citations. All the significant additions I have included either in the footnotes or in the appendices, and I have also noted significant deletions in the footnotes. I have been greatly helped by the edition of the

---

[37] See Appendix C.
[38] It is noteworthy that both these calls to war were expressed in chapters added to the original composition.

1598 text, *Della ragion di stato di Giovanni Botero con tre libri delle Cause della grandezza delle città, due Aggiunte e un Discorso sulla popolazione di Roma*, edited by Luigi Firpo (Turin, 1948), and two translations: *The Reason of State*, translated by P.J. and D.P. Waley with an introduction by D.P. Waley, and containing also Robert Peterson's 1606 translation of *The Greatness of Cities* (London, 1956); and the recent excellent French translation, *De la raison d'État (1589–1598) par Giovanni Botero*, translated and edited by Pierre Benedittini and Romain Descendre, with an introduction by Romain Descendre (Paris, 2014). I have drawn extensively on the notes from this edition.

Botero uses the word *virtù* in three senses: to designate "virtue" in the traditional moral sense, to designate talent or skill along with virtue, and to designate talent or skill alone. I translate the first sense with "virtue"; for the other two I leave the Italian "*virtù*."

Dedication

To the Most Illustrious, most Reverend Lord, most Respected Lord Wolfgang Theodore, Archbishop and Prince of Salzburg.[1]

These past years, for different reasons, partly my own and partly of my friends and patrons, I have found it expedient to undertake various journeys and to frequent more than I would have wanted the courts of kings and great princes, both here and beyond the mountains. There among the other things that I have observed I have marveled greatly at the mention nearly every day of reason of state and in this context to hear cited now Niccolò Machiavelli now Cornelius Tacitus, the former because he provides precepts for the government and rule of peoples, the latter because he describes in a lively fashion the arts employed by Tiberius Caesar to obtain and then to preserve his position in the Roman Empire. It struck me then as worthwhile (since I have often found myself among people who reflect on such matters) that I learn myself also to give some account of them. So, having begun to page through one and then the other author, I found that, in short, Machiavelli based reason of state on little respect for conscience, and Tiberius Caesar cloaked his tyranny and cruelty in a most barbarous law of majesty[2] and in other ways that would not have been tolerated by the most cowardly women in the world nor even by the

---

[1] Some editions have different dedicatees, for example *RS* 1596 is dedicated to Philip Emmanuel, Prince of Piedmont, and *RS* 1598 to Federico Quinzio, Royal Fiscal for His Catholic Majesty in the State of Milan.

[2] Tiberius restored the *lex majestatis* aimed at crimes of lèse-majesté. But contrary to ancient practice, where the law looked to actions against the majesty of the Roman people, Tiberius following Augustus applied it to protect his own reputation; see Tacitus, *Annals*, I.72.2–4. He applied it "atrociously" according to Suetonius, *The Twelve Caesars*, "Tiberius," 58.

I

Romans if C. Cassius had not been the last of the Romans.[3] So have I been greatly astonished that such an impious author and such wicked, tyrannical means are so esteemed as to be held, as it were, as the norm and the pattern of the way that states ought to be administered and governed. But that which arouses in me wonder as much as contempt is to see accredited such a barbarous style of government that is so shamelessly opposed to the law of God to the point of saying that some things are licit by reason of state and others by conscience. One cannot say anything more irrational nor impious because whoever withdraws from the sphere of conscience its universal jurisdiction over all that transpires among men, in public as well as in private matters, demonstrates that he has neither soul nor God. If all animals have a natural instinct that inclines them to what is useful and holds them back from what is harmful, should the light of reason and the dictates of conscience given to man to know how to discern the good and the evil, be blind in public affairs and defective in matters of importance? Induced by I do not know whether contempt or zeal, I have often had a mind to write of the corruption introduced by these two men into the government and counsels of princes which has given rise to all the scandals in the Church of God and to all the disorder in Christendom. But after considering that a treatise on corruption would have no credit or authority unless I first showed the true and royal way that a prince ought to follow in order to become great and to govern his people successfully, I have put off the first project to another time, to outline at least the second in this book of the reason of state which I send to your most Illustrious Lordship.[4] The noise of the court and the obligations of service (plus my limited ability) make it so that I do not dare to say that I have described it even in part much less to have embodied it. But desirous that it pass through the hands of men with some greater distinction than it has received from me, I have boldly presumed to honor it with the most eminent name of Your Most Illustrious Lordship. (Not to speak of the antiquity of Your most extensive House, adorned as it has been at all times by ecclesiastical and secular titles, by the singular valor of His Lordship your father in military campaigns,[5] by

---

[3] Cassius along with Brutus led the plot against Julius Caesar in 44 BCE.

[4] In some editions, from "But after ... to another time" has been omitted and replaced by "whence I have been prompted to outline at least a few things in these books of the Reason of State." See Giovanni Botero, *Della ragion di stato*, ed. Chiaro Continisio (Rome, 1997), 4, n. 2 and xxvi–xxvii.

[5] Hans Werner von Raitenau was a military man in the service of the Habsburgs.

the supreme authority of His Lordship Cardinal Altemps,[6] your uncle, in the Christian Church), I have not been able to find a prince who has either greater knowledge of matters of state or who takes greater pleasure in them or with greater wisdom and judgment administers them and puts them into practice. The Divine Majesty has given Your Most Illustrious Lordship a most extensive and wealthy state, both spiritual and temporal. You, in the heyday of your life, govern your people with such justice and religion and moderate in such a way severity with grace in a noble and amiable fashion that you are equally feared and loved. You unite in such a rare fashion the solicitude of the pastor with the *gravitas* of the prince, and so you elicit the greatest reverence for you in your subjects and a stellar reputation among all. Finally, you bear yourself so in every action in such a way that it makes one wonder which state you maintain with greater dignity, that of prince or prelate. I trust that the reasons that have moved me to send to you and to dedicate to you my modest efforts will also move your Most Illustrious Lordship to accept and appreciate them with the magnanimity and courtesy that is proper to you. The lowliness of this topic that would perhaps have held others back leads me to present it to you with greater assurance of your favor; for it is proper to a great prince (so imitating the Most High God) to raise up base matters and to magnify small matters with kindness and favor. I pray to the Lord God for the well-being of Your Most Illustrious Lordship, and I most humbly kiss your hand.

Rome, 10 May 1589

From the most humble and most devoted servant of Your Most Illustrious and Most Reverend Lordship, Giovanni Botero

---

[6] Cardinal Mark Sittich von Hohenems (Marco Sittico d'Altemps), 1533–95, was a nephew of Pius IV and son of Clara de' Medici, sister of the pope.

Book One

1 What is Reason of State

Reason of state is knowledge of the means suitable to found, conserve, and expand dominion. It is true that speaking absolutely, it encompasses all three of the above; nevertheless it appears that taken more strictly it designates conservation more than the other two, and of the other two more expansion than foundation. The reason is that reason of state presupposes a prince and a state which are not at all presupposed by foundation and only in part by expansion; rather they are preceded by them as is clear.[1] But the art of founding and expanding is the same because he who expands wisely has to establish a foundation to which he adds and where he establishes a foothold.[2]

[1] This sentence is unclear. They, that is, the prince and the state, are preceded by them, that is, by foundation and expansion.

[2] In *RS* 1596 Botero added at the start "A state is a firm rule over people." The addition reads in Italian: "Stato e un dominio fermo sopra popoli." I am grateful to Professor A. Enzo Baldini of the University of Turin for clarifying this for me. In it there seems to be an echo of the opening lines of *The Prince:* "Tutti li stati, tutti e' dominii che hanno avuto et hanno imperio sopra li uomini, sono stati e sono o republiche o principati." In *RS* 1596 he also reformulated and expanded the last four lines thus: "The reason is that reason of state presupposes the prince and the state (the former as the artificer, the latter as the material), which are not presupposed at all by foundation and in part by expansion; rather they are preceded by them. But the art of founding and expanding is the same because the principles and the means are of the same nature. And even if all that which is brought about by the above-mentioned causes is said to be brought about by reason of state, nevertheless this is said more of those things that cannot be reduced to ordinary and common reason." This final clause was probably also added in response to critics who contended that this was the normal understanding of reason of state. See, for example, Scipione Ammirato, *Discorso sopra C. Tacito* (Florence, 1594), book 12, chap. 1 (pp. 228–42). See *BD*, 67, n. 1 and 68, n. 3.

2 Division of Dominions

Dominions are of many types: ancient, new, poor, rich, and of other similar qualities, but coming more to our point, we say that some dominions possess superior power, others do not, some are natural, others acquired. We call natural those of which we are masters by the will of the subjects, either expressly as happens in the election of the king of Poland, or tacitly as is the case with legitimate succession in a state, and the succession is either clearly lawful or doubtful. By acquired we mean those that are obtained by purchase or the equivalent or by arms; by arms they are acquired either by sheer force or by agreement; agreement is either at the discretion of the conqueror or by treaty.[3] Furthermore, some dominions are small, others large, some middle-sized, and of these some are not absolutely such but in comparison to and with respect to those bordering them; so that a small dominion is such that it cannot exist by itself but needs the protection and support of another, as is the case with the Republic of Ragusa or Lucca; middle-sized is that which has the forces and sufficient authority to maintain itself without needing the support of another, as is the case with the dominion of the Venetian lords, the kingdom of Bohemia, the duchy of Milan, and the county of Flanders. We call those states large which have a notable advantage over their neighbors, such as the Turkish Empire and the Catholic King. Beyond this, some dominions are unified, others are not. We call those unified whose members are continuous and who touch one another, we call those dispersed whose members do not form a continuous body and are not of one piece as was the empire of the Genoese when they governed Famagusta[4] and the Ptolemais,[5] Faglie Vecchie,[6] Pera,[7] and Caffa,[8] or of the Portuguese with their states in Ethiopia, Arabia, India, and Brazil, and that of the Catholic King.

3 Of Subjects

The subjects, without which dominion cannot exist, are by nature settled or transient, peaceful or warlike, dedicated to trade or to the military, of

---

[3] The following is added in *RS* 1590 and later editions: "And their state is so much the worse as the resistance to the acquisition was greater."
[4] On the island of Cyprus.
[5] The town of St.-Jean-d'Acre, now Acre on the Israeli coast.   [6] Not known.
[7] A Genoese colony opposite Constantinople, today Galata.
[8] A Genoese colony in the Crimea, today Theodosie.

our faith or of some other sect; and if of another sect, completely infidel, or Jewish or schismatics or heretics; and if heretics, Lutheran, Calvinists, or of some other form of impiety.[9] In addition, they are all subjects of one type with the same law and form of subjection, or with different ones, as the Aragonese and the Castilians in Spain, the Burgundians and the Bretons in France.

4 Of the Causes of the Ruin of States

Works of nature fail through two types of causes, some intrinsic, some extrinsic; intrinsic I call excess and corruption of its early qualities, extrinsic fire, sword, and other forms of violence. In the very same way states are ruined by internal or external causes; internal are the incapacity of the prince, either because he is a child, because he is inept, because he is impious, or because he has lost his reputation which can happen in many ways. States are also ruined intrinsically by cruelty and licentiousness toward subjects which sullies the reputation of noble and generous men; this it was that chased from Rome the king and the Decemvirs, brought the Moors into Spain, and forced the departure of the French from Sicily. Dionysius the Elder,[10] having learned that his son had carried on with the wife of an honored citizen, reproved him harshly, demanding to know whether he had ever seen him do such a thing. And because the youth responded, "If you did not do it, it was because you were not the son of a king." "Nor will you be father of a king," he replied, "unless you change your ways." It is often disputed whether more states come to ruin because of the licentiousness of princes or because of their cruelty. To resolve this is not difficult. Cruelty gives birth to hatred and fear of him who uses it. Licentiousness generates hatred and contempt, so that cruelty leads to hatred which makes for opposition and to fear which makes for support – weak support however, because it lasts only a short time, whereas licentiousness does not in any way generate support but only hatred and contempt. Beyond this, cruelty weakens or kills the one subject to it, which licentiousness does not do. Other intrinsic causes of the ruin of states are envy, rivalry, discord, ambition among the nobles, frivolousness, instability and the furor of the multitude, the

---

[9] Added here in *RS* 1590 and subsequently: "And they ought to be held for more evil to the degree that they are of a more distant sect and further from the truth."

[10] Tyrant of Syracuse, 405–367 BCE.

inclination of the barons and the people for a different government.[11] External causes are the deceptions and power of enemies. So the Romans destroyed the Macedonians, the barbarians Roman grandeur. But which causes are more destructive? Without a doubt, the internal; rarely does it happen that external forces ruin a state which internal causes have not first corrupted.

From these two types of simple cause arises another which one can call mixed, when subjects consort with the enemy and so betray their country or their prince.

5 Which is the Greater Work, to Expand or to Conserve a State

Without a doubt the greater work is to conserve; human affairs proceed as it were naturally, now declining now growing after the manner of the moon to which they are subject, so that to hold them in place and, when they are growing, to sustain them in such a way that they neither fail nor crash is an enterprise of singular and nearly superhuman achievement. In making acquisitions opportunity plays a great part as does the disorder of enemies and the work of others, but the retention of what has been acquired is the fruit of an excellent *virtù*. One acquires by force but preserves with wisdom; force is found with many, wisdom with few. Moreover, whoever acquires and expands his dominion worries only about the external causes of the collapse of states whereas he who conserves has to deal with the internal and the external. The Lacedaemonians, wishing to demonstrate that it was a greater thing to conserve one's own than to acquire another's, punished those who had lost not their sword but their shield, and the Romans called Fabius Maximus "the shield" and M. Marcellus "the sword of the Republic," and there is no doubt that they made more of Fabius than Marcellus. Aristotle was also of the same opinion when in his *Politics* he wrote that the principal task of the legislator is not to constitute nor fashion a city but to see to it that it can maintain itself secure for a long time.[12] And Theopompus, king of

---

[11] The following is added in *RS* 1590 and subsequently: "Ambitious princes with little sense often ruin their own states by scattering their own forces, desirous of encompassing more than they can control; one can see this in the ventures of the Athenians and the Lacedaemonians and especially in Demetrius, king of Macedonia [r. 294–288 BCE] and Pyrrhus, king of Epirus [r. 295–272 BCE]."

[12] Aristotle, *Politics*. This is a free interpretation of the *Politics* which does not seem to be found in any particular passage (*BD*, 72, n. 5).

Sparta,[13] having added to the royal office the senate or council of ephors, responded to his wife who accused him of having weakened his rule that "it would be greater the more stable and firm that it was." But how does it come about (someone will ask) that those who acquire are considered greater than those who conserve? Because the results of him who increases his rule are more evident and more popular, make for a greater din and excitement, have more visibility and novelty of which people are beyond measure fond and desirous, so that it happens that military enterprises produce more delight and amazement than the arts of conservation and peace which, inasmuch as they have less turmoil and novelty, require more judgment and sense from him who maintains them. And so if rivers of great length are more noble than torrents, nevertheless many more people stop to admire a dangerous torrent than a tranquil river, so he is more admired who acquires than he who conserves.

6 Which States are More Lasting, the Large, the Small, or the Middle-Sized

It is certain that the middle-sized states are more apt to survive because the small due to their weakness are more easily exposed to the forces and affronts of the large states which, as birds of prey feed on the small and as the big fish on the small ones, devour them, and rise through their ruin. So Rome expanded through the destruction of neighboring cities, and Philip of Macedon through the oppression of the Greek republics. Large states stir up jealousy and suspicion in their neighbors which often leads them to ally, and many united accomplish what one cannot do. But there are also many more subject to the internal causes of ruin, because with size riches increase and with them vices, luxury, arrogance, licentiousness, avarice the root of all evil,[14] and the kingdoms which frugality has led to the heights fail because of their opulence. Besides this, size brings with it confidence in one's own forces, and confidence leads to negligence, leisure, disdain for subjects and for enemies, so that such states often survive more through their reputation based on past events than through present courage and principles. And as alchemy seems to the eye to produce gold but the gold loses its value at a closer look, so such states enjoy a great reputation but have little substance, similar to some high and great trees that are hollow and rotten and to some men

---

[13] From the late eighth to the early seventh century BCE.   [14] 1 Timothy 6:10.

with large bodies but little spirit, as experience makes evident. Sparta, so long as it remained within the borders prescribed by Lycurgus, flourished beyond all the other Greek cities in substance and in reputation. But when it expanded its imperium and subjugated the cities of Greece and the kingdoms of Asia, it then declined in such a way that the city, which before Agesilaus[15] had never seen the smoke nor even the forces of the enemy, after defeating the Athenians and despoiling Asia saw its citizens flee before the Thebans, a vile people and of no account, and hasten back to their own delightful environs and commit every crime under their own walls. The Romans after conquering the Carthaginians remained in fear of the Numantines for fourteen years. After conquering so many kings and subjugating so many provinces to their rule, they were torn to pieces by Viriatus in Spain[16] and by the banished Sertorius[17] in Lusitania, and by Spartacus in Italy; and they were besieged from every side and starved out by pirates.

Courage opens the way through difficulties to greatness but, once arrived there, it is immediately smothered by riches, weakened by culinary delights, deadened by sensual pleasures. It holds up through the wildest tempests and most dangerous storms on the high seas but it perishes and suffers shipwreck in port. Benevolent thoughts, high-minded intentions, honorable enterprises cease and in their place ascend pride, arrogance, ambition, the avarice of magistrates, and the insolence of the mob. No longer do captains find favor but buffoons, not soldiers but charlatans, not the truth but flattery. No longer is virtue esteemed but riches, not justice but bribes. Simplicity yields to deceit and goodness to malice, so that as the state grows the foundations of its strength are undermined, and as iron generates rust which eats it away and ripe fruit of itself produces worms which spoil it, so great states produce certain vices which little by little or sometimes at one stroke lay them low or give them as prey to their enemies. So much suffices for great states.

The middle-sized states are the most lasting because neither by great weakness are they vulnerable to violence nor by their great size are they exposed to the envy of others, and because their riches and power are moderate, their passions are also less vehement and ambition does not receive the same encouragement, nor does licentiousness find such stimuli as in the great states. The suspicion of neighbors holds them in check,

---

[15] Agesilaus II was king of Sparta from roughly 400 to 360 BCE.

[16] A rebel in Spain, 149–141 BCE.

[17] Sertorius, a Roman general during the civil wars, 121–72 BCE.

and if tempers fly and stir up trouble, they also quiet down and are easily calmed. Rome exemplifies this. There so long as it was a middle-sized state, few revolts lasted and at the sound of foreign wars they grew quiet and in every way subsided without bloodshed, but after the greatness of their empire opened the field for ambition and factions took root while enemies were lacking, and the wars and spoils of Numidia and the Cimbrians[18] fell to Marius, of Greece and Mithridates to Sulla, of Spain and Asia to Pompey, and of Gaul to Caesar, and they acquired a following and reputation and the means to maintain it, then war was no longer conducted with stools and chairs as in past rebellions but with fire and sword, and the struggles and wars ended only with the defeat of the contrary factions and of the Empire itself. So we see that some middle-sized powers have endured much longer than the largest ones. This is the case of Sparta and Carthage, and above all of Venice whose mid-sized dominion has been more stable and steady than any other. But even if middling size is more suitable for the endurance of a state than expansion, mid-sized states nevertheless do not long endure because princes are not satisfied and want to advance from a mid-sized to a great and even to the greatest state. So surpassing the limits of mid-size they expand beyond secure boundaries, as happened with the Venetians who wanting to encompass so much more than a mid-size state required, in the campaign against Pisa took on a huge debt without turning a profit[19] and in the league against Ludovico Sforza[20] came close to causing their own ruin. But should a prince realize the limits of a mid-sized state and be satisfied with them, his rule should long endure.

7 Whether United States or Dispersed Ones are More Lasting[21]

Dispersed states are separated into territories either in such a way that the territories are unable to assist one another because between them

---

[18] The Cimbrians were a Germanic tribe that migrated from the Jutland Peninsula and fought the Romans from 113 to 101 BCE.

[19] From 1496 to 1499, Venice took Pisa under its protection against Florence.

[20] At the end of 1498 Venice allied with the king of France against Ludovico il Moro, duke of Milan, until the duke fell from power in 1500.

[21] This is the title of the chapter as given by Botero. But one also might entitle it "Whether compact or composite states are more lasting." On the concept of the "composite state," see J.H. Elliott, "A Europe of Composite Monarchies," *Past and Present*, 137 (1992): 47–71, and the ensuing literature.

there lie powerful principalities either hostile or unreliable, or in such a way that they can assist one another and this in three ways: with the aid of funds, but this can be of great difficulty; through an understanding with the princes through whose lands it is necessary to pass; or, easily, through naval forces if all the territories of the state have a sea coast. Furthermore, the territories of a dispersed state are either so weak that they cannot maintain themselves nor defend themselves against their neighbors, or so great and powerful that they are superior or equal to their neighbors.

Now I would say that a great empire is without doubt more secure from the assaults and invasion of an enemy because it is large and united, and the union means greater vigor and force. But on the other hand it is more subject to the internal causes of ruin because size leads to confidence, confidence to carelessness, and carelessness to contempt and loss of reputation and authority. Power brings forth riches which are the mother of all pleasures, and pleasures the mother of every vice. And this is the reason that states fall from the summit: with their increase in power courage grows less and with great wealth virtue declines. The Roman Empire was at its peak under Caesar Augustus. Pleasures and licentiousness began to overwhelm virtue under Tiberius, and successively then under Caligula and the others. Vespasian reversed this trend somewhat with his courage, but Domitian worsened the situation with his vices. Matters returned to their pristine state with the goodness of Trajan and some few emperors who followed but after that they successively went hurling downward precipitously until they ended in ruin, and if sometimes they were assisted and kept standing, this happened not because of Roman valor but because of foreign emperors and captains. These emperors were Trajan who was Spanish, Antoninus Pius French, Septimus Severus African, Alexander Mamaean,[22] Claudius Dardanian, Aurelian of Moesia, Probus from Sirmium, Diocletian Dalmatian, Galerius Decian, Constans, who was the father of the great Constantine, Dardanian, Theodosius who can be said to have restored the Empire, Spanish. The same can be said of those captains who demonstrated some merit: Stilico, Ullin, and Aetius were Vandals, Castinus Scythian, Boniface Thracian, Ricimer, who defeated Beorgor King of the Alans, a Goth.[23]

---

[22] Changed to "Syrian" in later editions. This is probably an allusion to Alexander Severus, emperor from 222–235 CE, who was born in Caesarea of Lebanon (*BD*, 77, n. 1).

[23] These were all generals of the late Roman Empire.

So we see that Roman virtue, enfeebled and corrupted in such a way by pleasure, was not able to stand on its own feet or keep its head up without foreign assistance. And because their own interests and particular designs dictated the aid of the barbarians, and it often came with treason and betrayal, the Empire finally collapsed. An empire that does not possess internal strength cannot long survive in face of the plots and assaults of its enemies. So Spain, generally corrupt, fell to the power of the Moors within thirty months, and the Empire in Constantinople was subjugated by the Turks in a few years. Besides this, if in a united state there arises discord among the barons or an uprising among the people, or dissoluteness among the one and the other, it easily spreads like the plague or some other contagious disease to the healthy parts because of their nearness. And if the prince is given over to laziness and is inept, the compact state will more easily become demoralized and infected than the disunited one, and consequently it will become weaker in the face of its enemies.

On the other hand, the dispersed state is weaker against foreigners than the united one, because the disunity alone weakens it, and if its parts are so weak that each of itself is helpless against the attacks of its neighbors, or they are divided in such a way that one cannot come to the aid of another, a state so created will not long endure. But if the parts are able to aid one another and each is large and strong enough that it does not fear invasion, such a state ought not be considered less stable than a united one, because, first of all, if the parts are able to reciprocally assist one another, one cannot say that they are in fact dispersed, and even if the dispersed state is by its nature weaker than a united one, it yet has many advantages, first of all because it cannot be attacked all at once. And this so much the less the further one part is from another because one prince alone will not be able to do this and many together will unite only with difficulty. So it follows that when a state is attacked in one part, the others that remain undisturbed will always be able to come to the aid of the one that has been attacked, as we see in the way that Portugal has so often aided its state in the Indies. Moreover, the dissension of the barons and the insurrections of the people are not as widespread because the factions in one place do not predominate in the other, and the families, the friendships, the loyalties, and the networks do not extend so far, and it is easy for the prince with the loyal part to punish the rebels, and similarly other forms of corruption do not spread so far nor so rapidly through a dispersed state as through a united one, nor with such force, because the lack of unity interrupts the course of disorders and the distance among locations reduces the speed of their spread, and time always favors a legitimate prince and justice, and because it rarely happens that external causes bring about the ruin of a state which has not first become internally corrupt. *Nulla enim quamvis minima natio potest ab adversari perdelere, nisi propriis simultatibus se iosa consumperit* (For not even the least element can be destroyed by enemies unless it has first been undermined by its own enmities) says Vegetius.[24]

I do not consider less secure nor enduring dispersed states under the following two conditions that unite them, in this case the kingdom of Spain. First of all, the states that belong to this crown have sufficient forces that they are not alarmed by every movement of arms by their neighbors, as is attested by Milan and Flanders, which have been threatened so many times in vain by the French, and so also Naples and Sicily. Furthermore, even if the parts are distant from one another, one ought not in fact to consider them dispersed because, beyond the fact that the funds of which that crown has an abundance are available to all, they are united by the sea. There is no state that is so far that it cannot provide assistance, apart from Flanders due to the opposition of England, and the Catalans, the Biscayans, the Galicians, and the Portuguese so excel as mariners that one can truly say that they are masters of seamanship. Now the naval forces that these peoples have at hand create an imperium that otherwise seems disunited with its parts cut off from one another. But it ought to be considered united and as it were continuous, so much the more now that Portugal is united with Castile. These two nations, the former extending from the west toward the east and the latter toward the west, meet in the Philippine Islands and throughout such a grand tour touch upon islands, kingdoms, and ports at their command because they belong to their empire or to friendly princes, clients, or allies.

8 On the Ways to Conserve [a State]

The conservation of a state consists in the peace and quiet of the subjects, and this is of two types, as it is also in the case of a disturbance or a war; a disturbance arises either from your own [subjects] or from foreigners. Disturbances from your own subjects arise in two ways; either they fight among one another, and this we call civil war, or they fight against the

[24] Cf. *Concerning Military Matters (De re militari)*, 3, 10.

prince, and this we call an uprising or a rebellion. Now one avoids each of these through the use of those arts which gain for the prince love and reputation from his subjects because just as natural things are preserved by the same means whereby they were generated, so the causes of the preservation and foundation of states are the same. Now, in those first centuries there is no doubt that men set out to create kings and to give the principality and government of themselves to others, moved by the affection that they bore to them and by the highest esteem (which we call reputation) that they had for their valor; these two features, it is necessary to say, maintain the subjects in obedience and in peace. But what has the greater influence in the election of a king, reputation or love? Without a doubt it is reputation which leads people to give the government of the republic to others, not to please or show favor to them but for the good and the welfare of the community. So it follows that they elect not the more gracious and more friendly candidates but those in whom they recognize valor and *virtù*. So the Romans in perilous times entrusted their campaigns not to young and charming favorites but to mature personages of much experience: to the Manlii, the Papiri, the Fabii, the Decii, the Camilli, the Pauli, the Scipioni, the Marii. Camillus, hated and so banned from Rome, was in time of danger recalled and made dictator. M. Livius was many times scorned and condemned by the people and so for a long time, because of the ignominy and dishonor he received, he avoided the eyes of his fellow citizens; but in a time of extreme danger to the republic, he was created consul and then general against the brother of Hannibal, while all those were passed over who with every type of ambition sought to acquire the love and favor of the people. Reputation called L. Paulus to the Macedonian campaign, Marius to the Cimbrian, Pompey to the campaign against Mithridates. Reputation also gave to Vespasian, to Trajan, and to Theodosius the Empire in Rome, to Pepin and to Hugh Capet the kingdom of France, and to Godfrey and others that of Jerusalem.

But what is the difference between love and reputation? Both are based on *virtù*, but love is content with a mediocre *virtù* while reputation is obtained only through excellence. When the goodness and perfection of a man exceed the ordinary and arrive at a certain eminent level, however much he may be beloved inasmuch as he is good, nevertheless his lovability remains surpassed as it were by his excellence which brings him not so much love as esteem. And if this esteem is rooted in religion and piety, it is called reverence; if in the political and military arts, it is called reputation. If those things that are suited to make a prince beloved in the manner of his government are also suitable to make him esteemed, they will always possess a certain divine excellence. What is more beloved than justice? The excellence of Camillus's justice when he sent back that schoolmaster who had brought his students before him obtained for him such a reputation that it enabled him to open the gates of the Falerii when arms had not been able to do so.[25] Similarly Fabricius, when he returned to King Pyrrhus the doctor who had betrayed him, this so filled the king with wonder and amazement that he set aside thoughts of war and turned completely to negotiations for peace.[26] What is more beloved than honesty? Nonetheless, that outstanding action of P. Scipio when he returned that most beautiful young woman untouched to her husband, did not make him so much beloved as admirable, and it gained him such esteem and reputation with all that the Spaniards held him to be nearly a god descended from heaven.[27]

9 How Great Must the Excellence of the *Virtù* of a Prince Be

The fundamental principle of every state is the obedience of the subjects to its superior, and this is based on the eminence of the prince's *virtù*. As the elements and the bodies of which they are composed obey without opposition the movements of the heavenly spheres because of the nobility of their nature, and in the heavens the inferior follows the motion of the superior, so peoples submit voluntarily to the prince in whom shines forth some preeminence of *virtù* because no one refuses to obey or be subordinate to one who is superior to himself but he does do so to one who is inferior or even equal to himself. *Nec quemquam iam ferre potest Caesarumve priorem Pompeiusve parem* (Nor is Caesar able to bear anyone else as superior nor Pompey [anyone else] as equal).[28]

But it is important that the superiority of the prince not be exercised in irrelevant matters or those of little or no importance but in those which

---

[25] Camillus, 446–365 BCE, Roman general and statesman. When an enemy schoolteacher offered to Camillus a number of boys to be held as hostages by the Romans, Camillus sent them back to the enemy camp. See Machiavelli, *Discourses*, 3.20.

[26] See Machiavelli, *Discourses*, 3.20.

[27] By the laws of war at the time, Scipio might have kept her for himself. See Machiavelli, *Discourses*, 3.20.

[28] Lucan, *On the Civil War* (*Pharsalia*), 1.125.

elevate the spirit and the intelligence and which reveal a certain grandeur almost heavenly and divine, and that make a man truly superior and better than the others, because (as Livy says) *Vinculum fidei est melioribus parere* (The bond of loyalty is to obey one's betters)[29] and Dionysius, *Aeterna naturae legis est, ut inferiores praestantioribus pareant* (It is received as the eternal law of nature that inferiors obey those more excellent)[30] and Aristotle states that natural reason dictates that those who surpass others in intelligence and judgment should be princes,[31] and he says that nobles are to be honored because nobility is a certain virtue of family and blood and that it is likely that good men are born of good men and better men of better men;[32] for this reason tyrants fear good men more than evil ones and the large-hearted more than the cowardly because tyrants being unworthy and incapable of the rank assigned to virtue, with reason fear those who are deserving and worthy of it.

10 Of the Two Types of Excellence in the *Virtù* of a Prince

Now this excellence is either absolute or partial; it is absolute in those who in all or in most virtues surpass the level of mediocrity, partial in those who are ahead of others in those particular virtues that are proper to a ruler. In the first class among the emperors are Constantine the Great, Constans, Gratian, Theodosius, Justin, Justinian (if he had not been a Monothelite[33]), Tiberius II, Leo the Philosopher, Henry I, Otto I (if he had not persistently arrogated the authority to confer benefices), Otto III, Lothar II, Sigismund, Frederick III, Charles V, Ferdinand; among the kings of France are Clovis and Charles Martel (even if he did not have the title of king), Pepin, Charlemagne, Charles the Wise, Robert, and Louis VII and IX. Among the kings of Spain the most glorious have been Ricaredo, the first Catholic king of the Goths, Pelagius, Alfonso the Catholic, called such for having extirpated the Arians in Spain, Alfonso the Chaste, Ramiro, Alfonso the Great, Alfonso VII, Sancho,[34] who was

---

[29] Livy, *History of Rome*, 22.13. The citation is used in a sense a little different than in Livy (*BD*, 83, n. 3).

[30] Cf. Dionysius of Halicarnassus, *Roman Antiquities*, 1.5.

[31] Aristotle, *Politics*, 3.13 (1284b), 3.17 (1288a), 7.3 (1325b).   [32] Cf. ibid., 3.13 (1283b).

[33] Monotheletism was a heresy that asserted that there was only one will in Christ. It was condemned at the Third Council of Constantinople in 680–81.

[34] Sancho III (*c.* 1134–58), king of Castile.

as it were another Titus in Spain and was called "the Desired" as Titus
had been called the "World's Beloved," both of whom lived and reigned
only a short time, Alfonso VIII, James, king of Aragon, Ferdinand III,
Ferdinand called the Catholic.

Among the supreme pontiffs of the most eminent *virtù* were, after St.
Silvester, Julius I, Damasus, Innocent I, Leo the Great, Pelagius, Gregory I, and after him Boniface IV, Vitalianus, Adeodatus, Leo II, Conon
who because of the sanctity of his life was called "the Angelic," Constantine, Gregory II and III, Zacharias I, Stephen II, Adrian I, Leo III,
Pascal I, Eugene II, called the pope of the poor, Leo IV, Benedict III
made pope against his will, Nicholas I made pontiff in his absence and
also against his will, Adrian II, John IV, Leo IX who, chosen by Emperor
Henry, entered Rome as a private person and was there elected canon-
ically by the people, Nicholas II, Alexander II elected in his absence,
Gregory VIII[35] who restored the liberty of the church and the authority
of the Apostolic See after it had been persecuted by the emperors, Urban
II, author of that heroic expedition against the infidels, Pascal II, elected
against his will, Gelasius II, Callistus II, Anastasius IV, Alexander III, of
indomitable constancy against the schismatics and Emperor Frederick,
Clement III, and Clement IV who did not want to agree that his nephew
hold more than one prebend, Nicholas III called "the serene" because of
the integrity of his life and the moderation of his habits,[36] Nicholas V
elected against his will.

11 What are the Virtues that are Suited to Produce Love and Reputation

But although every virtue is suited to bring love and reputation to him
who is adorned with it, nevertheless some are suited more for love than
reputation, and some the contrary.[37] In the first class we place those
virtues which are totally aimed to benefit [others], humanity, courtesy,
mercy, and the others, which we are able to reduce to justice and liberality; in the other class we place those which contain a certain grandeur
and force of soul and ability, which are suited to great enterprises,
bravery, the military and political art, perseverance, vigor of soul and

---

[35] An error for Gregory VII.   [36] Probably an error for Nicholas IV (*BD*, 85, n. 4).

[37] This is corrected in *RS* 1590 to read "some more for reputation than love, and others, to
the contrary, more for love than reputation" (*BD*, 86, n. 1).

quickness of mind, all of which we include under the names of prudence and valor.

12 Of Justice

Now, the first way to benefit subjects is to preserve and to assure to each his own through justice, in which consists without a doubt the basis for peace and the establishment of concord among peoples. Christ Our Lord when instituting his Church as the best republic as it were, unified and fashioned it with charity, which is of such force and virtue that there justice is not necessary where it flourishes and reigns, because charity not only regulates the hand but unites the hearts, and where such a union is found, neither wrong nor injustice nor the occasion for justice is possible. But because men are ordinarily not perfect and charity regularly grows cold, it is necessary, to keep order in the city and to maintain peace and quiet in the community, that justice plant its roots there and make laws. Not even assassins and thieves are able to live together without some shadow of an excellent virtue; and the ancient poets said that not even Jupiter could rule the peoples suitably without the assistance of justice, and Plato entitled his books on politics *On Justice*. There is nothing more appropriate for a king than to render justice. So Demetrius, king of the Macedonians, after telling a woman who demanded justice that he did not have time to do so, received that memorable reply, "Then give up being king."[38] And there is no doubt that the first kings were created by the people for the administration of justice; the princes of the Jews, whom the kings succeeded, demanded to be called judges. And from the beginning all the cities of Greece (as Dionysius writes) were under the kings who decided disputes and rendered justice according to the laws.[39] So Homer called kings ministers of justice.[40] But when kings limited in their authority began to act as absolute and to abuse their authority, a large part of Greece changed its form of rule and government. But because in some cases the magistrates did not maintain the clear laws of the land nor were these adequate to uphold the reputation of the magistrates, they returned to a royal authority but under another name. The Thessalians called the

---

[38] Botero here confuses Demetrius with Philip of Macedon; see Plutarch, *Sayings of Kings and Commanders*, "Philip," 32.

[39] Dionysius of Halicarnassus, *Roman Antiquities*, 5.74.   [40] *Iliad*, 1.238–39.

supreme magistrates "archons," the Lacedaemonians "harmostes" (governors), the Romans dictators and, being horrified by dictatorial majesty, made Pompey only a consul, giving him the extraordinary authority of a dictator but the ordinary title of consul. The kings of Egypt were so concerned about justice that they made magistrates swear that they would never obey their commands if they knew them to be unjust, and Philip the Handsome, king of France, prohibited judges to take account of or show respect for royal letters that pertained to justice if they did not consider them to be lawful.

13 Two Types of Royal Justice

There are two types of royal justice, the one between the king and his subjects and the other between subject and subject.

14 Of the Justice of a King toward his Subjects

Peoples are obligated to give to their prince all those powers that are necessary for him to maintain justice among them and to defend them from the violence of their enemies, so that he, satisfied to remain within these limits, will not scourge or torment his subjects with unaccustomed impositions out of proportion to their ability to pay, nor will he permit that ordinary and suitable impositions are harshly exacted and increased by rapacious ministers because peoples burdened beyond their strength will either leave the country or revolt against the prince or go over to his enemies. So Emperor Tiberius responded to a minister who proposed unaccustomed means to raise money that a good shepherd ought not to skin the sheep but be satisfied with shearing them. And I do not want to leave out recounting what Polydore Vergil writes about St. Edward, king of England; having been presented a huge sum of money collected avariciously by his ministers, gazing at it he saw a demon sitting upon and reveling in it; for this reason, filled with fear and horror, he commanded that it be immediately returned.[41] No less should he keep from spending the income wastefully (which is nothing else than the sweat and

---

[41] Polydore Vergil, *Historiae Anglicae libri XXVII* (Basel, 1555), ed. Dana F. Sutton (The Philological Museum, 2010), www.philological.bham.ac.uk/polverg (accessed April 17, 2015), 8.8.

blood of his vassals), because there is nothing that more afflicts and more torments the people than to see their prince throw away needlessly the money that they with such labor and hardship provided him for the support of his grandeur and the maintenance of the republic. And because vanity has neither limit nor measure, it follows that he who spends needlessly falls into disorder and hardship, and in order to escape it, turns to fraud, iniquity, and assassination of the innocent. So Caligula, having in one year gone through sixty-seven million scudi which Emperor Tiberius had over many years with inestimable diligence accumulated, and lacking any measure to his expenditures, resorted to robbery and every sort of cruelty. Solomon spent a good part of the one hundred and twenty million left him by his father on the construction of palaces and parks, on feasts and incredible pomp. Even if he did not find himself reduced to necessity, he burdened his kingdom with so many taxes that, unable to bear them any longer, the greater portion of the population rebelled under his son Roboam.

It also belongs to this type of justice to distribute rewards and honors proportionately, balancing burdens with benefits and easing charges with recognition. Where labors and services are recognized and rewarded virtue takes root and valor flourishes because everyone desires and seeks comfort and reputation (the lower classes more comfort, the upper classes more reputation), and they seek these by the means which they see to be valued by the prince, with virtue if he is pleased with it, with adulation if he is vain, with ceremony if he is pompous, with money if he is avaricious. But nothing is more harmful to a king than to assign titles and offices on the basis of favor rather than merit because, beyond the fact that this is an affront to virtue, the outstanding men, seeing that the unworthy are preferred, abandon his service and frequently obedience to him too, and the people who are governed by such men see themselves as little valued and revolt against the prince himself because of hatred of his minister, and if the prince wants to support him, he himself loses credit and reputation and brings himself into a labyrinth from which he can emerge only with difficulty. And there is no other way to conserve his reputation than to assign magistracies and offices to competent and worthy persons. No less dangerous is the invidious distribution of his favor because as soon as a disproportionate grace comes to light, envy works in such a way in the souls of the common people and contempt in those of the high-minded that they begin to think about abandoning him. They will not hesitate to oppose the king by bringing down the favorite, as happened in England to Edward II because of the excessive favor shown to a certain steward, Hugo,[42] and in Brittany to Duke Francesco because of the unlimited confidence he had in Peter Landais; the nobility conspired against him and forced the duke to give that wretched man into their hands whom they then strangled.[43] And in Naples the favors shown foolishly by Giovanna II to Pandolfello Alopo and Giovanni Caracciolo were the cause of so many troubles,[44] so much the more since one who is favored more than his rank and merit dictate, exercises restraint only with difficulty. This increases the envy already felt toward him and adds, as we are accustomed to say, fuel to the fire. Because it has no foundation in merit and valor he is necessarily fearful for his own high position, and he opposes virtue with all his power and keeps far from the eyes and grace of the king all those who through the labors that they have endured and the services they have performed have merited of him. He considers the rise of another his own downfall. Since the good are excluded in this way, who does not recognize that matters devolve into the hands of low types and those more quick to flatter with their tongue than to work effectively with their hands? Those promoted to judgeships and to governmental offices will not be persons who look to the service of the prince and the benefit of the people but to the satisfaction and favor of those who appointed them. So the court is filled with factions, the kingdom with dissension, the barons with rancor, and the cities with grumbling.

15 Of Justice between Subject and Subject

It is especially the task of the prince to see that justice prevails among his subjects which consists in maintaining the country and the cities free of violence and fraud. Exiles, thieves, assassins, and murderers cause violence. They ought to be kept in check by vigorous and intimidating measures. It is of little benefit that enemy armies and forces are kept at a distance if those who perhaps do more harm are active at home. Fraud, even if it receives little notice, does not for that reason cause insignificant damage: to manipulate weights and measures, to falsify testaments and contracts and to counterfeit money, to lessen commerce with monopolies, to steal provisions, and to do similar things which after the manner

---

[42] The influence of Hugues Spencer on Edward II caused a large number of the barons to rebel and compelled the king to abdicate in 1327 (*BD*, 90, n. 1).

[43] Landais was the favorite of Francis II, duke of Brittany (1433–88).

[44] These two lovers of Giovanna were assassinated.

of underground mines destroy concord and peace. If the prince will put a stop to such abuses he will gain incredibly the love and affection of the people. Louis XII of France was called "father" by the people for the care he took and the solicitude he showed to help them and to defend them from oppression by the nobles. But there is no matter to which the prince ought to pay more attention than usury, because it is nothing other than larceny, or even worse. The usurer was condemned by the ancients, as Cato wrote, to pay quadruple if he took more than twelve per cent, the robber only to pay double.[45] This plague often caused disorder and greatly endangered the republic of Athens and the city of Rome because of the extreme misery usurers created for both peoples, and the kings of France have more than once been compelled to expel the Italian bankers. And how does it help the prince if he does not burden his vassals immoderately but allows them to be ruined by the avarice of the usurers who without working nor contributing any benefit to the republic consume the wealth of individuals? So much for individuals. Usury also destroys the public treasury and ruins the public income. Customs and taxes create adequate income when real commerce flows, entering and exiting your states and as it passes through paying tribute at seaports and river crossings, at city gates and other suitable locations. Now commerce is not able to flow properly if money is not invested in it. And who does not know that those who want to grow rich through usury give up trade because one cannot engage in it without risking one's wealth and without exertion of body and mind, and with a piece of paper selling partly time and partly the use of money, draw interest from money and so enrich themselves without effort? They are like certain wasps who without exerting themselves or being of any use, invade a nest of bees and devour the fruit of their industry and labor. So in this way, since everyone prefers to earn without effort, the town squares are necessarily deserted, the arts are abandoned, commerce is interrupted because the artisan abandons his shop, the peasant his plow, the nobleman sells his inheritance and changes it into money, and the merchant, whose calling requires him to travel untiringly from one country to another, remains at home. Inasmuch as the cities lose whatever they have that is beautiful and good, taxes decline, customs produce no income, and the treasury is depleted, and the people, reduced to extreme misery and desperation, desire a change in the state. So Asia twice went over to Mithridates

---

[45] Cato the Elder, *De agricultura*, preface, 1.

with a great slaughter of the Romans because with their infinite usury the Romans had destroyed their wealth in the manner of Harpies.[46] In Athens Solon gained praise for ending or at least moderating usury, as did Lucullus in Asia, and Caesar in Spain. The riches of a prince depend upon the wealth of individuals. Their wealth consists in their posses-sions and in the real exchange of the fruits of the earth and of indus-try, in imports and exports, shipping from one place to another either within a kingdom or from other countries. The usurer not only does none of these things but, fraudulently taking in money for himself, takes from others the means of doing business. We have in Italy two flourish-ing republics, Venice and Genoa. Of these two Venice is way ahead of Genoa both in its government and in its greatness. If we seek the reason for this, we will find it to be the case because the Venetians, engaging in commerce, become moderately rich as individuals but infinitely so in common whereas the Genoese, active in banking, have increased private wealth beyond measure but have greatly impoverished public revenues.

16 Of the Ministers of Justice

Because it is not fitting that a prince himself decide cases or hand down sentences, it is necessary that he provide sufficient competent ministers who act on his behalf. So he ought to use great care in selecting them and then in retaining them in office. Let him choose, with the partic-ular care that has always been employed by wise republics and princes, men endowed with the knowledge and experience necessary for the task that he wants to give them as well as with incorruptible virtue. Emperor Alexander Severus, before sending governors into the provinces, pub-lished their names many days ahead of time, so that if some vice of theirs should come to light, he would be able to change the appointment and assign the office to another. Those princes fail notably who sell magistra-cies; this is nothing other than to promote avarice rather than justice to tribunals. It is difficult for a judge who receives gifts to be fair in his judg-ment (because, as God says, gifts blind even wise men);[47] how much less so one who buys the office and enters not as it were a field of thorns and brambles but into a most fertile and abundant possession? Louis XII, king of France, was accustomed to say that those who purchased their

---

[46] Asia here is the Roman province of Asia Minor.
[47] Deuteronomy 16:19, Ecclesiastes 20:31.

offices sold at a higher price retail what they had purchased at a lower price wholesale. Aristotle criticized the laws of Lycurgus because they provided that a magistracy had to be sought by the one who was judged worthy of it rather than assigned to one deserving of it even though he did not want it.[48] What would he have said if he had seen it given to the one who bought it? Polybius preferred the Romans to the Carthaginians. In Carthage one obtained honors openly through gifts; this was considered a capital crime in Rome. The two republics recognized virtue differently, and so the qualities necessary and the means used to obtain rewards differed greatly in them.[49]

But because I said that practical knowledge is sought in officials, I do not want to fail to say that the kings of China assign magistracies according to a particular order, first to beginners at the lowest rank and then gradually to those of higher rank, so that after gathering experience at the first level they rise to a higher one. With us these processes are established not by laws but through the diligence that ought to be employed in the election of magistrates. A wise prince will be able through different means to acquire knowledge of the competence and integrity of the persons that he wants to promote for the administration of justice and the government of the people. Among these means are evaluations by worthy men because the judgment of a person without passion or interest cannot go wrong. The illustrious actions and as it were heroic bravery of someone amount to a powerful argument because such deeds result from outstanding *virtù* and demand that a man not do anything unworthy of the reputation that he has acquired. Knowledge of past conduct in grave matters also helps because on the basis of past actions one can draw highly probable conclusions about the future. It helps to have modesty and moderation of spirit, which are revealed by a consistency of life; from a well-composed spirit one can expect only well-regulated actions. Liberality and beneficence help; one who is generous and kind will not easily be led to act unjustly toward another. A weighty argument is public opinion and reputation because it rarely deceives, and it leads to office more than virtue, reputation, and standing. So the Spartans in choosing their officials put a few men in a room near the place where the people were assembled. Then in an order determined by lot they called out the names of the candidates, and then they listened with attentive ears to the applause and approval that each elicited. They then chose the candidate

---

[48] *Politics*, 2.9 (1271a), 12–13.　　[49] *The Histories*, 6.56.

who in this way was understood to enjoy the greatest regard and reputation of the multitude, because it rarely happens that he who receives
the approval of the common opinion of men is not truly that for which he
is taken to be. Here it should be noted that the poor provide a much more
trustworthy testimony of the virtues of persons than the rich because the
rich are motivated by ambition and design, the poor more by respect for
virtue and zeal for the common good. On this point it occurs to me that
a Japanese named Bernardo happened to be in Rome at the time of the
creation of Pope Marcello[50] and was then walking through the city at the
precise time of his election. Immediately he said that it had been a good
choice. When asked how he knew this, he replied, "Because the poor celebrate and rejoice." Age is also a factor as in many other matters, because
the vehemence of their passions renders young men incapable of governing others because he who does not govern himself will not be able to
rule others well. Ancient legislators allowed only rich citizens to become
magistrates because they thought that the poor and needy would only
be able to refrain from extortion with difficulty; but this is a matter
of little importance. It is necessary that interior virtue and conscience
restrain the spirit and the hand; otherwise there will be no effective remedy because, if avarice takes root in the soul, it will transport the rich
man much further beyond limits than the poor man, because if the latter
wants to grow rich, the former will do everything to become very rich,
and if necessity induces the poor man to some improper action, cupidity,
the root of all evil, will induce the rich man to something much worse.

Of greater consideration is whether a judge or other official ought to
be a native of the country or a foreigner. Foreign judges were brought
into Italy in Florence, in Lucca, and in Genoa, and in several other cities
of Italy, to deal with the factions of these peoples, divided as they were
in Guelph and Ghibelline. Two foreign judges were elected for Florence
to remove the mistrust and dissatisfaction that usually arose over judgments between the parties after the city had recovered its liberty following the death of Frederick II,[51] and the factions and civil wars had
been reduced to a degree. They adjudicated the differences among the
citizens. One was called captain of the people and the other *podestà*.[52] The

---

[50] Pope Marcello II reigned only from April 9 to May 1, 1555, when he died.

[51] December 13, 1250.

[52] In reality the institution of the *podestà* had existed for a long time in Florence; only the
captain of the people was introduced after the death of Frederick. Both offices had political
and military as well as judicial functions (*BD*, 97, n. 4).

disadvantage with a citizen judge is that he allows himself to be easily swayed by the interests of his friends and relatives. A foreign judge, realizing the weakness of his position, will seek support from the leading citizens in order to maintain and defend it. Hence it would please me to have neither a foreigner nor a native of the place exercise the office, but someone from another area subject to us where the factions of the city in which the tribunal is located do not rule. For this reason Marcus Aurelius ordained that no one govern his own native place and Philip the Fair of France that no one be a judge in the territory where he was born.

17 On the Retention of Magistrates in Office

But it is not enough to take great care in the selection of magistrates. It is also necessary to take every precaution, after they have been promoted, that they remain incorrupt because many doves become crows and lambs wolves, and there is nothing that more reveals the interior of a man than a magistracy because it places power in his hand, and that man is truly virtuous who has the opportunity to do evil but does not do it. Of Vespasian one reads that he employed such diligence and care restraining the officials of the city and the prefects of the provinces that they were never more moderate nor just. Today, the means to ensure their integrity are diverse. The first is to pay them and to threaten them with serious punishments for accepting presents. The kings of China do this in a singular way; they provide judges with provisions and living quarters, furnishings, aides, servants, and all that belongs to their comfort and status, so that no other thought remains for them than to attend with their whole mind to the administration of justice and to the office committed to them. They are enjoined with such severity and strictness that they are able to enter the court room or give an audience only when they have fasted, and if permission is granted to a weak person to take a cordial or something similar, he is not permitted to drink wine. It is important also, to assure the good administration of justice, that the prince does not allow his ministers, however grand might be their rank, the final judgment and the absolute power to make laws, but that he subjects them as much as possible to the prescriptions of the laws, reserving final judgment to himself because he is sure of the laws but not of the judgment of another who is subject to various passions. He who has complete authority in giving judgment often does not make use of that diligence which is proper to master the case and to understand the applicable laws. But let us move on. The Romans were restrained by the fear of being accused themselves because in that city, so full of ambitious rivalry, there was no one so powerful that he did not have an adversary who sought every opportunity to bring him down and humble him. Not only did private feuds come to light but public wrongs also were avenged. A few severe prosecutions of those who act unjustly suffice because the punishment of one deters thousands of others. Cambyses, king of the Assyrians,[53] having found a judge named Sisami to be at fault, had him skinned alive, and he covered with his skin the seat of judgment on which he had wanted his son to sit and hold court. Of what importance do we believe was this severe and almost cruel example in making others restrain themselves? Some princes make use of syndics or visitors as they are called, but there is great danger of corruption in this remedy. So Cosimo, Grand Duke of Tuscany,[54] made use of several secret spies who, happening to be present on various occasions as persons beyond suspicion, informed him of everything that they had heard about the actions of his officials. This method appears to me to be better than syndics because one syndic is easily corrupted and two without great difficulty; many are a financial burden to the prince and to the people. Not so with spies. They are not known, and they do not wish to be known, and because they are not able to reconcile their reports, they are not able to deceive the prince, and they cost little. Some princes visit their states themselves, listening to the complaints of the people, learning about the progress of the ministers, and, finally, reviewing everything that has been done. This Trajan undertook more than any other emperor, visiting nearly the whole Roman Empire. Aritperto, king of the Lombards,[55] celebrated for his exercise of justice, was accustomed to travel about in disguise and cleverly to spy out whatever was spoken ill of him or his ministers. And in truth it is necessary that princes either hear or see for themselves what is going on, because all the other methods are more or less corruptible as well as the officials themselves. The ways to deceive a prince who makes use only of the eyes and ears of others, and the tricks to get him to take black for white are so great that it is not humanly possible to defend himself from all of them. A gentleman with great practical experience of courts told me that for a king to understand the truth of things it would be necessary for him to

---

[53] Cambyses, the son of Cyrus the Great, ruled from 530–522 BCE.
[54] Duke of Florence 1537–69, Grand Duke of Tuscany 1569–74.
[55] Aritperto reigned from 653–61.

be deaf not to be deceived by thousands of false reports but rather, standing on the top of a high tower, to see everything through a looking-glass. But since this is not possible, let him make use of spies, intervene himself often in the courts, visit in disguise now one place now another, and listen to the truth from one who has no fear. Tiberius Caesar was accustomed, either seated or walking, to speak to his judges, warn them and remind them of their office, their obligation to obey the laws, the burden on their conscience, and the importance of the cases with which they dealt. The doges of Venice did the same. Caesar Augustus read various books and was accustomed to note in them all that pertained to good government, and he then sent a copy to his magistrates according to the needs of each which he knew from the evaluations that each had received.

18 Words of Caution regarding the Administration of Justice

There are many things that ought to serve for the administration of justice, but let us speak of two, more as words of caution than as precepts. The first is that it be uniform and the second that it be speedy. We have spoken above about how a prince is able to keep his ministers in check. But it is not enough that the minister keeps the balance straight and steady if he boldly bends and distorts it by pardoning one who deserves punishment and grants life and continued residence to one who deserves a thousand deaths and a thousand exiles. Truly, to show mercy belongs to the prince. The judges are bound to proceed according to the law. Only the prince can moderate its rigor and temper its harshness with equity.[56] But he should not pardon when it results in prejudice to justice or to the republic. Not to justice, because it ought to be the rule and the norm of every political government, and to pardon one whose crime cannot be excused by ignorance or by righteous grief is not to show mercy but to commit iniquity. Nor to the republic, because the principal purpose for which the people pay tribute and taxes to the prince is so that he maintain peace and quiet through the administration of justice. Pardon granted without respect to equity or the public good upsets everything and from this there often follows the ruin of states because God punishes

---

[56] Botero is here dealing with the classical moral issue of equity or *epikeia*; he disagrees with Thomas Aquinas, *Summa theologiae*, 2.2, q. 120, ad 3, who seems to allow the practice of *epikeia* to other than the ruler.

in princes the sins of those guilty of murder or unscrupulous business practices whom they have pardoned, as can be seen in the cases of Saul and Ahab.[57]

I do not want to omit saying that one ought never to easily dispense from the nature of a punishment. When Giovanni di Vega was viceroy of Sicily,[58] he was persistently implored that a grandee of that kingdom who was condemned to death for parricide be put to death secretly (and he was offered thirty thousand scudi for this). He responded with those memorable words, justice does not take place if it is not carried out in its proper place.

The other condition is that it be speedy. Everyone desires this. But there is no end to the supplications and memorials made to the prince and magistrates; the prolongation of the case in this way wears down even the party in the right so that when sentence is pronounced in its favor it takes no pleasure in the outcome because the expense involved is frequently greater than the funds at issue. I remember a case in Paris where six scudi were at issue; he who lost the case was condemned beyond this to pay sixty scudi in expenses. Now when such an expense is required to obtain justice, the poor desire and seek it in vain and turn instead to give up their right rather than litigate it. Now, a suitable way to make justice expeditious and to cut off such delaying tactics would be to commit the matter to a committee of nobles. I do not believe that this would be impossible. Julius Caesar, a figure of great valor in wars, did not judge this consideration unworthy of himself whereby, because the administration of civil law was scattered here and there and had almost disappeared, he entrusted to outstanding men the task of shaping it and of selecting the laws most necessary and useful. Vespasian made a great effort to ensure that suits were decided expeditiously, and he chose some outstanding persons to whom he gave the authority to provide summary justice. Titus, his son, because of his desire to shorten lawsuits, prohibited *de eadem re pluribus legibus agi et quaeri de cujusdam defuncti statu ultra certos annos* (that many laws deal with the same matter and that suits regarding the property of a deceased person be introduced after a certain number of years).[59] And the Catholic King wrote recently to the senate of Milan that it would be a great service if someone would propose a more brief and more expeditious way of administering justice and bringing lawsuits to an end. The

---

[57] 1 Samuel 15:9 and 1 Kings 20:34.   [58] 1547–57.
[59] Suetonius, *Twelve Caesars*, "Titus," 8.14.

laws are infinite but this would be of little import if subtlety of mind had not found so many at least apparent contradictions, so many diverse and contrary interpretations, and finally, so many ways to obscure the truth and call into question the certain, so that the administration of justice has never been in a worse state. There is nothing worse than the multitude of doctors who continually write and who, even if they always show little judgment, add to the number. He wins not who speaks better but who cites the most. And still the truth ought not to be found by authority but by reason, nor by the number of opinions but by the force of the proofs.

19 On Liberality

One also does good by liberality, and this in two ways: one is to free the needy from misery, the other to promote *virtù*.

20 On Freeing the Needy from Misery

There is no work more royal nor more divine than to aid the poor. Nothing is more praised in Scripture over everything else than the mercy of God and the care and protection that he has for the suffering and the poor, and he recommends the same most strictly to princes, and one cannot imagine anything more suited and effective to win over the minds of the populace and to bind them to their lord. The Jews take it as a maxim that almsgiving preserves their families and contributes to their greatness. So we see that the most famous Christian princes have been the most liberal toward the needy: the Constantines, the Charlemagnes, the Theodosiuses, and others. I do not want to leave out Robert, king of France,[60] who with the abundance of his alms stabilized the kingdom and crown of France in the house of Hugh Capet, whose son he was, by feeding a thousand poor and also providing them with carriages so that they might follow the court and pray for him. Nor do I want to omit Louis IX,[61] who reigned happily for forty-four years; he regularly supported one hundred and twenty poor people, during Lent one hundred and forty. And what will I say about Louis, duke of Savoy,[62] so kind toward the poor and so generous toward the needy, who engaged in no

---

[60] Robert the Pious, king of France (r. 996–1031).
[61] Saint Louis reigned from 1226–70.
[62] Duke of Savoy and Piedmont (r. 1440–65), called "the Generous."

other pastime than to feed the hungry, clothe the naked, and provide aid to whomever had need of it? And if liberality always becomes a prince, yet is it of greater efficacy through the effect of which we speak at times of public calamities when hunger or want or plague or earthquake or fires or floods or the scourges of enemies or war or any other such event afflicts or torments them. Titus, who was an example of a most friendly prince and for this reason was called "the delight of mankind," in times of plague or other disasters showed not only the care of a prince but the affection of a father toward the afflicted, consoling them with letters and helping them effectively in every way that he could. And if the disasters are so great that little can be done to help them, he at least ought to demonstrate sympathy, as Caesar Augustus did after the slaughter of Varus's army in Germany, and as the king of the Jews did in the attack on Jerusalem when there was extreme hunger. He put on sackcloth in order to placate God's anger and to show that he shared the distress of his people. Indeed, public disasters provide the appropriate situation and the best occasion that a prince can encounter to win over the souls and hearts of his subjects. At that time it is necessary to sow seeds of benevolence and to plant love in the hearts of subjects which will grow and return with interest of one hundred per cent. This he ought to do so much the more promptly the more that his rank and his office require it, because the need of a private person can be met by an individual but the disaster of a community requires the remedy from its prince. Besides, it is not expedient that when a private individual wants clearly to provide a remedy, he allows him to become involved, because it does not contribute to its security when a community becomes so indebted to a private man. The Romans knew this when they killed Cassius, Manlius Capitolinus, and the one and then the other Gracchus because they created a bond with the Roman people that was not proper for a private citizen partly through their generous distribution of grain during a time of famine and partly with laws that benefited the multitude. It is highly effective to encourage love for a prince if he gives up something himself in order not to burden or cause hardship for the people.

21 The Promotion of *Virtù*

Liberality serves not only to raise the poor man out of his poverty but even more to foster and promote *virtù* because this sort of generosity, beyond the fact that it does not create envy since it is directed toward persons who merit it, fosters talent, supports the arts, allows the sciences to flourish, and adds luster to religion which is the supreme ornament and splendor of states and binds the people closer to their prince. Outstanding men, in letters or in other areas, are as it were leaders of the multitude that depends on their judgment; they remain indebted to the king because of the favor and benefits they receive from him, and they bind the rest to him. So all outstanding princes have fostered outstanding talent as well as virtue. Alexander wanted never to be portrayed except by Apelles nor sculpted except by Lysippus. Even though he favored all artists, Caesar Augustus did not much like that his name be celebrated except in a serious way by outstanding persons, and he commanded the presidents of the provinces not to permit that his name be used in the competitions among poets and other writers so that it not be degraded. Theodosius, in order to promote the sciences and liberal studies, founded, as some claim, the studium of Bologna, and increased the number of professors and stipends at the school of Rome. Emperor Justinian, although not only unlearned but illiterate, showed prudence when he greatly fostered letters and the liberal arts. Charlemagne, king of France, was unique in this respect. Besides an infinite number of Latin and Greek schools that he founded throughout his realm, he founded the universities of Paris and Pavia, restored that of Bologna, worked to discover outstanding talent, praised the arts, stimulated *virtù* so that during his time learning and morals flourished marvelously. With the arts no less than through his military valor he gained for himself the title "the Great." Emperor Constantine Ducas,[63] although with no knowledge of letters, favored enthusiastically the sciences and learned men, and he was accustomed to say that he would desire to be ennobled rather for his learning than for his imperial title. Although still a youth, Otto III earned the admiration of the whole world by the favor that he showed to letters and to the lettered.

22 Words of Caution about Liberality

Three cautions deserve mention. The first is that one not give to the unworthy because the gift, beyond the fact that it is poorly invested when given to one who does not merit it, wrongs worthy persons and beyond this, it wrongs *virtù*. So it happens that subjects seeing their prince generous toward those without merit, disdain *virtù* and embrace

---

[63] Emperor of the East (r. 1059–67).

every other means to obtain his favor and secure rewards which although they are owed only to *virtù*, are given more readily for everything else. Because his predecessor had badly misused the public income and funds, Emperor Basil the Macedonian[64] sent into exile those who had received money from him as a gift until they made restitution. The second caution is that he not give immoderately because this cannot last long before the prince extends his hand where he ought not to do so, turning to robbery and becoming a tyrannical king. In fourteen years Nero gave away more than fifty million scudi but, in order to give to his flatterers and other similar types, he assassinated good men, ruined the rich and the honorable in order to enrich the rascals and the worthless. Galba revoked all the gifts bestowed by him.

Finally, one ought not to give at once all that one intends to give but to do so little by little, so that he who receives is bound to the giver by the hope of receiving more. But he who receives all at once withdraws and is satisfied with this, so that as a gentle rain waters and sinks further into the earth, so liberality exercised with measure and reason is more effective for eliciting and preserving the good will of him who is benefited.

---

[64] Basil I, emperor of the East (r. 867–86).

Book Two

1 Of Prudence

We now come to those things that lead to reputation; they are principally two: prudence and valor. These are the two pillars on which every government ought to rest. Prudence serves the prince as his eye, valor as his hand. Without the former, he would be as a blind man, without the latter he would be powerless. Prudence aids counsel and valor power. The former commands, the latter executes; the former perceives the difficulties of an enterprise, the latter overcomes them; the former draws up a plan, the latter puts it into effect; the former refines the judgment, the latter emboldens the heart of great personages.

2 Of the Knowledge Suitable to Sharpen Prudence

For no one is it necessary to know more things, as Vegetius says, than for a prince whose knowledge is useful and advantageous to his many subjects.[1] But in particular not only useful but necessary for him is the knowledge of all those things regarding affections and behavior about which the moral philosophers write abundantly, and of the methods of government which the political writers explain; moral philosophy communicates knowledge of the common passions and politics teaches how, with rules of good government, to moderate or encourage these passions and the effects that follow from them in the subjects. And because war also is the responsibility of the prince, he ought to have complete

---

[1] *Concerning Military Matters,* 1, Proemium.

knowledge of military matters, of the qualities of a good captain, of a good soldier, of the way to choose them, to draw them up in battle formations, to improve them, and also knowledge of the subjects that are related to military science, geometry, architecture, and all that is related to mechanics in which Julius Caesar stood out. But I do not intend that he attend to these matters as an engineer or as a craftsman but as a prince, that is, that he have enough knowledge of them that he know how to distinguish the true from the false and the good from the wicked, and from the many proposals made to him, to choose the best. It is not his responsibility to construct bridges or engines of war, nor to emplace or handle artillery nor to design or build fortresses but to make good use of those who make profession of such skills.

But because the arts of peace and the military arts are not well served without an eloquence that soothes tempers, quiets the republic, and leads the people, he must stand out in it. Because eloquence is not able to be vigorous, effective, noble, without knowledge of the natural world, which is the foundation for things artificial, it would be well for him to understand enough for him to be able to make judgments and to speak intelligently about it. To have knowledge of the disposition of the world, of the order of nature, of the movements of the heavens, of the qualities of simple and compound bodies, of the generation and corruption of things, of the essence of the soul, of its powers, of the properties of herbs, plants, rocks, minerals, of the affections and as it were of the behavior of animals, of the production of imperfect substances, rain, clouds, hail, thunder, snow, lightning, rainbows, of the origins of springs, rivers, lakes, winds, earthquakes, the ebb and flow of rivers and the various movements of the sea, they all stimulate the intelligence, enlighten judgment, and raise the soul to great things. From all this is born judgment in administration of the republic and magnanimity for undertakings, as we know of Alexander the Great, and a certain grandeur in speaking and talking as one reads of Pericles who, shining brightly and thundering, turned Greece upside down, winning over the people to courses they had opposed. This outstanding personality learned eloquence not from the rhetoricians but from the greatest philosopher of his times.[2] Nor ought a prince to be terrified by the variety and greatness of the matters that we propose to him, nor fail to trust in his intelligence or in the times, for what is difficult for a private person, and perhaps impossible, ought to easily stir a prince to

---

[2] Anaxagoras.

action. And among the other means to achieve outstanding success, one is to have near him persons scarce in every profession: mathematicians, philosophers, captains, soldiers, outstanding orators from whom at table and elsewhere he is able to learn in a few words what is learned in the schools in many months. Let him put to these men questions for discussion while walking, riding, and on every other occasion. Let him keep them on their toes in such a way that they come into his presence prepared and with a desire to converse about notable and rare happenings. Spending time with them that others spend with jesters he will acquire notably superior knowledge that will be of the greatest moment for the perfection of his intellect and the governance of his people. Who was ever more occupied with perpetual projects than Alexander the Great and Julius Caesar? They never abandoned the study of the sciences, and they never took less account of the pen than of the sword. Who was busier than Charlemagne? But he never lacked time to listen to men outstanding in doctrine in whom he took great pleasure. And no less so Charles the Wise of France of whose favor for the literati and the study of Sacred Scripture one cannot say enough. And so also of Alfonso X, king of Castile,[3] who, besides his other studies, claimed that while attending to his other duties he had read the whole of the Sacred Scriptures with commentaries forty times; and Alfonso I of Naples,[4] than whom no king ever faced more difficulties, was accustomed to say that an illiterate prince was a crowned ass, and, with the value that he placed in letters, filled his court and his whole kingdom with men outstanding in every profession, as did Francis I the kingdom of France. Trajan, emperor of such great fame, was not ashamed to ask Plutarch to write out for him instructions on how to govern the Empire in a praiseworthy manner and with authority, adding that he would be highly pleased if he illustrated his instructions with examples.[5]

3 Of History

But there is nothing more necessary for the perfection of prudence and for the administration of the republic than experience, mother of the

---

[3] Alfonso the Wise, king of Castile and León (r. 1252–84).

[4] Alfonso I of Aragon reigned in Naples 1442–58.

[5] *Institutio Traiani*, attributed to Plutarch; it was integrated into the text of John of Salisbury's *Policraticus* of the twelfth century, a work on which Botero drew extensively for this chapter (*BD*, 117, n. 1).

above-mentioned *virtù*. Many things appear to be based on reason so long as one discusses them at leisure in the council room but then, when put into effect, do not succeed. Many appear easy to implement which practice then shows to be not only difficult but impossible. Now experience is of two sorts; it is acquired either directly by us or through others. The first is necessarily much restricted as to place and time because one is not able to be in many places nor to have experience of many things, but he ought to exert himself to extract the essence of prudence from what he sees and hears. The second way is of two types; one may learn from the living or the dead. The first, even though it is not very large as to time, can nevertheless encompass many places because ambassadors, spies, merchants, soldiers, and similar persons have been in many places and participated in many events, for pleasure, business, or some other reason. They are able to inform us about an infinite number of things necessary or useful for our office. But a much greater field from which to learn is that offered us by the dead with the histories written by them. These take in the whole life of the world in all its parts, and indeed history is the most vast theater that one can imagine. There, at the expense of others man learns what is useful for him; there he sees shipwrecks without dread, wars without danger, the customs of various peoples and the institutions of different republics, all without expense. There passes before one's eyes the principles, the means, and the ends and the causes of the growth and collapse of empires. There one learns the causes why some princes reign quietly, others face many troubles, some flourish with the art of peace, others with the valor of arms, others spend profusely without profit, others frugally with dignity. History is of such great utility that Lucullus, having been dispatched to the Mithridatic War, applied himself during the voyage, without any teacher, to reading about the past, and became one of the great captains of his time.[6] And, not to cite only our examples, Muhammad II, king of the Turks,[7] who was the first to have been called the Great Turk, continually had some ancient history at hand. Selim I[8] took great delight in reading of the deeds of Alexander the Great and Julius Caesar, and he had them translated into Turkish, so that he was much like the one and the other in the ardor and quickness of his campaigns.

[6] 118–56 BCE, Roman consul and general.
[7] Ottoman sultan from 1444–46 and 1451–81, the conqueror of Constantinople. Also known as Mehmed II the Conqueror.
[8] Ottoman sultan from 1512–20, who greatly expanded Ottoman holdings.

Nor is poetry to be overlooked. We read that Alexander the Great drew considerable inspiration from Homer. Even if the poets tell fictitious stories, they present them in such a way that they stimulate spirits and inflame them with a certain ardor to imitate the heroes that they celebrate. We read that Ferdinand, marquis of Pescara,[9] having read in his adolescence romances, was so set on fire by that desire for glory that he became a distinguished captain. I speak here of heroic and lyric poets who in an elevated and grave style celebrate the valor of great personages, such as Homer, Pindar, and Vergil. The others have for the most part with their immodesty and lasciviousness disgraced the Muses rather than ennobling and honoring them, and they are more suited to demoralize their readers than to rouse them to virtue.

4 Of the Knowledge of the Nature and Inclinations of Subjects[10]

Because nothing is more necessary for good government than to know the nature, the minds, and the inclinations of the subjects (because these ought to influence the form the government takes) we return at the start to the consideration of the above-mentioned topics. We say therefore that the nature, inclinations, and humors of persons can be learned from their location, their age, their fortune, their education. But because many have spoken of education, and Aristotle has spoken divinely of age and fortune in his *On Rhetoric*,[11] I will content myself with a couple of words about location.

5 Of the Location of a Country

With regard to location, one ought to consider whether it is north or south, facing the east or the west, flat or mountainous, subject to winds or not, because as in every matter the good lies in the middle, so in the

---

[9] Ferdinand Francis d'Avalos, called Ferrante (1489–1525), marquis of Pescara, husband of Vittoria Colonna, general in chief of the imperial army under Charles V.

[10] Botero turns here to an old topic (see Ptolemy of Lucca and his continuation of Thomas Aquinas's *De regimine principum*) which comes to the fore again in Machiavelli (*The Prince*, dedication and chap. 5) and in Jean Bodin (*Les six livres de la république*, edn. of 1583, 4.7 and 5.1), the knowledge of the nature or character of individual peoples. The theory of climate is important here; it postulates an interdependence of geographical zones, the customs of peoples, and their forms of government (*BD*, 119, n. 2).

[11] Botero may refer here to Aristotle, *Rhetoric*, 2.12–17.

universe. The peoples who have been placed between the north and the
south and between the hot and the cold are better qualified than the others because they are endowed in mind and spirit and most suited to rule
and to govern. So we see that the great empires have been placed in the
hands of such people, the Assyrians, Medes, Persians, Mongols, Turks,
Romans, French, Spanish. The northern peoples, but not those at the
extreme north, are spirited but without guile; on the other hand southerners are astute but lack boldness. The northerners have bodies similar
to their souls, that is, they are tall, heavy, and full of blood and vigor; on
the contrary the southerners are thin and dry and more suited to flight
than to resistance. The former have a simple, genuine spirit, the latter
are secretive and cunning in their ways. The former have much of the
lion in them, the latter much of the fox. The northerners are slow and
consistent in their actions, the southerners are impetuous and frivolous;
the northerners merry and subject to Bacchus, the southerners melancholic and subject to Venus. Those in the middle then, sharing in the
extremes, have modest and moderate ways, are not astute but prudent,
not ferocious but brave. So the northerners rely on power, and they govern themselves either as a republic or an elective monarchy as do today
the Transylvanians, the Poles, the Danes, and the Swedes. And even if
now the southern peoples live for the most part in hereditary principalities, this is not because their nature is such that they prefer absolute
monarchy but because monarchy is of such excellence that it transforms
all other forms of government into itself. But yet we see that even if the
French live under a king, they desire that he be peaceful, friendly, and
of such a manner that he be as their brother or at least, as they say, their
cousin. The Scots have had up to the present a hundred and six kings,
nearly an incredible number, more than half of whom they have murdered. It is known how many civil wars the English have had, how many
variations of government, how many changes of kings! The southerners,
much given over to speculation, often govern themselves in part through
religion and superstition; there astrology was born; there magic has its
origins; there priests, gymnosophists,[12] Brahmins, magicians are held in
esteem. The Empire of the Saracens, based completely on the vanity of a
highly foolish superstition and a most brutal law, which they think came
down from heaven, had its origins in Arabia. The Sharif, after deceiving

---

[12] "Naked philosophers," a name given in the West to Indian holy men given over to asceti-
cism and contemplation.

the people in the dress of a pilgrim or hermit, not long ago had himself made king of Morocco and Fez,[13] and the Great Negus, whom we call Prester John,[14] obtained as it were adoration from his followers because he shows them nothing else of himself but his foot. We see then that of the heresies that have afflicted the church of God those born more toward the south have had more of the speculative and the subtle; on the other hand, those of the north more of the physical and the coarse. To the south some have denied the divinity, some the humanity, others the plurality of wills in Christ, others the procession of the Holy Spirit from the Word and other such things. To the north they are not so concerned about things high and sublime; they have denied fasts and vigils, penitence and all the practices that prevent the increase of blood of which they have an abundance, the celibacy of priests, and other such things which, even if they deeply conform to reason and the Gospel, are repulsive to flesh and to the senses which largely hold them in sway. They deny the authority of the Vicar of Christ because, being of a large heart, they love liberty immoderately; and as they govern themselves temporally in a republic or under a king who depends upon their election and their will, so they would want a spiritual government of this type. And as the northern captains and soldiers make use of force in war more than artifice, so their ministers in disputes with Catholics rely more on curses than on reason.

But the peoples in the middle as they are located between north and south, govern themselves in a moderate manner, that is, with justice and reason. So they have established laws, created constitutions, and mastered the arts of peace and war. The peoples living in the extremes of north and south, in the excess of cold and heat, show much more of the brutish than others, and the one and the other are small of body and poorly dressed because the former are at home in the cold and the latter suffocated by the heat. In the one there is an abundance of phlegm which dulls them, in the other melancholy which nearly turns them into beasts. And that which I have said of the peoples on this side of the equinox

[13] The Sharif claimed to be a descendant of Ali, cousin and son-in-law of Muhammad, and the fourth caliph of the Arabs; in 1549 a Moroccan family claimed this descent, took the throne, founded the prosperous dynasty of the Sadiana, and expelled the Portuguese (Waley, 39, note).
[14] The Great Negus was the king of Ethiopia or Abyssinia; by this time he was identified with the mythical Nestorian Christian, Prester John, who was thought to be a ruler first in Asia and then in Africa.

should also be said of those in the same distance from it on the other side.

Those to the east are easy-going by nature and tractable, beautiful and stately persons; those to the west more proud and reserved. The peoples located to the east and to the south, such as the Tuscans and Genoese, possess a subtle mind and shrewd ways; on the other hand, those who look to the west and to the north possess a more open and simple soul. The inhabitants of lands subject to unpredictable and vehement winds have restless and turbulent habits, those who inhabit quiet and tranquil places take on the natural air with gentleness and consistency of manners. Mountain-dwellers tend to the fierce and the wild, valley-dwellers to the effeminate and the soft. In barren countries industry and diligence flourish, in fertile lands leisure and refinement. Maritime peoples through their considerable contact and dealings with foreigners show themselves to be shrewd and wise and successful in their business dealings; on the other hand, those who live inland are sincere, loyal, and easily contented.

6 Points about Prudence[15]

Let it be taken for a settled matter that in the deliberations of princes interest overcomes every other consideration, and so the prince ought not to trust any friendship nor relationship nor alliance nor any other bond with negotiating partners that is not based on interest.

Meet with vigorous measures the beginnings of any trouble because with time disorder increases and gathers strength. But when the trouble is too much for your forces, stall for time because with time matters change and vary as do their features, and whoever has time has life.[16] Do not ignore minor disorders because all troubles are small in their beginnings but in the course of time grow and threaten disaster as we see to be

---

[15] This chapter is a collection of political cautions in the style of the editions of the *Consigli e avvertimenti* of Francesco Guicciardini (later known as the *Ricordi*) published between 1570 and 1580 (*BD*, 123, n. 3). Botero has added important points to this chapter in subsequent editions. The following notes reproduce five additions that he inserted in *RS* 1598.

[16] *RS* 1598 adds: "Do not agree that anything be brought into council that includes any change or novelty in the state because those matters that are taken up in negotiations or in council acquire credibility and positive evaluation no matter how strange and pernicious they may be. The ruin of France and Flanders began with two memoranda." One was read by Gaspard de Coligny to Francis II that called for tolerance for the Reformed in 1560, and the second was presented in 1566 by Henri de Broderode and Louis de Nassau to Margaret of Parma, then governing the Netherlands for Philip II, that advocated the end of persecution for the Reformed and the recall of the Inquisitors (*BD*, 124, n. 2).

the case when imperceptible vapors gradually give birth to storms and horrible tempests.[17]

Do not undertake many enterprises of importance at the same time because he who undertakes much holds on to little.

Establish yourself well in acquired territories and do not attempt anything else before you have firmly secured your position; so it is the part of a wise king not to embark on a new enterprise in the first years of his reign. For this reason Ariosto, intending to praise King Francis, inadvertently charged him with imprudence when he said that he began the campaign in Lombardy "the first year of his happy reign when the crown was not yet firmly fixed on his head."[18] Ladislaus, son of Charles III, king of Naples,[19] not having yet established himself firmly in the paternal kingdom, went off to take possession of the kingdom of Hungary to which he had been summoned. But scarcely arrived in Zara he received the news that the Hungarians, having changed their mind, had placed Sigismund, king of Bohemia, on the throne, and that the barons of his own kingdom had revolted.[20]

It is the part of a wise man sometimes to yield to the weather and to avoid severe storms because there is no better way to take shelter against an overwhelming storm than to lower the sails. In this respect Philip, king of the Macedonians, was excellent. When at the start of his reign he saw an infinite number of enemies coming at him, he chose to come to terms with the more powerful at cost to himself, and he made war on the weaker ones. So he bolstered the spirit of his own people and demonstrated courage to his enemies. The Venetians when they were attacked by Louis, king of Hungary, and his allies wisely yielded and so secured their own position,[21] but not wanting to yield in the war made

---

[17] *RS* 1598 adds: "Do not think in your deliberations that it is possible to avoid all disdvantages because just as it is impossible that in this world something be generated without the corruption of something else, so to every good act is joined some evil. *Habet aliquid ex iniquo omne magnum exemplum; quod contra singulos utilitate publica rependitur* (There is an element of evil in every exemplary punishment imposed on individuals for the public good)." Tacitus, *Annals*, 14.44.4.

[18] Francis I of France invaded Italy in the first year of his reign, 1515.

[19] Ladislaus reigned 1386–1414.

[20] *RS* 1598 adds: "Do not clash with those more powerful nor carry on several wars at the same time because *ne Hercules quidem contra duos* (not even Hercules [could prevail] *against two*) [reported of Socrates by Plato in the *Phaedo*, 89c.]. The Romans kept their eyes carefully on this as have the Turks. Dissimulate injuries from the more powerful and offenses that cannot be punished."

[21] 1357–58. This alludes to the Peace of Zadar in 1358.

against them by Louis XII, king of France, they were on the point of losing everything.[22]

There is nothing more unworthy of a prudent prince than to entrust himself to the decision of fortune and chance; in this Tiberius Caesar was most firm. *Immotum adversum eos sermones fixumque Tiberio fuit non omittere caput rerum, neque se in casum dare* (Notwithstanding these remonstrances, it was the inflexible purpose of Tiberius Caesar not to quit the headquarters of empire or to imperil himself or the state).[23] Among modern captains are Prospero Colonna[24] and Ferrante of Toledo, duke of Alba,[25] to say nothing of Fabius Maximus and other ancients; but incomparable in this respect is Philip, king of Spain.[26]

Do not make sudden changes, because such actions have something of the violent, and violence rarely succeeds and never produces a lasting effect. Charles Martel, aspiring to become king of France, did not want as majordomo of the king suddenly to usurp the title of king but took the title of prince of the French nobility. His son Pepin then easily obtained the title of king and the kingdom. The Caesars from perpetual dictators became tribunes, then princes, and finally emperors and absolute masters.

Having prepared to undertake some campaign, do not put it off; when this happens the delay usually causes disorder among your forces and not among your enemy's. *Nocuit semper differre paratis* (It is always harmful to delay when you are prepared).[27]

Prefer old things to new and the quiet to the upsetting because this is to place the certain before the uncertain and the secure before the dangerous.

---

[22] The French and their allies in the League of Cambrai defeated the Venetians decisively at the Battle of Agnadello in 1509.

[23] Tacitus, *Annals*, 1.47.

[24] Prospero Colonna (1452–1523), a successful Italian commander in the Italian Wars who under Charles V became commander of the imperial army at the end of his career.

[25] Fernando Alvarez de Toledo (1507–82), 3rd duke of Alba, was considered by many the finest general of his age. He held many military and administrative offices under Charles V and Philip II, including the governorship of the Netherlands at the time of the Dutch Revolt.

[26] *RS* 1598: "He who has neighbors more powerful than himself should do everything to keep peace between them because should they go to war, if he helps the one he offends the other; if he assists both he spends his own resources without gaining anything; if he sides with neither, both consider him an enemy."

[27] Lucan, *On the Civil War*, 1.281.

Remember that saying of Demetrio Falareo to Tolomeo Filadelfo, that he would find in many beautiful secret books that which no one would dare to say to him.[28]

Do not break with powerful republics if you are not at a great advantage and so sure of victory because the love of liberty is so powerful and has such roots in the souls of those who have enjoyed it for a while that to conquer it and to extirpate it is nearly impossible; and the enterprises and counsels of princes die with them but the designs and deliberations of free cities are as it were immortal.[29]

Similarly, do not break with the church because it is difficult that such an enterprise be just, and it will always appear to be impious and will not advance anything. The dukes of Milan, the Florentines, the kings of Naples, and the Venetians all learned this; their wars with the church cost them much and benefited them nothing because the church never loses its claims, and even if one pope dissimulates them another will take them up and revive them.

Do not wage continued war with your neighbors because this will make them warlike and bellicose. After he was wounded by the Thebans, Agesilaus was told that he had received the reward that he deserved from that people whom he had taught how to manage their forces through his continuing wars with them. The Turk has practiced this art with Christian princes; he has never waged a long war against one of them but attacking now this one, now that one and having taken an important area from one and a kingdom from another, then, not to give them time to prepare their forces, has made peace or a treaty and then turned elsewhere. Likewise he has not given time to peoples to become spirited and bold through the continuation of the war but after taking from them some city or state, has readily granted them peace or a treaty. So it happens that their troops have always been veterans and ours always new because he has continually waged war with one of our princes and none of them has warred continually with him.

But much less does it make sense to carry on a war with your subjects, especially your natural subjects, because they become embittered and ever more alienated. And if in the beginning they were stirred by

---

[28] This is a citation of a comment of Demetrio Falareo (345–282 BCE), a Peripatetic philosopher, to Ptolemy II, Philadelphus, Ptolemaic king of Egypt (r. 285–246 BCE), regarding the translation of Jewish religious texts. It is found in Flavius Josephus, *Jewish Antiquities*, 12.

[29] Machiavelli, *The Prince*, 5.

resentment, in the long run they break out into open rebellion as happened to King Sigismund in the war of Bohemia[30] and to the Catholic King in the war of Flanders. No people is so shameless that at the first moment without warning it revolts against its prince, because the words treason and rebellion mean infamy and hatred; but once the swords are bloodied and the pretense and the care to proceed justly has been torn away, a complete break and rebellion are the result. Alexander, king of the Jews,[31] after warring with his subjects for a period of six years during which fifty thousand persons were killed, because he did not see any end to the campaign, asked finally how it would be possible to reach some form of a good peace. "Not otherwise," they responded, "than with your death." He did at the end what he should have done at the beginning.

Do not trust so much in a peace when you disarm because a peace with disarmament is weak.

Take it for sure that in campaigns quickness is of much greater importance than force because it strikes without warning whereas force is usually foreseen; quickness throws the enemy into disorder, force crushes, and it is easier to stir up disorder and then crush than to crush that which remains well-ordered.

In the same way take it for certain that major campaigns are brought to a successful conclusion by patience not by force; force presses ahead with violence, patience weakens by taking advantage of opportunity and time, and it is easier to weaken and then wear down than to overcome at one stroke.

Study to recognize the proper time for campaigns and for negotiations and embrace them at the right moment. Nothing is of greater importance than a certain period of time which is called opportunity; it is nothing other than a combination of circumstances that facilitates an endeavor that before or after that point would be difficult. In this Philip II, king of Macedon, stood out; in an admirable fashion he took advantage of the weakness and discord of the Greek city-states in order to achieve his goal. No less shrewd than he in this respect was Amoratto I, king of the Turks,[32] who, in order to enlarge his empire in Europe exploited the differences among the Greek princes. In the last resort neither forces nor cleverness are of much use if they are not favored and guided as it were by opportunity.

---

[30] This refers to the Hussite Wars, 1419–36.
[31] Alexander Jannaeus (Jonathan), *c.* 126–76 BCE, king of Judaea.
[32] Murad I, Ottoman sultan (r. 1360–89).

Do not admit into your council of state any person dependent upon another prince because the advice of one who has at heart the interest of another cannot be sincere.[33]

Do not entrust the execution of a campaign to one who in the council was not of the opinion that it should be undertaken because the will is not able to be effective when it is not moved by the intellect. On the day of Lepanto, Occhiali, who did not share the view that they should engage in combat, avoided the battle.[34]

Consult carefully about undertakings but do not prescribe the method of carrying them out because this depends in large part on the opportune time and the situation at that time, all of which change continually. To limit his execution of the plan is nothing other than to cripple the minister and bungle the outcome.

Do not think to avoid labors and dangers by fleeing them but by going out to meet them and putting them to flight because if you flee they run at you and increase in number, but if you go out to meet them, they withdraw and dissolve into nothing.

Be careful not to show yourself partial to the nobility rather than to the people or vice versa, because in this way you will become not a prince but the head of a party.

Do not trust anyone who has been offended by you or who thinks that he has been offended by you;[35] the desire for revenge is extremely powerful and it is awakened when the opportunity presents itself as the example of Count Giuliano[36] and Charles of Bourbon[37] shows.

The ministers who are present with you at court will look after themselves. Take care of those who are absent because they usually incur more expenses and endure more hardship than the others.

---

[33] *RS* 1598: "and there is nothing that enters through more ways into the councils of princes and of others and more subtly than interest."

[34] Occhiali or Uccialli was the name in Italy given to the notorious Ulug Ali, corsair and captain in the Ottoman navy. Of Calabrian origin and a convert to Islam, he died in 1587. Contrary to what Botero writes, he inflicted heavy losses on the Christians at Lepanto and returned to Istanbul (*BD*, 131, n. 2).

[35] Machiavelli, *Discourses*, 3.17.

[36] According to partially legendary accounts, Count Julian, the Christian governor of Ceuta, encouraged and aided the Omeyyades to conquer the Iberian Peninsula in 711; the Spanish king, Roderick, had violated his daughter (*BD*, 132, n. 1).

[37] The High Constable of France, Charles de Bourbon (1490–1527), took revenge on Francis I for attempting to seize a part of the Bourbon inheritance by becoming the leading general of Charles V (*BD*, 132, n. 2).

Do not oppose the multitude directly. You will not easily conquer them, and if you do, this will happen with a great loss of affection. But after the manner of a good sailor, take your direction from the wind, and appear to want and to give that which you cannot prevent or take away.

7 Of Secrecy

There is nothing more important for him who carries on negotiations of peace or war than secrecy. It facilitates the implementation of plans and the management of campaigns which if discovered would have encountered many substantial difficulties. Just as mines, if they are hidden, produce marvelous effects but otherwise do harm rather than bring benefits, so are the counsels of princes, so long as they remain secret, effective and more easily implemented but this is not the case if they suddenly come to light. Then they lose all their force and are more difficult to carry out because their enemies or rivals seek to oppose or to counter them. Grand Duke Cosimo de' Medici, a prince of outstanding judgment, considered secrecy to be one of the principal features of the government of states. But the way to keep things secret is to communicate them to no one, which that prince was able to do with confidence because he had so much experience of affairs and so great judgment that he was able to make decisions himself. So one reads was Antigonus, king of Asia,[38] who once upon being asked by his son Demetrius when he wanted to summon the army out of its quarters, responded angrily, "Do you alone think that you will not be able to hear the sound of the trumpets?" So too was the Macedonian Metellus[39] who responded to one who asked about his plan for the contest in Spain, "Be content," he said, "not to know, because if I thought that the shirt on my back knew what I have in mind, I would right away throw it in the fire." Peter of Aragon[40] made the very same response to Martin IV who wanted to know to what purpose he had assembled the great armada with which he took Sicily from the French. But if the prince does not possess the valor to make the decision himself or if the business at hand requires the input of others, this should be done with a few and secretly because a secret known to many

---

[38] Antigonus the One-Eyed, a general and satrap under Alexander the Great, founded the Antigonid dynasty in Macedonia, where he ruled from 306–301 BCE.

[39] Metellus Macedonicus (210–115 BCE), a Roman consul and general under whom Macedonia became a Roman province, hence "Macedonicus."

[40] Peter III of Aragon (r. 1276–85) conquered Sicily.

will not long remain secret. And because councillors, ambassadors, secretaries, spies are usually ministers who ordinarily share the secrets, persons ought to be chosen for these offices who either by nature or by effort are slow to speak and very shrewd. Dissimulation helps here. Louis XI, king of France,[41] saw in it an important feature of the art of rule, and Tiberius Caesar prided himself on nothing more than the art of dissimulation of which he was a master. Dissimulation means to pretend not to know or to care about that which one does know or care about, as simulation is to pretend and to take one thing for another. Because there is nothing more contrary to dissimulation than the force of anger, it is expedient that the prince moderate this passion above all in such a way that he does not blurt out in words or in other signs his mind and his feelings. Alfonso, duke of Calabria,[42] while in Lombardy for the war with Ferrara, often allowed to come from his mouth that upon his return to Naples he would straighten out matters in the kingdom by punishing some. These words, reported, were the cause of the rebellion of Aquila and the barons. Passerino, lord of Mantua,[43] after threatening Louis Gonzaga, was forestalled and murdered with his son. Francesco d'Orso of Forli because he saw himself to be threatened by Count Geronimo Riario,[44] anxious about this, murdered him in his room; threats are the arms of the threatened.

8 Of Counsels

Because I have mentioned counsels and designs above, I do not wish to omit saying what the counsels of the prince ought to be.

First of all, he ought to profess not astuteness but prudence. Prudence is a virtue whose function is to seek and recover suitable means to reach the goal; astuteness tends to the same goal but differs from prudence in that in the choice of means prudence seeks the honorable more than the useful, while astuteness takes account only of interest.[45]

Counsels ought not to be valued because they have more of the subtle and the shrewd; for the most part these do not succeed because inasmuch as their subtlety is greater, their execution must be more right

---

[41] 1461–83. The dictum "qui nescit dissimulare nescit regnare" is usually attributed to him.

[42] Alfonso II of Aragon (1448–95), duke of Calabria and son of Ferdinand I of Naples, became king of Naples from 1494–95.

[43] Ronaldo Bonacolsi, called "Passerino," lord of Mantua and Modena, was overthrown by Louis Gonzaga in 1328.

[44] 1443–88, Lord of Imola and Forlì.

[45] This paragraph disappeared from *RS* 1590 and subsequent editions.

on the mark. This cannot ordinarily be achieved because grand projects require for their execution many means and, as a result, meet with many unanticipated situations. And so as the more intricately a clock is put together and assembled, so much the more easily it fails to work and to tell time accurately, so designs and projects that require a certain minute subtlety for the most part do not succeed. Nor ought those projects be recommended that have more of the grandiose and magnificent instead of those with more simplicity and security, because the former usually result in embarrassment and harm. So it was with the plan of Antiochus the Great[46] when he caused to be buried with much honor and pomp the Macedonians who died in the battle between King Philip and Q. Flaminius.[47] This did not at all win him the favor of those peoples and was the reason that he broke completely with the king. On this Livy wrote that due to their nature and their vanity, kings are accustomed ordinarily to embrace counsels that appear to be good but have little substance.[48] Much less ought one to commit to vast plans that include nearly immense features for which he is not able to supply either the funds, the life, or the forces and which require such great resources. Such were ordinarily the plans of Emperor Maximilian I.[49] Also dangerous are plans of great boldness which, even if in the beginning they exhibit I do not know what spirit and bravado, encounter in their implementation enough difficulties and troubles and end up in misery and desperation. So in their place they ought to follow well-founded and mature counsels subject as little as possible to chance. Although this ought always to be observed, nevertheless, when it is a question of acquiring and mounting a campaign against enemies, sometimes one can risk something (because he who does not risk does not gain) and demonstrate boldness because ardor is more suited to him who attacks. But where it is a question of preserving what one has and retaining what one has acquired, nothing is less expedient for a wise king than to take a risk, because the loss would be much greater than any useful gain. Long consultations are appropriate for great princes because they ought to attend more readily to conservation than to acquisition; prompt and rapid deliberations are more suitable for those who look to increase their territory rather than to preserve it and, because recognition of the value of counsel does not depend

---

[46] Antiochus III, the Great, Seleucid king of the Hellenistic Syrian Empire (r. 223–187 BCE).
[47] This probably refers to the Battle of Cynoscephalae in Thessaly in 197 BCE in which the Roman general Quinctius Flaminius defeated Philip V of Macedon.
[48] *History of Rome*, 36.8.   [49] Reigned 1493–1519.

less on practical knowledge than on speculation, the advice of practical men ought not to be less valued than that of persons of great intelligence because, as Aristotle says, judgment is no less in practical men than in the learned.[50] So one ought not to easily trust in new inventions if experience has not first warranted it.

9 Of Not Introducing Novelties

Nothing is more hateful in governments than to change things which have acquired esteem through their antiquity. *Nihil motum ex antiquo probabile est*, says Livy, *veteribus, nisi quae usus evidenter arguit, stari malunt* (No movement away from the ancient is acceptable; they prefer to remain with the old unless usage evidently convinces otherwise).[51] This is always to be avoided especially in the beginnings of a government. So Saul waited two years after he was elected king and anointed by Samuel, a private man as it were, without a court and without a guard; so he thought to avoid envy and rivalry.[52] Caesar Augustus, in order to lessen the novelty of his principate, did not want to be called emperor or king but established the Empire with the title of tribune, and he based his laws and ordinances as much as possible on examples from the past. But there was no one who made greater use of antiquity than Tiberius Caesar; he also covered and as it were honored with ancient expressions the crimes and tyrannies that he introduced from day to day, not only his praiseworthy statutes and orders. The novelty brought forth hatred, and the change of deep-seated customs was not possible without resentment. Vonones, king of the Parthians, was chased from the kingdom because he lived there in the manner of Rome where he had been for a long time.[53] More serious was the blunder of Louis XI, king of France;[54] after succeeding to the kingdom, he deprived of their office and rank all those who had enjoyed the favor and esteem of his father. Because he was new to government and so had neither the knowledge nor experience of affairs, he should have at least retained the former ministers because if the prince and ministers are all likewise newcomers, changes necessarily follow as Louis himself showed when he found himself more than once in serious trouble. And if they have to make changes, it is necessary that they proceed little by little and as it were imperceptibly imitating nature which

[50] *Metaphysics*, 1.1.980. [51] *History of Rome*, 34.8. [52] 1 Samuel 13–15.
[53] Vonones II (d. 51 CE). [54] Reigned 1461–83.

does not move directly from winter to summer nor from summer to winter but places two temperate seasons between them, that is, spring and autumn, so that their pleasant character renders tolerable the passage from cold to hot and the return from hot to cold. *Nec res hunc tenerae possent perferre laborem, si non tanta quies inter frigusque caloremque iret, et exciperet coeli indulgentia terras* (Nor could the tender beings endure the world's harshness did not between the seasons of cold and heat come such repose, and earth receive the blessings of a tender sky).[55]

10 Of Valor

Valor consists in prudence and vigor of spirit, which two things united in one man produce marvelous deeds. And for the maintenance of states valor is of much greater importance than power. Aristotle proves this with the example of princes who acquire a state and rarely if ever lose it as their descendants do who have not acquired *virtù* along with the power of their ancestors.[56] Here we will speak of valor only inasmuch as it consists of courage. Now courage proceeds partly from the spirit, partly from the body, and partly from external forces of which we will speak in their place. And if the spirit is the principal source because it often prevails over the infirmity of the body, governs it, and keeps it on its feet, nevertheless the unhealthy or ill-formed body will ordinarily drag down the spirit. So it is desirable that the prince be a person well put-together and with a healthy and hardy constitution, and nature ought to be helped by those arts which preserve and promote good health. Sobriety and moderation in food preserve health; the vices of gluttony, drunkenness, and excess fill the body with ill humors and indigestion from which come gout and other sicknesses which make life miserable and no less tedious than for others. Continence helps the preservation of health and of strength; unbridled lust weakens beasts as well as men, hastens old age, enfeebles spirits, wears down nerves, weakens sight, and opens many paths to gout, drooling, and death. Exercise then increases strength, and it ought to be such that stimulates and moves all the members as do ball games especially recommended by Galen, and the hunt. To secure this result it also helps to accustom oneself to diverse and contrary conditions, to cold and to hot, to keeping watch, to hunger, to thirst, to water

[55] Vergil, *Georgics*, 2.343–45, trans. H.R. Fairclough (Cambridge, MS, 1916).
[56] *Politics*, 3.14 (1286b). This citation does not seem to address directly the issue that Botero is discussing.

and wine, and to every variety of life and food. In this way a man secures his health and fortifies his members and strengthens his person and so makes himself ready and able for every accident and for any obstacle. If the training of the prince requires him to face an infinite number of situations, his body hardens and is disposed so that no obstacle is new or arduous for him. But because sometimes the weakness of nature overcomes every aide whatever be the condition of the body, it is necessary that the spirit at least be filled with vigor and courage and a certain vivacity that readies it to face all difficulties and dangers to which necessity summons it. He ought finally to overcome the trials of the body with the greatness of spirit of which Charles V gave us an outstanding example in the War of Germany where even though he was tormented by the gout in such a way that he was not able to keep his foot in the stirrup and so supported it with a sling, nevertheless he stood the whole winter, a bitter one, amid snow and mud and supported the weight of his body with his vigor of spirit. Now, the ways to keep the spirit awake and alert are all those that foster health, that hinder melancholy, that incite a man to the desire for honor and glory: to speak about the virtues proper to a prince and about the campaigns of great generals, to read the lives of some emperors and persons of great valor, to converse with men no less courageous than prudent, and finally to consider his duty. This brings to my mind the memorable saying of Emperor Vespasian who at the final moment of his life while bleeding said *Imperatorem stantem mori oportere* (An emperor ought to die standing up).[57]

11 Of the Ways to Preserve Reputation

Up until now we have discussed the virtues that give birth to reputation: prudence and valor. Now we discuss some particular ways by which it can be maintained and further increased.

The first is astutely to hide his weaknesses because many princes, although they are weak, preserve their standing and reputation as powerful by hiding their lack of power instead of building fortifications. Building fortifications often reveals their weakness which otherwise is not known.[58] To increase reputation it helps to show off forces but without ostentation. Ludovico Sforza stood out in this respect more than

---

[57] Suetonius, *Twelve Caesars*, "Divine Vespasian," 8.24.
[58] The sentence "Building fortifications ... not known" is omitted in later editions.

in their use whereas Alfonso of Aragon, king of Naples,[59] stood out in both respects. And even if Hezekiah was reproached for this, it happened because instead of giving the infidels to understand that he trusted not in himself but only in God, he showed that he trusted in his own wealth.[60]

It also helps to have more deeds than words because the former are more valued than the latter and as a result, so are men who show deeds rather than those who profess words. So men who are more reserved in speech and of a melancholy disposition are more highly regarded than those who are cheerful and talkative. And reputation calls for gravity and firmness in speaking and for promising less than what one is able to do and for not allowing out of one's mouth words of boasting and bravado. In this Scipio Africanus was admirable. Livy writes that while speaking to the ambassadors of the Spanish cities *Loquebatur ita elato ab ingenti virtutum suarum fiducia animo, ut nullum ferox verbum excideret, ingensque omnibus quae ageret cum maiestas inesset, tum fides* (He spoke with such confidence and trust in his own qualities that no arrogant word escaped him, and supreme dignity and confidence marked everything that he did).[61]

Avoid in discussion embellishments and the use of hyperbole because they undermine belief in what you say and argue little experience of affairs, so that it is women and children who naturally use them.

It is of no little importance to keep your word because this proceeds from firmness of spirit and judgment; and it secured glory in Flanders for lord Alexander Farnese, duke of Parma.[62]

Also of great importance is perseverance in adversity because it indicates greatness of heart and vigor and moderation in prosperity because it argues a spirit superior to fortune. In both the one and the other situation the Romans were marvelous in the Second Punic War and in the campaign against Antiochus to whom they proposed the same conditions before their victory as if they had already won and after the victory as if they had not conquered.

Guard against attempting an enterprise that is beyond your strength, and do not enter into a negotiation nor into a business that is not certain

---

[59] Alfonso I reigned in Naples from 1442–58 (and as Alfonso V, the Magnanimous, was king of Aragon from 1416–58).

[60] 2 Kings 20:12–19.   [61] Livy, *History of Rome*, 26.19. This citation is inaccurate.

[62] Alexander Farnese (1545–92), duke of Parma, served as governor of the Spanish Netherlands from 1578–92. He is known especially for his campaigns against the Dutch, and many consider him the outstanding general of his day. He was for Botero the counterpart of Cesare Borgia for Machiavelli.

to succeed honorably; in this regard the Spaniards are without a doubt wary, so much the more so that they almost never want to win a battle unless decisively. A prince ought not invest in trivial and unworthy campaigns because that which does not have something grand about it cannot augment reputation. Campaigns ought to be grand especially at the start of a reign or government because by these will the rest of the reign be judged, and the beginning constitutes half, and as Plato says, even more than half of the work. But once having begun an honorable enterprise, he ought not easily to abandon it in order not to show that he had demonstrated little judgment in entering upon it and little spirit in withdrawing from it. As Marcello said to Q. Fabio, during the siege of Casilinum, *Multa magis ducibus sicut non aggredienda, ita semel aggressis non dimittenda esse, quia magna famae momenta in utramque partem fiunt* (Just as there are many instances when the commanders ought not to have attacked, so once having attacked they ought not to withdraw, because in each case they gain much in reputation).[63]

No less important is not to show himself dependent on the counsel or the work of anyone whoever it might be, because this is to admit a superior or an equal in the administration of affairs and to reveal your incapacity and weakness.

He ought not to make profession of anything that does not befit a prince, expressed in those verses of Vergil: *Tu regere imperior populos, Romane, memento, parcere subjectis et debellare superbos; hae tibi erunt artes, pacique imponere morem* (Remember, Roman, yours is to govern peoples by your power, to spare subjects and to tame the proud; these are your arts, to impose the rule of peace).[64] Therefore, it is not appropriate for a prince to perform or write verse as did Nero, to draw the bow as did Domitian, to make lamps as did Aeropos, king of Macedonia,[65] or images of wax or clay as did Emperor Valentinian. It is scarcely compatible to make machines of wood for use in war as did King Demetrius,[66] or to hunt the whole day as did Charles IX, king of France, or to cast artillery as did Alfonso I, duke of Ferrara, or to attend to astrology with such zeal as did Alfonso X, king of Castile. Philip I, king of Macedonia,[67] having begun to discuss with an excellent musician about his profession and

---

[63] Livy, *History of Rome*, 24.19. Casilinum was near Capua; the siege took place during the Second Punic War.

[64] *Aeneid*, 6.851–53.   [65] Reigned 397–394 BCE.

[66] Demetrius, king of Macedon (r. 294–288 BCE).

[67] Philip I, king of Macedon (r. 640–602 BCE).

desirous, after some disagreement, that the musician yield to his position, the musician said "O Philip, may God protect you from being able to compete with me in the study of music," wishing to imply that in a prince it shows a lack of judgment to engage in such studies.

Also of great importance is secrecy because beyond the fact that it makes him similar to God, it makes men who are ignorant of the prince's thoughts stand in suspense in great expectation of his designs.

He ought not allow that his affairs be managed by other than outstanding men; Alexander the Great, in order not to derogate from his greatness, wanted no one but Apelles to portray him and no one but Lysippus to sculpt him. Augustus Caesar disdained that his name be celebrated other than by unusual talent and in a sublime style and seriously.

He should not carry on negotiations through base or weak men, as did Antiochus, king of Syria, who made use of his doctor, Apollofane, as head of his council of state, and Louis XI, king of France, who made use of his doctor as chancellor and his barber as an ambassador. The baseness of the means degrades the negotiations and weakness spoils them. But he should make use of honorable subjects, men of prudence and valor joined to dignity.

He ought not to converse nor become familiar with every sort of person, not with talkative and gossipy persons because, making known what ought to be kept secret, they will discredit him with the people. He should not appear daily in public nor on every occasion but on grand occasions and with dignity.

Let him wear sober rather than showy apparel, reserved rather than ostentatious.

Let him avoid extremes, neither hasty nor slow, but mature and moderate, and rather slow than hasty because slowness is more similar to prudence and haste to rashness than which nothing is more contrary to reputation.

Severity also helps because, as Menander says, it is more salutary for cities than pleasantness, as bitterness is more wholesome than sweetness.[68]

Let him see to it that all his possessions are of excellent quality and are made to fit their surroundings. Aemilius Paulus[69] did not acquire

---

[68] This saying cannot be found among Menander's fragments (*BD*, 146, n. 3).
[69] Lucius Aemilius Paulus (229–160 BCE), Roman consul and general who conquered Macedonia.

less reputation by the banquet that he gave at Amphipolis for the Greek ambassadors than by his defeat and capture of the Persian king.

Let him show magnificence in every operation by supporting generously causes widely held to be honorable; and honorable are those that pertain to the worship of God or the benefit of the state, and on extraordinary occasions.

He should show magnanimity, and with this virtue adorn all the others. Let him carry himself in a grand manner with dignitaries and in a humane manner with equals. Let him take greater account of the truth than of opinion.

Let him not be concerned to do many things but few that are excellent and glorious.

Let him show in every action something of the lofty and heroic; in this Scipio Africanus was admirable as well as Alfonso, king of Naples, and "il Gran Capitano."[70]

He should maintain the obedience and subjection of his subjects and dependence on him in important matters.

He should not share with anyone that which pertains to his grandeur, his majesty, or supremacy: such as the authority to make laws and grant privileges; to declare war or to make peace; to appoint the principal magistrates and officials for peace and for war; to grant pardons to those who have been deprived of life, honor, or possessions by judicial process; to coin money and to establish weights and measures; to impose burdens or taxes on the people, or to name the commanders of fortresses, or other like things that concern the state or his majesty.[71] Remember the words of Sallustius Crispus: *Eam condicionem esse imperandi, ut non aliter ratio constet quam si uni reddatur* (The one condition of rule is that it cannot be maintained unless it is conferred on one person alone),[72] and those others, *sit summus severitatis et munificentiae* (let him be the height of severity and munificence)[73] and of Tiberius Caesar, *ceteris mortalibus in eo stare consilia, quid sibi conducere putent, principum diversam esse sortem quibus praecipua rerum ad famam dirigenda* (it is the business of other mortals to attend to their own interests; but the lot of princes is different, for their main concern is what leads to fame).[74]

---

[70] Gonzalo Fernández de Cordoba (1453–1515), Spanish general in Italy.
[71] Here are listed the marks of sovereignty developed by Jean Bodin in chap. 10 of the first book of the *République* (*BD*, 147, n. 5).
[72] Tacitus, *Annals*, 1.6.   [73] Ibid., 1.46, from memory.   [74] Ibid., 4.40.

Finally, let him hold for certain that reputation depends on being, not on appearing.

12 Of those Princes who because of their Greatness or Reputation have been Said to be Great or Wise

We have said that reputation is based on wisdom and valor. Let us now see with what qualities some outstanding rulers acquired the title "Great" or "Wise," so that ours, imitating them, aspire to the same greatness. But we should not think that those with these titles have shown more valor or wisdom than all the others because neither Scipio nor Hannibal nor Marius nor Julius Caesar nor Trajan nor Severus were inferior to any of those who have been called Great even though they did not have this title of Great. It suffices that in those who have the title the light of a singular valor and prudence shines, absolutely or in part.

The first of this celebrated rank who acquired this glory by virtue of the incomparable greatness of his deeds was Alexander, king of Macedonia; in little more than ten years he conquered the whole East and filled the whole universe with the fame of his victories. Antiochus, one of his successors, had the same honor more from the greatness of the states that he lost when conquered by the Romans than because of his valor. Fabius Maximus was called thus not because of his deeds in war but because he tactfully suppressed the tumult and the danger to the republic arising from the libertine multitude. Pompey had the title Great much earlier in life because of the cheers of the soldiers given a victorious young man (as with the Gran Capitano of our days) rather than because he had really conducted a campaign worthy of the title. Mithridates, king of the Parthians,[75] and another king of Pontus[76] were celebrated as Great, the former because of the extent of his conquests, the latter because of the length of the war that he waged against the Romans. Herod I was called Great, I think, because of the skill and notable valor with which he rose from private person and foreigner to become king of the Jews and maintained this position amongst the most dangerous misfortunes and threatening ruin caused by the hatred of Cleopatra and the contempt of Antony and then of Octavius Caesar, and no less because of the cities that he enlarged, some founded by him and others restored,

[75] Mithridates II, the Great, king of Parthia (r. 121–91 BCE).
[76] Mithridates VI, the Great, king of Pontus (r. 120–63 BCE).

and the various buildings he constructed in a grand style. Because of the greatness of his victories and of his empire Genghis, king of the Tartars, was given the title of Great, and this title has remained hereditary with his successors who are all called the Great Khan.[77] The innumerable victorious campaigns of Muhammad I earned him the title of Grand Turk; he conquered two Christian empires, twelve kingdoms, and two hundred cities. This title has remained for his successors; he had it because of his valor, they through inheritance as it were.[78] For the same reason the kings of Egypt are called the Great Sultan, but he who first acquired it for himself and for his successors I have not yet found out. The same title was held by Tamerlane because of the size of his armies and campaigns, the most memorable of which was the capture of Bajazet, king of the Turks.[79] Muhammad, his successor in our time, with eight hundred thousand soldiers, partly infantry partly cavalry, conquered the East and extended his empire infinitely between the Ganges and the Indus.[80] He is called the Great Mogul because his people are called Moguls. Because of the greatness of his campaigns and for his conquest of Persia, Ismail is called the Great Sophy.[81] The Spaniards gave the same title of Great to Mansour, king of Africa and Spain.[82]

But let us come to Christian princes. The first of these to obtain this glorious title was Emperor Constantine because of the greatness of his empire and of the help that he gave to the universal propagation of the faith. Under him the Empire, then divided into many parts, was reunited and our holy faith incredibly increased throughout its extent. After him I found Emperor Theodosius to be called Great, though not with the same eminent fame, because he liberated the Empire from most powerful tyrants and dangers. But no one ever acquired such greatness in his name more gloriously than Charles I, king of France, because of the greatness of his enterprises, in peace and in war, the propagation of the faith, the favor with which he embraced and as it were revived letters and sciences, but chiefly because he was the first emperor of the West. Michael

---

[77] *c.* 1162–1227, founder and Great Khan of the Mongol Empire.

[78] This should be Muhammad II or Mehmed II, the Conqueror, Ottoman sultan from 1444–46 and 1451–81.

[79] Bajazet I reigned as Ottoman sultan from 1389–1403.

[80] The Mogul conquest of India began in 1525.

[81] Ismail was the first of the Persian dynasty, the Safavids, that came to the throne in the early sixteenth century. In the West the Persian kings were called the Sophy.

[82] Al Mansour (931–1000?), a Muslim hero, ruled the kingdom of Cordova and later captured Santiago de Compostela.

Comnenus Paleologus was called Great either because he drove the Latins out of Constantinople and Greece and recovered the Empire for the Greeks or because in the Council of Lyons he united the Greek Church with the Latin.[83] Emperor Otto obtained the same title by virtue of his many victories over the princes of Germany, Bohemia, and Hungary and against Berengarius who was first conquered and then driven out of Italy, and further, because he most zealously promoted the faith which under his reign as emperor expanded infinitely in the northern provinces.[84]

Among the kings of Spain Ferdinand III attained the title of Great, because he was the first to unite under one crown the kingdoms of León and Castile and because with his outstanding valor he took large states from the Moors; moreover, he was no less glorious because of his justice and his religion than for his military and his victories.[85] Alfonso III was honored with the same title because of the supreme valor with which he conquered rebels and seized many cities from the Moors, and built churches and palaces in a grand style and, among other things, enriched and enlarged the structure and income of the church of Saint James of Compostela.[86]

Among the kings of France beyond Charles I, Francis I was called Great. I do not know whether this was to distinguish him from his nephew Francis II whom the French call "Little King Francis,"[87] or because of the greatness of his campaigns which were for the most part unsuccessful, or because of the many good laws by which he reorganized the administration of justice and revived the study of letters in France.

Among the kings of Poland Casimir II had this glorious greatness not so much because of his many victories as for the cities that he rebuilt, for the castles that he fortified, for the churches that he enriched, and for other similar works of peace.[88]

Nor should we leave out Matteo Visconti, called Great, no less for having with patience overcome fortune than for having with valor acquired the incomparable duchy of Milan for himself and his descendants;[89] nor Can Grande della Scala, illustrious with the same title for the states that he acquired in Lombardy that made him feared by his neighbors.[90]

---

[83] Reigned 1261–82.   [84] King of Germany 936–73, Holy Roman Emperor 962–73.

[85] King of Castile 1217–52, king of León 1230–52.

[86] King of León, Galicia, and Asturias (r. 866–910).   [87] Francis II (r. 1559–60).

[88] Botero errs here. Casimir III (r. 1333–70) was called "Great."

[89] Lord of Milan (r. 1287–1322).   [90] Lord of Verona (r. 1308–29).

Alfonso I, king of Naples, was called not Great but Magnanimous because of the nobility of his deeds in the conquest as well as in the administration of the kingdom, no less in adversity than in prosperity.

In the house of Medici where political prudence has always flourished in a singular fashion, there are three who have acquired the title of Great: Cosimo the Elder, Lorenzo, and Grand Duke Cosimo: Cosimo the Elder because as a private person he accomplished the works of a king; Lorenzo because with his valor as head of the Florentine Republic he made himself arbiter of the affairs and rulers of Italy; Cosimo, because to the great wisdom with which he established in his house the principality of Florence and added to it Siena, he joined outstanding religion for which he was honored by Pius V (a pontiff than which I know no greater for his prudence and sanctity) with the title of Grand Duke[91] which his son Don Francesco inherited and which Don Ferdinando presently holds by every right of inheritance and of his own valor.

Among the Roman Pontiffs Leo I and Gregory I have had this honor, Leo because with zeal and marvelous rhetoric he made Attila, filled with rage and fury against the city of Rome, turn back and because with his authority, in a council of 630 bishops celebrated at Chalcedon,[92] he condemned the heresy of Nestorius and Eutyches, and cast down the pride of Dioscurus; Gregory because of the sanctity of his life, the loftiness of his doctrine, the extirpation of heresies, the reform of ceremonies and of every area of ecclesiastical discipline, and for the conversion of the English.[93]

From what has been said, one can understand that of those who have been called Great, some have acquired this honor by the size of the territories that they have united under their crown when circumstances have ordinarily played a greater role than valor; others by the greatness of their undertakings in peace and in war. The undertakings are considered to be great either by their importance or because you have been the first to carry them out.

13 Of the Wise

The first to acquire this title among the kings, after Solomon, was Alfonso X, king of Castile, not because of his wisdom in governing or

---

[91] Cosimo I, who reigned in Florence from 1537, acquired the title of Grand Duke of Tuscany in 1569.
[92] In 451. [93] Reigned 590–604.

his political prudence but because of his private study which led him to philosophy and chiefly to consideration of the heavenly movements to which his astronomical tables testify.[94] After him Albert, archduke of Austria, was given the title Wise, I think, because of his skill in negotiations and in the enrichment of his own.[95] Charles V, king of France, received the title, and with greater reason, not so much because he was a great patron of letters and of the literati but because, without sallying forth into combat and bearing arms, he waged war most successfully against the English through his ministers and retook from them all that his father had lost.[96] I do not want to pass over Otto III who, even though he was called neither Great nor Wise, had a greater honor; he was named a miracle of the world (*miracolo del mondo*) because of the shrewdness and valor he showed even at a young age.[97]

14 Of the Virtues which Preserve the Aforementioned Qualities

The virtues which we have up to this point discussed and on which love and reputation depend do not long endure if they are not assisted and maintained by two others; these are religion and temperance. The republic is as it were a vine which cannot flourish nor bear fruit if it is not favored by heavenly influences and helped by human industry which trims and cuts away what is superfluous. Religion procures the maintenance of the state with the supernatural aid of the grace of God; temperance keeps at a distance effeminacy and all that feeds the vices that lead to ruin.

15 Of Religion

It is most certain that in heroic times princes were responsible for sacred matters, as Aristotle teaches,[98] not because they themselves offered sacrifices, although Methusale[99] was at the same time king and priest, but so that with their help sacrifices would be celebrated magnificently. And the same Aristotle says that it is proper that the supreme magistrate sacrifice in a grand manner and magnificently.[100] The Romans did not undertake

---

[94] King of Castile, León, and Galicia (r. 1252–84).   [95] Reigned 1330–58.
[96] Charles V the Wise (r. 1364–80).   [97] Otto III, Holy Roman Emperor 996–1002.
[98] *Politics*, 3.14 (1285b).   [99] Probably an error for Melchisedech.
[100] *Nicomachean Ethics*, 4.2 (1123a).

any campaign or public business without first deliberating about how to obtain omens and to placate the anger of the gods or to win their favor or to thank them for benefits. Finally, they held religion to be a principal feature of their government nor did they allow that this be changed in any way, much less broken off. Diotimus writes that there are three things necessary for a king:[101] piety, justice, and an army, the first for his own perfection, the second to control his own office-holders, and the third to keep enemies at a distance. And Aristotle advises even the tyrant to appear to be religious and pious:[102] first, because considering him to be such, they will not fear being treated badly by one whom they think reveres the gods, and they will be careful not to rise up and cause disturbances against him whom they think to be dear to the gods. But it is difficult that he who is not truly religious be considered so because there is nothing that lasts less than simulation.[103] Therefore the prince ought to humble himself with his whole heart before the Divine Majesty and acknowledge that the kingdom and the obedience of his subjects come from him; and the more that he is placed in a higher rank over others, so much the more ought he abase himself in the presence of God, nor set his hand to any negotiation, nor undertake any campaign or anything else which he is not certain to be conformed to the law of God. God himself commands the king that he have near him a copy of his holy law and that he observe it carefully; and God does this with words that, because they are of such importance, will not be difficult for me to set down here. He says *Postquam autem sederit in solio Regni sui, describet sibi Deuteronomium legis hujus in volumine, accipiens exemplum a sacerdotibus leviticae tribus, et habebit secum, legetque illud omnibus diebus vitae suae, ut discat timere Dominum Deum suum, et custodire verba et ceremonias eius quae in lege praecepta sunt, ne elevetur cor eius in superbiam super fratres suos, neque declinet in partem dexteram vel sinisttam, ut longo tempore regnet ipse et filius suus super Israel* (When he is enthroned in his kingdom, he shall have a copy of this law made from the scroll that is in the hands of the levitical priests; and he will have it with him and will read it all the days of his life, so that he learn to fear the Lord, his God, and to heed and fulfill all the words and ceremonies which are prescribed in the law. Let him not raise his heart in pride over his countrymen, nor turn aside to the right or to the left from these commandments, so that he and his son may reign a long

---

[101] There is no Diotimus to whom this saying can be traced.   [102] *Politics*, 5.11 (1314b).
[103] Machiavelli advises the ruler to appear to be religious (*Prince*, 19).

time over Israel).[104] For this reason it would be necessary that the king never bring to the council anything for deliberation that was not first vetted in a council of conscience to which outstanding doctors of theology and canon law belonged. Otherwise he will burden his conscience and do things that he will later have to undo if he does not want to damn his soul and the souls of his successors. Nor ought this to appear strange. If the Romans did not attempt anything without the advice and approval of the auspices and the augurs, if the Turk does not start to wage war or to do anything of importance without consulting the mufti and obtaining his judgment in writing, why should the Christian prince close the door of his privy council to the Gospel and to Christ and follow a reason of state contrary to the law of God as though it were a rival altar? O how can he hope that things ought to have a happy outcome if they have been deliberated without any respect to the author of all happiness? Who was ever more religious and more successful in wars than Constantine the Great who placed all his confidence in the cross? Of Theodosius, Nicephorus writes that he obtained many victories more rapidly through the fervor of prayer than through the valor of his soldiers.[105] The greatness of the princes of Austria was born of their outstanding piety. According to the story, Rudolf, count of Habsburg, was hunting during a great rainstorm when he encountered a priest walking alone. He asked the priest where he was going and what led him to journey at such an inopportune time. The priest responded that he was bringing the Most Holy Viaticum to a sick man. Immediately Rudolf dismounted, and humbly adoring Jesus Christ hidden under the species of bread and wine, placed his cloak over the shoulders of the priest, so that the rain would not pour down on him and so he might carry the Most Sacred Host with greater dignity. The good priest, admiring the kindness and piety of the count, gave him immortal thanks and beseeched His Divine Majesty that he reward him with an abundance of his divine graces. A miracle! Within a short time Count Rudolf became emperor, his successors archdukes of Austria, princes of the Low Countries, kings of Spain with the monarchy of the New World, lords of infinite states and of immense countries. The Carolingians acquired the kingdom of France through the protection and favor that they accorded to religion and to the vicar of Christ. The Capetians

---

[104] Deuteronomy 17:18–20.
[105] Nicephorus Callistus, *Historia ecclesiastica*, Book 4 (in Migne, *Patrologia Graeca*, vol. 146, col. 1066).

acquired the same kingdom through the same means of piety. Religion is the foundation of every principality because every power comes from God, and because the grace and favor of God is not acquired by any other means than religion; every other foundation will collapse. Religion renders a prince dear to God, and what can he fear who has God on his side? The goodness of a prince is often the cause of the prosperity of peoples. But because God often permits misfortunes and deaths of princes, revolutions in their states, and the ruin of their cities because of the sins of the people, and because this fosters the glory and service of His Majesty, the king ought to employ every effort and all diligence to introduce religion and piety and to increase it in his state. For this reason William, duke of Normandy, after he acquired the kingdom of England, in order to stabilize and firmly establish his rule there, summoned a great synod at Winchester, with the authority of Alexander II. Here he saw to it that the best laws were issued to reform the corrupt customs of clergy and people and that all matters regarding religion and the worship of God were properly ordered.[106] In the time of Emperor Arnulf[107] and the following years, religion died out because of the bad example and the faults of the emperors who were extremely insolent toward the church. All virtue disappeared and Italy was ravaged by the Saracens and finally ruined by the barbarians to the point that Sergio II, who was a man of great holiness of life and of a great religious spirit, and Emperor Henry II[108], who was of great valor in war and of no less piety in every aspect of his life, once again lit up the world and led the church back to its ancient splendor. Religion is as it were the mother of every virtue. It renders subjects obedient to their prince, courageous in campaigns, bold in times of danger, generous in time of scarcity, alert to every necessity of the republic because they know that in serving their prince they render service to God whose place he holds.

16 Of the Means to Propagate Religion

Religion is of such power for government that without it every other foundation of the state wobbles. So all those who have wanted as it were to establish new empires have also introduced new sects or renewed old ones, as did Ismail, king of Persia, and Sharif, king of Morocco, Louis,

---

[106] In 1070.   [107] Reigned 896–99.
[108] King of Germany 1002–24, Holy Roman Emperor 1014–24, subsequently canonized.

prince of Condé, Gaspard de Coligny, Admiral of France, and William of Nassau who by their heresies brought scandal to the faith and upset Christianity.[109] But of all the laws none is more favorable to princes than the Christian because it submits to them not only the bodies and faculties of subjects where this is appropriate but the souls and consciences as well, and it binds not only the hands but even the affections and thoughts, and it prescribes that obedience be given to wicked princes as well as to ordinary ones and that everything be endured in order not to disturb the peace. And there is nothing that dispenses a subject from obedience owed to the prince unless it is against the law of nature or of God. And in these cases the Christian law prescribes that everything should be done before it comes to an open break. The Christians of the primitive church give a powerful example of this because, even though they were persecuted and tormented with every cruelty, nevertheless nowhere do we read that they rebelled against the Empire or revolted against their princes. They endured the wheel, the sword, and fire, as well as the inhumanity and fury of tyrants and executioners, for the sake of public peace. Nor should we think that this happened because they had no forces because entire legions threw down their arms and allowed themselves to be tortured cruelly and, what amounts to a minor miracle, with all this they prayed daily for preservation of the Roman Empire. And in our times we see that Catholics are oppressed everywhere in Scotland, in England, in France, in Flanders, and in many areas of Germany. It shows the truth of the Catholic faith that renders these subjects obedient to their prince and binds their conscience to them, makes them desirous of peace and enemies of rumors and scandals. But Luther, Calvin, and the others, distancing themselves from evangelical truth, sow everywhere weeds and revolutions in the states and the overthrow of kingdoms. Now, because of the great importance of religion for the successful government and peace of the states, the prince ought to favor it and make efforts for its expansion. And it is necessary first that he avoid the extremes which are simulation and superstition, the former because, as I have said, it cannot last and, once discovered, entirely discredits the simulator, the latter because it causes contempt. Let him be genuinely religious against pretense and intelligently pious against superstition. God is truth, and wants to be adored in truth and in sincerity of soul.

---

[109] Louis de Bourbon, prince of Condé (1530–69), and Gaspard de Coligny, Admiral of France (1519–72), were prominent Huguenot leaders in France; William of Nassau (1533–84), "the Silent," Prince of Orange, was a leader of the Dutch Rebellion.

Given this foundation, let him pay due honor to the Vicar of Christ and to the ministers of the sacred and give an example to others. Let him be persuaded that there is nothing more foolish, nothing that so reveals extreme meanness of spirit than to fight with popes and religious persons. If you honor them for the sake of God whose place they hold, but do not yield to them, you are impious; if you do not honor them for the sake of God but because of qualities that they possess, you are foolish. In this respect one cannot adequately praise Hernán Cortés, conquistador of New Spain, because this most excellent personage, with the incredible reverence that he bore toward priests and religious, accorded the highest esteem and repute to the faith and the Christian religion in those lands. His example carried such force that up to the present day there is no place in the world where the clergy are more respected and religious persons more revered than in New Spain. And it is not possible that you esteem the religion without taking account of the religious because how can you honor the religion, which you do not see, if you do not esteem religious whom you have before your eyes?[110]

Select religious persons of excellent doctrine and virtue and accord them the greatest credit with the people that you are able, listening to them often if they are preachers, making use of their prudence if they are persons of practical knowledge, participating in the divine office in their churches whose ministers give a good example, honoring them occasionally at your table, asking their opinion on some matters, submitting to them some types of memoranda or supplications regarding conscience, assistance of the poor, or some other pious works, finally providing them the material and an occasion to use their talents for the common good. And because a great part of the spiritual assistance for the people depends on preachers, see carefully to it that you have an abundance of them, and give support not to those who with a certain type of florid and wandering speech, which is ineffectual and vain, are more entertainers than preachers but those who scorn this type of pompous and as it were shameless speech and in their preaching breathe into the souls of their hearers and as it were infuse into them spirit and truth, reprove vices, detest sin, inflame souls with the love of God, and finally, preach not themselves but Jesus Christ *et hunc crucifixum* (and him crucified).[111]

He should not permit that ecclesiastics be contemned because of their begging because there is nothing that more degrades religion and the

---

[110] Religious here are members of religious orders.   [111] 1 Corinthians 2:2.

worship of God among the common people than the need and misery of his ministers.

In the construction of churches let them display grandeur, and consider nothing more worthy of a Christian prince than to restore ancient churches rather than to build new ones because restoration will always be a work of piety but in the construction of new churches vainglory often plays a hidden part.

Finally, let him foster the worship of his Creator in every way possible. David in the midst of wars prepared all that was necessary for the construction of a most magnificent temple; he introduced an improved order for the service of the tabernacle; he improved and increased the instruments and the voices for the divine office. Charles the Great brought up from as far as Rome excellent musicians for the divine office, and he ordered a diligent search for the sermons of the Holy Fathers and the lives of the martyrs, and their circulation; he provided an opportunity for Paul the Deacon to write about the deeds of the saints and for Usuard to draw up his *Martyrology*.[112] Constantine the Great ordered, for the sake of understanding religion, that at his own expense the books scattered by past persecutions be collected and that extensive libraries be built.

But as far as government is concerned, leave freely to the prelates the judgment of doctrine and the direction of customs and all the jurisdiction that the good government of souls requires and that the canons and laws concede to them, and promote their observance with authority or with power or with money or with deeds because the more the subjects will be accustomed to and fervent in the way of God, so much the more manageable and obedient will they be to their prince.

17 Of Temperance

Religion is the mother and temperance the wet nurse of the virtues, for without its cooperation and assistance prudence becomes blind, courage becomes weak, and justice becomes corrupt, and every other good loses its force. "Gluttony, sleep, and idleness"[113] banish from the world whatever there is of the honest and the generous, debauchery dulls intelligence, diminishes vigor, and shortens life, delicacies and excessive comforts give birth to effeminacy. But the evil does not end here; in order

---

[112] Usuard was a French Benedictine monk of the ninth century whose *Martyrology* was later a source for Cardinal Cesare Baronius's *Ecclesiastical Annals*, 12 vols. (1588–1607).
[113] Petrarch, *Canzoniere*, 7.1.

to be able to surpass their equals and to equal their superiors, in the magnificence of their table, the elegance of their dress, and in every luxury and vanity, not satisfied with the income from their own possessions and profits from their own business, men stretch out their hands toward sacred things and give themselves over to every kind of wickedness, and so private persons go bankrupt, the public interest is ruined, and lacking any foundation, states collapse. Whoever wants to consider the causes of the collapse of the Roman Empire will find it to have been softness and display because after pleasures came to Rome from Asia and Greece and began to delight the people of Mars, their spirits hitherto unconquered by the sword were overcome by pleasure, and Roman men became women, and the most just lords became the most cruel assassins of the peoples subject to them; each one desiring to live as a king despoiled the cities entrusted to their government. So valor died out smothered by pleasures, and the affection of the peoples was lost because of the oppressive violence of the governors. These developments encouraged the barbarians to enter the provinces and then to assault Rome itself. Pleasures entered Rome with the triumph of Scipio Asiaticus and Manlius Vulso[114] and gradually diffused their poison to the point that having lost their greatness of spirit and ancient nobility, the Romans were not ashamed to support the horrible tyranny of Tiberius, the bestiality of Caligula, the inhumanity of Nero, and the indolence of Heliogabalus, and to obey such monsters of the human race without showing any noteworthy signs of resentment. If some of these were in fact killed, it was as if the women were more responsible than the men, the barbarians rather than the Romans, private citizens rather than the senate; nor was there ever a people in the world that allowed themselves to be so freely oppressed and outraged by tyrants as these. All this shows that their virtue vanished in the theaters, wasted away in the villas of Lucullus, drowned in the fish ponds of Messala,[115] enfeebled in leisure and pleasures. So it was easy for Alaric, king of the Goths, Ataulf[116] and Genseric, kings of the Vandals, Odoacer, king of the Heruli, Theodoric and Totila, kings of the Visigoths,[117] to take Rome, sack it, burn and reduce it to dust and ashes,

---

[114] Scipio Asiaticus was the younger brother of Scipio Africanus; he led the Romans to victory over Antiochus the Great of the Seleucid Empire at Magnesia in 190 BCE. Manlius Volso, consul in 189 BCE, defeated the Galatian Gauls of Asia Minor that year.

[115] Probably Marcus Valerius Messala Rufus (104–26 BCE), Roman senator.

[116] Ataulf, king of the Visigoths (r. 410–15 CE).

[117] Theodoric the Great was king of the Ostrogoths from 475–526 CE, Totila from 541–42.

while the provinces left without spirit became the prey of the barbarians. Of such a nature is human greatness which at its peak generates the worms of pleasure and the rust of luxury which consume it and gradually destroy it.

The kingdom of Portugal provides a great example of this in our day, ruined not by the Moors but by the delights of India. There is no project more difficult than to remedy this. Those who would be able to provide a remedy are the first to be ensnared and give themselves over to sensual pleasures, and rarer than white crows are those whom victories do not leave licentious, prosperity does not blind, and power to do evil does not make vicious. The Roman Empire itself would have fallen much earlier if the valor of some princes had not upheld it to a degree; as Cato said, how could that city last for a long time where a fish was sold for more than an ox? Caesar Augustus endeavored to moderate the excesses in the cost of buildings, and to this purpose, in a public edict called all to consider a fine speech on this topic by P. Rutilio. Tiberius reformed his household furniture and his table, and by his example greatly fostered public frugality; in the formal banquets that he gave he often served the leftovers of the previous day such as half a wild boar remarking that it was the same as the whole pig. Vespasian significantly moderated intemperance with the simplicity of his clothing and the frugality of his table. His son Domitian prohibited the use of litters, purple garments, pearls, and other similar things except for some few persons of a certain age and on certain days. But no one attended more to this than did Aurelian and Tacitus who did not make use of nor want others to make use of garments made completely of silk. Aurelian aimed to eliminate gold from clothing, from rooms and furnishings, and from every other place; this use of gold he said was wasteful. But there is nothing for which greater care must be taken than to limit the display and adornment of the ladies; the unseemly dress of the ladies, according to Aristotle, not only has in itself a certain indecency and ugliness[118] but it awakens the desires of men and leads them toward an evil course of action. Since ladies are much more apt to corrupt men than men are to restrain the ladies, few husbands are masters of their wives. Display foments ambition and vanity, and I will also say that the lust and lewdness of that sex causes the ruin of the property and patrimony of the husband, and as the display increases, so do the trousseaus and the dowries. Therefore, require that expenses for food and

---

[118] *Politics*, 2.9 (1269b–1270a).

for clothing be limited. This can be done in two ways. The first is to prohibit completely the use of certain types of cloth and ornaments for dress
as the Portuguese and Genoese have done. The second is not to prohibit
these things but to burden them with such heavy taxes and impositions
that they become very expensive; in this way only the prince and nobles
will be able to wear such adornments, and there will be some benefit for
the prince. All the above things do infinite harm to temperance and as
a result to the preservation of states. They also are the reason that frequently huge quantities of gold and silver are taken out of your country.
Since pearls, jewels, perfumes, and fragrances and other such things are
in the hands of foreigners, they are sold at their price, and because of the
sensibilities and idle talk of women your state is emptied of true riches.
You ought not to take little account of all this, because it is most certain
that all the great empires have been ruined because of two vices, luxury
and avarice, and avarice is born of luxury, and luxury of women.

Book Three

1 Of the Ways to Divert the People

Up to this point we have discussed in general the virtues with which a prince can win the love of his subjects and a good reputation among them; these two things are the foundation of every state. We speak now a little more about some of the means to this end. The first are abundance, peace, and justice; the people who without fear of foreign or civil war, who without fear of being assassinated in their own houses through violence or fraud, who have the necessary food at a good price, are not able not to be content and are not concerned about anything else. The people of Israel showed this in Egypt where, although they were under a bitter servitude and were harshly treated by the ministers of the pharaoh-king so that they scarcely had time to breathe, nevertheless because of the plentiful food that they had there, they did not think about liberty. On the contrary, when they progressed through the desert, at every least lack of water or some other similar thing they murmured and complained beyond measure against him who had taken them out of Egypt. And all those in Rome who aspired to the kingship attempted this by gratifying the people with the distribution of grain, with the concession of plots of land for cultivation, with agrarian laws, and with all that was suited to satiate the Roman people; so proceeded the Cassii, the Melii, the Manlii, the Gracchi, Caesar, and all the others.[1] Vespasian, once he secured

---

[1] Spurius Cassius Vecelliunus, executed in 485 BCE; Spurius Maelius, decapitated in the fifth century BCE; Marcus Manlius Capitolinus, executed in the fourth century BCE; Tiberius Sempronius Gracchus and Caius Sempronius Gracchus, executed in the second century BCE.

the Empire, took no greater care of any other business than of abundance, and Severus with great solicitude and diligence saw to it that at his death he left for the people of Rome in the public storehouses enough grain for seven years. In order that provisions be sold at a better rate Aurelian increased the weights by an ounce; he judged, as he wrote in a letter, that there was nothing in the world happier than the Roman people when they were well-fed. Experience has taught us in Naples and in other places more than once that there is nothing that more moves and exasperates the people than scarcity of provisions and shortage of bread.

But an abundance of provisions does not help if it cannot be enjoyed either because of the violence of enemies or the injustice of the providers; so it is necessary to join it with peace and justice. Also, because the people are by nature unstable and desirous of novelty, it happens that if they are not entertained in various ways by the prince, they will seek it on their own even with a change in the state and the government. As a result all wise princes have introduced some popular entertainments which the more they stimulate virtue of the mind and of the body, the more suitable they will be. The Greeks have shown more judgment in their Olympic, Nemean, Pythian, and Isthmian Games[2] than the Romans in their Apollinarian, secular, and gladiatorial games and in their comedies, hunts, and other similar things in which the Roman citizens exercised neither their mind nor their body so that they served as pure entertainment.[3] But the games of the Greeks served also as exercise. However that may be, Caesar Augustus, a prince of great prudence, appeared in person at the games, in order to give status to the performances and satisfaction to the people, and to demonstrate the care that he took for their recreation and amusement. These entertainments, interrupted for many years by the floods and wars with the barbarians, were revived by Theodoric, king of the Goths, a prince (if he had not been an Arian) of outstanding prudence.[4] He rebuilt the theaters and amphitheaters, the arenas and artificial lakes for sham naval battles; he introduced the ancient games and spectacles, to such delight of the crowds that they had no concern for a change of government.

---

[2] These were the four Panhellenic competitions.
[3] Starting in 212 BCE, the Apollinarian Games were celebrated every year in Rome, the secular games only rarely.
[4] Theodoric, king of the Ostrogoths, ruled Italy from 493–526.

Matteo and Galeazzo Visconti[5] operated in the same style in Milan, and Lorenzo and Piero de' Medici[6] acquired the love and benevolence of the people with various tournaments, jousts, and other similar inventions. Such spectacles ought to take place without danger to life because beyond the fact that they offend the law of God, it is also against the nature of the game to risk serious injury or loss of life for anyone. Zizim[7], the brother of Bajazet, when asked what he thought of a tournament at which he was present, responded that these contests amounted to little if one truly fought but they were excessive as an amusement because of the dangers that they ran. Furthermore, the men who are accustomed to see the wounds, blood, and death of others in a game necessarily become fierce, cruel, and bloody, and from this there easily follow brawls, homicides, and other scandals in the city. For this reason the gladiatorial contests were suppressed by the Emperor Honorius[8], as some writers claim because a certain monk was sent to condemn this impious custom; the people used to being amused every day by the sight of the wounds and deaths of men, pursued and killed him.

To the extent that the above-mentioned spectacles will be more decent and more serious, so they will have greater force to attract, delight, and entertain the people. The happiness at which these entertainments aim consists of two elements, namely pleasure and moral conduct. For this reason I would praise tragedy more than comedy because comic material is ordinarily such that morality has no part in it, and the actors more readily play the part of ruffians than comic actors. For this reason the church canons do not allow them to be baptized nor to receive the sacraments of penance or the Eucharist without first giving up this infamous practice. But why do I cite the church canons? Scipione Nasica, fearing that comedies and farces would infect the Roman people with vices, advised the senate to destroy a theater that was under construction.[9] Ecclesiastical

---

[5] Matteo II (1319–55) and Galeazzo II (1320–78) Visconti; they were co-rulers of Milan along wih their brother Bernabò.

[6] Lorenzo de' Medici, the Magnificent, governed Florence from 1469–92, his son Piero from 1492 until the French invasion in 1494.

[7] Zizim (1459–95), brother of Bajazet (Bayezid) II, sultan from 1481 to 1512, a pretender to the throne, fled to Rhodes and was held prisoner in Italy and France at the request of the sultan.

[8] Honorius Flavius, Roman emperor in the West from 393–423; after the sack of Rome in 410, he moved his capital to Ravenna.

[9] Publius Cornelius Scipio Nasica died in 141 BCE.

spectacles have more of the serious and the marvelous than do secular spectacles because they participate in the sacred and the divine. For this reason Aristotle advised the prince to offer sacred sacrifices,[10] and we have seen Cardinal Borromeo entertain the innumerable population of Milan with feasts celebrated religiously and with ecclesiastical activities undertaken by him with ceremony and incomparable gravity, in such a manner that the churches were always filled from morning until evening nor were the people ever happier, more content, and more quiet than were the people of Milan in those days.

2 Of Honorable and Great Enterprises

The works and honorable and magnificent enterprises of princes provide great diversion, very serious and nearly heroic; they are of two kinds, some civil, others military. Of the civil are buildings which are amazing either for their size or for their utility, such as the Propylaeum constructed by Pericles,[11] the lighthouse built by Ptolemy,[12] the port of Ostia made by Claudio and expanded by Trajan, the aqueducts, the bridges over rivers or streams, the reduction and improvement of swampy areas, the roads for use within the city and beyond such as were the Emilian, the Appian, the Cassian and others, the redirection of rivers for the benefit of navigation and agriculture such as the canals of Milan, the hospitals, monasteries, cities; we will mention here also the ships of marvelous grandeur like that of Alfonso I of Aragon, and the engines of war such as the one built for the siege of cities by Demetrius.[13] But with similar works it is necessary to guard against two drawbacks. One is that they do not become in fact useless. The other is that the people are not excessively burdened by them. In this the kings of Egypt deserve blame because for the sake of a foolish show of their infinite riches, they created immense structures. And what will we say of the vanity of Semiramis who had a statue sixteen stadii high set on a mountain?[14] Little more useful was the Colossus of Rhodes[15] so celebrated by the ancients. Nor merit less blame

---

[10] *Politics*, 3.14 (1285b).
[11] The Propylaea atop the Acropolis in Athens, built in 437 BCE.
[12] The lighthouse of Alexandria, begun under Ptolemy Philadelphus (r. 285–246 BCE).
[13] Demetrius I, Poliorcetes, king of Macedonia (r. 294–288 BCE).
[14] It was found on a crag in Bagistan between Babylon and Ecbatana; in reality it rose only 166 meters. Semiramis had her own image carved into the lower section of the statue.
[15] A statue of the Greek titan-god of the sun, Helios, erected on the island of Rhodes in 280 BCE and destroyed in an earthquake of 226 BCE.

perhaps the palaces and pleasure villas built by King Solomon at infinite expense and, consequently, an intolerable burden for the subjects. It is not fitting when building such things for the diversion of the people and to preserve them in peace, that they suffer abuse and are reduced to desperation. In order to keep them content and quiet, buildings and other such things will better serve the purpose the more they will produce greater common utility and pleasure; this will ease the tasks, render the hardships agreeable and the labors mild because interest pacifies all.

3 Of Enterprises of War

But military enterprises occupy the people much more because there is nothing that more engages the spirits of the people than important wars that are undertaken either to secure the borders or to extend rule and to acquire justly riches and glory, or to defend allies or to benefit friends or to preserve religion and the worship of God. All those who can contribute something either with their hands or with counsel usually come to participate in such enterprises and there they vent their feelings against the common enemy. The rest of the people follow the camp in order to provide provisions or perform some similar service or they remain at home where they pour out prayers and offerings to the Lord God in order to win victory or they stand held in suspense by expectation and by the course of the war in such a manner that there does not remain in the souls of the subjects any room for revolts so much are all taken up in deed and in thought by the enterprise. At times of sedition on the part of the plebs the Romans ordinarily resorted to this remedy as a last resort; they led an army in campaign against enemies, and so they put to rest the ill will against the nobles. Cimon, seeing that the Athenian youth did not know how to remain peaceful, armed two hundred galleys and led them out to prove their courage against the Persians.[16] And if we will consider well why in our times Spain remains in complete peace and France is involved in perpetual civil wars we will find that this results in part from Spain's investment in foreign wars and in campaigns in remote areas, in the Indies, in the Low Countries, against heretics, against Turks and Moors. These occupy partly the hands and partly the minds of the Spaniards, so their homeland has enjoyed the greatest peace and diverted elsewhere every peccant humor. France, on the other hand, at peace with

---

[16] Cimon (510–450 BCE) was an Athenian statesman and general.

75

foreigners, has revolted against itself, and since it has no other pretext has taken that of the heresies of Calvin and of a new Gospel which, wherever it is heard, announces not joy but mourning, not peace but horrible war, and fills souls not with good will but with furor and madness. The Ottomans also with a perpetual course of the greatest campaigns and victories have not only extended their dominion but even more, which is not of little importance, have secured their acquisitions and kept their subjects at peace.

4 Whether it is Expedient for a Prince to Go to War in Person

It will not be outside our purpose to discuss whether it is good for a prince to go in person on military campaign; it is a matter of great dispute, by example and by reasoning, for one side and then the other. On the one hand it more easily happens that among the captains and barons given to arms there are one or more with excellent judgment and valor, and that these qualities are not always found in the prince. In this case it is better that he manage campaigns through others rather than in person. If he does not have those qualities that are sought in a captain, his presence will be more likely to upset the proper decisions and to impede their execution rather than to facilitate the former and to expedite the latter. Without leaving Constantinople, Justinian, making use of the prudence and valor of excellent men, liberated Italy from the Goths and Africa from the Vandals, held at bay the boldness of the Persians, and was considered fortunate thanks to the *virtù* of Belisario,[17] Narses, and the other ministers that he had. In the same way, Charles VI, king of France, while remaining in Bourges, chased the English out of his kingdom by means of his outstanding commanders, and so he received the title "the Wise."[18] On the other hand, if the prince is such as we have described, by going personally to war he will bring with him all those qualities that a minister would bring and in addition the advantage of his reputation and authority which will double the vigilance of the captains and the ardor of the

---

[17] Flavio Belisario (505–65 CE) was considered the most famous general of the Byzantine Empire.

[18] There is a misprint or error here. Charles V of France (r. 1364–80) was given the title "the Wise," not Charles VI (r. 1380–1422). Botero got this right above, *RS*, 2.13, p. 61. Charles VII (r. 1422–61) ended the Hundred Years' War.

soldiers because *urget praesentia Turni* (the presence of Turnus spurs them on).[19]

But because as much as a prince with the proper qualities can be greatly desired, only God, no other, can make one, it remains for us only to demonstrate which campaigns require absolutely the presence of the prince and which do not. Let us therefore first of all suppose that the prince ought not to move except for important wars or campaigns. Now such campaigns are undertaken either for defense or for offense and the acquisition of another's [territory]. Defense is either of your own principal state in which you have your residence, or of some other separate and distant member. Let us say then, that if an enemy will come with great force to assault you at home, it would be good for the prince to go out to encounter him personally because besides the reputation that he will bring to the campaign and to the following of the nobility and the people who will accompany him voluntarily and in competition with one another, he will also inspire the soldiers with his example and compel them by force of necessity to fight courageously for the defense and salvation of the king and the kingdom; this applies to offense, not only to defense. Furthermore, the defense and preservation of the state is of so great and universal a benefit that the prince should not act as though there were an obligation to any other than himself for it; otherwise he runs the risk of [losing] the state as happened to Childeric, king of France.[20] Abdimar, king of Spain, entered that most noble kingdom with 450,000 Saracens. While Childeric, occupied with the delights of his palace like a Sardanapalus,[21] gave himself over to good times and to plunging still further into sensual pleasures, Abdimar with terror and dispersion of the people put to fire and sword all that he encountered throughout the delightful country of Saintonge and Poitou. But Charles Martel was not sleeping. Having assembled a powerful army which included the sinews and flower of the nobility and people of France, he defied the barbarians with great spirit and in an awe-inspiring feat of arms killed 375,000 of them. This valiant defense had such an effect and with such general approval placed the souls of the French universally under obligation to Martel that the king counted

[19] Vergil, *Aeneid*, 9.73.
[20] Botero here mistakes Childeric for Theodoric IV, king of the Franks, when Charles Martel defeated a Saracen army near Tours in 732.
[21] Sardanapalus, the last king of Assyria, reigned from 667 to 626 BCE; he lived isolated in his palace and became proverbial for his soft and lascivious life.

for nothing, so that it does not surprise that Pepin his son was so readily acclaimed king of France in 752.[22]

And not only did the people bind themselves to him who defended the state and the temporal [power] but no less to him who maintained the spiritual and religion because this anchor is a benefit of the greatest importance that belongs to all. And in this same kingdom of France one sees how great was the love and reputation that some princes acquired through the protection that they always provided the faith and the cause of God. But it is not necessary that the prince always be under arms; it is sufficient that he sometimes approach the army and the battlefield, and finally that he do this in such a way that it is recognized that the safety of the state depends in whole or in great part upon his judgment, counsel, vigilance, magnanimity, and valor. The same ought to be observed in offensive wars of importance that are fought nearby, because proximity increases the grace and favor of him who conducts the enterprise to its end, and the benefit appears, truly, greater. The king of León and Castile and, successively, the other kings of Spain were personally present in all the campaigns against the Moors, and in particular Ferdinand, king of Aragon, and Isabella, queen of Castile, his wife, in the campaign and capture of Granada.[23] But if the war is fought far from home, the prince ought not to leave the heart of his states from where his authority and his power radiates to all around him. Tiberius Caesar diligently followed this policy. When in a situation of great danger the legions in Germany were rioting and it seemed to most that the prince, in order to quiet the rebels with the majesty of his presence, ought to journey there, he firmly resolved not to heed the murmurings of the common people nor the judgment of whoever it might be. He considered that it did not befit a great prince to depart without necessity from the seat of his empire and the place from which originated his government of the rest.[24] To the same point Herodotus wrote that it was not allowed the king of Persia to depart for war outside the kingdom without leaving at home, in order to avoid civil wars, a vicar with the insignias and title of king.[25] The Ottomans do not easily go on maritime campaigns. Suleiman, alone among all of them, in the campaign of Rhodes crossed over the little bit of sea that separates that island from land.[26] I wonder that Machiavelli counsels his

---

[22] Pepin was acclaimed king of the Franks, not of France, in 751 and anointed king the following year at Soissons.

[23] Granada was taken on January 2, 1492.   [24] Tacitus, *Annals*, 1.46–47.

[25] Herodotus, *Histories*, 7.2.   [26] Suleiman conquered Rhodes in 1522.

prince or tyrant, which ever he is, to move the residence of his person into lands that he has acquired.[27] This is nothing other than to endanger his natural subjects for the sake of his acquired ones and the substantial for the sake of the accessory. Nor is the example valid that he adduces of the Grand Turk, Muhammad I, who moved his residence from Bursa to Constantinople. The Turk has no natural subjects, and the site of Constantinople is much more comfortable than what he would be able to find in the midst of his states.[28]

[27] *Prince*, chap. 3.
[28] Botero errs here; it was Mehmed II (Muhammad II), not Muhammad I, who conquered Constantinople in 1453 and moved his capital there.

Book Four

1 Of the Way to Avoid Rumblings and Rebellions

Therefore it is not enough to possess the art of distracting the people, because this is misleading; more is necessary to see to it that they are not able, or at least ought not to have reason, to rise up and disturb the public peace and the majesty of the prince. Above all, it is necessary to remove the occasion and the easiness of revolts.

2 Of the Three Types of Persons who Make Up the City

In every state there are three sorts of persons: the rich, the poor, and those in the middle between the two extremes of these three types. Those in the middle are ordinarily the most quiet and the easiest to govern. The extremes are more difficult because the powerful, on account of the opportunity that their riches supply them, refrain from evil only with difficulty, and the poor because of the necessity in which they find themselves are similarly accustomed to be more prone to vice. So Solomon prayed to God that he would not give him great riches nor permit him to fall into great poverty.[1] Furthermore, those who abound in riches and thrive on nobility, family connections, and clients do not know how to be subject to others because of the refinement of their upbringing nor do they wish to be so because of their proud spirit. On the contrary, the poor are prepared to obey in dishonorable as well as in honorable matters. The

---

[1] Proverbs 20:8.

former give themselves over to violence and take pleasure in overbearing conduct; the latter become malicious and fraudulent. The former offend their neighbor openly, the latter work and grouse secretly. The rich do not know how to govern themselves because of their prosperity. This is why Plato, when asked by the Cyrenians to give them laws by which to govern themselves, did not wish to do so, saying that it was difficult to give laws to the Cyrenians who lived in such great prosperity.[2] The poor are not able to live under laws because the necessity in which they find themselves knows no laws.[3] But those in the middle have enough that they do not lack what is necessary for their state of life; they are not so powerful that they are able to take it to heart to plan and to undertake great enterprises. Ordinarily they are friends of peace and content with their state; ambition does not raise them up nor does desperation bring them down and, as Aristotle says, they are most suited to virtue.[4] And so it happens that great cities, because they have a large number of persons of modest means, are less subject to rebellions than the small ones.[5] Supposing therefore that those in the middle are by nature calm, we will discuss the extremes and the way to see to it that they do not break out in disorder and tumult.

3 Of the Great Ones

There are three types of persons whose authority and power are able to rouse the prince's suspicion: relatives who by reason of their blood have a claim to the crown or who are able to make the claim with the people; lords of important fiefs or of strategic locations; and personalities who because of their valor in war or their skill in peace-making have acquired reputation and credit with the people.

4 Of the Princes of the Blood

Nothing is more a cause of jealousy than [the rule of] states; often it leads princes to fury and rage. The ambition and jealousy of which we speak

---

[2] Plutarch, *Morals*, 50.1.

[3] This is a translation of the juridical adage *necessitas non habet legem*. Its usage here is original; it does not indicate exceptional situations which dispense from the law but identifies necessity with poverty and so the difficulty for the poor to be integrated into the juridico-political order. (See *BD*, 184, n. 6.)

[4] *Politics*, 4.11 (1295a–b).   [5] This sentence is suppressed in later editions.

can be so great in the souls of those whom it tyrannizes that it despoils them of their human nature or at least of their humanity. Alexander the Great, wanting to set out on his campaign in Asia, had all his relatives killed. The Turks as soon as they accede to the Empire have all their brothers killed. Murad III who now reigns had the throat cut of a concubine of his father who was pregnant.[6] The kings of Ormuz, before that kingdom fell to the Portuguese, blinded their relatives, which some emperors in Constantinople were also accustomed to do. The kings of China, abhorring this cruelty, were content with a more humane measure, to lock up those of the blood in some large and spacious places filled with every comfort and amusement. The kings of Ethiopia did the same, confining their relatives on a high and most pleasant mountain called Amara where they remained until fate called them to the succession to the crown. This mountain is so steep that it can be said to be an impregnable fortress. One can only climb up it by means of an extremely narrow path, and at the top there is a large arable field that can support a brigade with its produce, so that it is easily protected from attacks and need not fear to be starved out by a siege. But returning to our theme, let us say that neither the kings of China nor the emperors of Ethiopia by confining their relatives nor the Turks by killing them nor the Moors by blinding them secured their states from sedition or uprisings. Neither the Chinese nor the Ethiopians were able to do this because even when their relatives remained calm and well-ordered, it could happen that the people and the barons, led on by anger and passion or moved by fear of punishment or the desire of vendetta, sought to win over those confined and by bribing or overcoming the guards free them from their prisons or places of confinement and install them in office as the rebellious Communeros of Spain tried to do with the duke of Calabria who was then a prisoner in the fortress of Jativa.[7] But I do not deny that the customs of the Chinese and the Ethiopians have less of the barbarian and the unjust, because custom has the force of law and it is rational that, to free the kingdom from danger and also from suspicion, the relatives of the king are content with this peaceful confinement. But there is not that total security that one

---

[6] Murad III, sultan from 1574–95.

[7] Ferdinand of Aragon, the duke of Calabria, son of Frederick the deposed king of Aragon, was imprisoned in 1512 by Ferdinand II, the Catholic, at Jativa in Valencia. He had been there nine years when the Communeros wanted to liberate him and make him leader of their revolt; he refused (*BD*, 187, n. 1).

thinks because in China many kings have been murdered and many of the cruelest tyrants, even women, have ruled there, and in Ethiopia not many years ago Abdimilec was called to the Empire not from Mount Amara but from Arabia whither he had retired.[8] But much less secure is the cruelty of the Turks who murder or of the Moors who blind their brothers and relatives because in the other kingdoms a spirit eager for honor and for rule has no other stimulus that moves him to cause an uproar and take to arms than ambition, which can be variously ensnared or restrained or turned away and diverted elsewhere. But among the Ottomans and the Moors, beyond ambition there is the reputed necessity to preserve one's own life; so nowhere have there ever been more civil wars or more revolutions than in Ormuz, Tunis, Morocco, and Fez, and among the Turks, as demonstrate the wars between Orkhan and Musa and between Musa and Mehmed,[9] between Bajazet and Zizim, between Selim I and his father Bajazet II, between him and his nephew Alemschah,[10] between Suleiman and his son Mustapha, and between Selim II[11] and his brother Bajazet, who finally fled to the court of Tahmasp, king of Persia,[12] where he was murdered by his host for a million in gold promised him. The knowledge that he would have to be killed by whoever acquired the Empire makes each one consider his own situation and take up arms with the help of subjects and foreigners. So Selim I used to say that he deserved pardon even if he murdered so many, his brothers, cousins, nephews, and relatives of every sort, because the lowest member of the Ottoman house who rose to this rank would have treated him the same way.

On the contrary we see that in the kingdoms of Spain, Portugal, and France, and in the principalities of Germany and in the other states of Christendom, even if there are and have been many blood relatives and many princes with a claim to the throne, there do not arise so many wars and lengthy revolutions as among these barbarians because cruel laws and customs make men cruel and humane ones human. Why are there so many princes of the blood in the house of Austria, more brothers

---

[8] There is perhaps confusion here between the negus in power from 1578–97, Sarsa Dengel, who took the name Malak Sagad I, and the sultan Saadien of Morocco who reigned from 1576–78 after retiring not to Arabia but to Turkey (*BD*, 187, n. 4).

[9] During the period called the "Interregnum," Musa, brother of Mehmed (Muhammad) I, broke his alliance with him, to proclaim himself sultan of Edirne in 1410.

[10] Once on the throne in 1512, Selim I had all his brothers and nephews killed.

[11] Orhan, Mehmed I, Bajazet II, Selim I, Suleiman the Magnificent, and Selim II are Ottoman sultans from the fourteenth to the sixteenth century.

[12] Shah Tahmasp I of Persia (r. 1524–76).

and more cousins? But they have never offended against affection or disturbed the commonwealth by ambition; indeed they yield to one another their rights and their pretensions and live together most harmoniously as if many bodies were animated by one spirit and governed by one will. In France, even if there have always been many princes of the royal house, the succession has never been disturbed among the descendants of Charlemagne, Hugh Capet, or Merovech who preceded them. But is the sweetness of rule able to be so strong, the satisfaction so great, the contentment so complete that it ought to be purchased with the death of brothers and the extermination and ruin of relations? Or what kingdom is so rich and happy that one can enjoy it with good cheer and delight without having near a person of the same blood to whom one can communicate the benefits and a share of the prosperity? The way then to maintain the quiet and peace of states on the part of the prince who has the right of succession is justice and prudence. With these and a knowledge of the nature and the humors of the people, avoidance of insults, removal of the material for envy, than which there is no passion more vehement and more tempestuous, the state will remain quiet because as ferocity and cruelty embitter and infuriate the spirits of the great, so do peacefulness and suitable conduct keep them faithful to their duty and acting reasonably. The Turks, because they aim to kill their brothers, compel them to take up arms. In contrast Antoninus the Philosopher[13] took as his companion in rule Lucius Verus, his brother, and Valentinian did the same for his brother Valens, which resulted in nothing other than love and the redoubling of benevolence.[14] Gratian divided the Empire with Theodosius who was not related to him; nor was there ever a greater union of souls than between these two princes.[15] And I do not want to omit saying that the most probable cause of the future fall of the Turkish Empire is their cruelty toward relatives. The reason is that the Ottomans take as many women as they want and so they generate sons beyond number (it is said that one son of the present Amurat had fifty within two years)[16], all certain to be put to death by the one who acquires the kingdom, and it is likely in the long run that civil wars should arise in that Empire which

---

[13] Marcus Aurelius, emperor 161–80 CE.

[14] Valentinian governed the Empire in the West from 364 –75 CE; his brother Valens governed the Empire in the East from 364–78.

[15] Gratian, Roman emperor from 375–83 CE, son and successor of Valentinian, raised the general Theodosius to the imperial dignity in 379; he ruled until 395.

[16] This parenthetical sentence was suppressed in later editions.

would weaken its forces and divide the state into more parts, and in this way open the way for enemies to attack and subject it. Nor should anyone wonder that this has not yet happened because not many centuries have passed yet since Osman who died in 1328 founded the Turkish Empire at the time of Benedict XI;[17] but we have already seen the most vicious wars among them which make credible this my prediction.

5 Of Feudal Barons

There are both good and bad in the individual lords of a kingdom; the evil is authority and power inasmuch as it is suspect to the sovereign prince because it is as if it were both a support and a ready refuge for him who would want to mutiny or to rise up or for him who would attempt to start a war or to attack the state as have the princes of Taranto and Salerno and the dukes of Sessa and Rossano in the Kingdom of Naples.[18] The good is that these lords are as the bones and the firmness of the states which, deprived of them, would be as it were bodies composed of flesh and pulp, without bones and nerves which in the case of a great battle in war, the rout of an army, or the death of a king would easily collapse. Without any persons of lofty birth or inveterate authority who would stand out among the others and so qualify to be leaders, the people become confused and, deprived of decisive leadership and council, yield to the enemy, as has been seen more than once in Egypt and would be seen in Turkey if it should please God that the enemy for once should be defeated in battle. On the other hand we see kingdoms where a numerous nobility is as it were immortal, as France and Persia show. Having fallen nearly completely under the kings of England, France was revived by the efforts of its infinite nobility. Persia, similarly subjected either by the Tartars or by the Saracens, survived because of the valor of its abundant nobility. And was Spain not liberated from the servitude of the Moors by the valor and efforts of its nobility? Now someone will say that the titled lords are good for the conservation of the country and the state but not for the king because if they are apt for maintaining the country and inspiring the multitude, so they also can frustrate the prince and make him work. Who doubts this if the prince should be weak for the burden that he bears or incapable of greatness or unworthy of his

[17] Osman I died in 1325 during the pontificate of John XXII.
[18] This alludes to the plot of the barons against Ferdinand of Aragon in 1485.

fortune? If he does not have eagerness for justice, nor the light of counsel, if finally he will not be such as we have described? In this case he
will be not only tormented by the barons but deceived by his councillors
and untrustworthy persons, and he will serve not as a king but as a pawn
as did Childeric and Charles the Simple[19] in France (under whom the
fiefs began in that kingdom where because of the ineptitude of the king,
each feudal lord usurped those cities and places that he governed), and
Wencelaus in Germany,[20] Ramiro in Spain,[21] Andreasso in Naples,[22] and
Maximilian Sforza in Milan.[23] No sort of security will be good for such
a man because he lacks the advice and the judgment to make use of it.

6 Of Those who are Great because of their Courage

The third sort are those whose power can be suspect and those who, even
if they are not illustrious because of their blood, nor great because of their
riches or the number of their vassals, possess great authority either by
their handling of great matters or by their courage in various situations in
peace and in war. And truly nothing is more dangerous to republics than
the sovereign greatness of an individual; the Athenians rid themselves
of them by ostracism. Nor is he any less dangerous for all monarchies;
Aristotle thought that the conservation of the principality required that
no one rose disproportionately over the others either in authority or in
riches[24] because few are those who know how to be moderate in prosperity and to lower the pole of their boat in the face of favorable winds. One
can remedy these drawbacks first by not making use in important matters
of arrogant or notably bold people because such men are by nature always
planning something new, and boldness joined with power is restrained
with difficulty. Much less ought you to trust astute and brooding people
such as were C. Cassius,[25] Lorenzino de' Medici,[26] and in our time, Gaspard de Coligny, a man of little spirit but much malice, and William of
Nassau, more timid than a sheep and more fraudulent than a fox. The
bold presume enough on their bravura just as the astute have confidence

[19] Reigned 879–929.
[20] Probably Wenceslaus II (1271–1305), king of Bohemia (*BD*, 191, n.4).
[21] Probably Ramiro II, king of León and Galicia (r. 931–51).
[22] Andrew of Hungary, murdered by his wife Joanna of Naples in 1345.
[23] Duke of Milan (r. 1512–15).   [24] *Politics*, 4, 11 (1295b–1296b).
[25] Cassius instigated the plot against Julius Caesar.
[26] Lorenzino murdered his cousin Alexander de' Medici in 1537. Cassius and Lorenzino
were seen in sixteenth-century Italy as typical republican assassins.

in the superiority of their intelligence. But no one is less suitable to trust than the unstable and frivolous because these like reeds turn this way and that at the least whiff of hope or fear and are the joke of the bold and the astute. It is good not to install magistrates with jurisdiction and power close to the supreme authority because the sweetness of command leads men beyond the limits of the honest and the just, and if such magistrates already exist, they ought quietly to be suppressed as have been suppressed more than once the office of the Grand Constable in France and the Grand Masters of St. James of Alcantara and Calatrava in Spain. If it is not possible to suppress them, it will be good to weaken them and cut back part of their authority and power, especially by shortening their time in office because power joined with long continuance in office makes men, having forgotten their condition, aspire not to what they ought but to what is possible or to what they think is possible.

So I marvel that in the greater number of the kingdoms of Christendom the greater and more important offices are perpetual as are the Constables, the Admirals, and the Marshalls. Besides these in France the government of provinces is given to the great princes for life so that they become masters as it were; at the least it is not in the power of the king to remove them from government of the province without an uproar and suspicion of some rebellion or innovation. By perpetuating the government of the richest provinces for life in the hands of those who hold it and by passing it from father to son, they acquire so many friends, clients, and partisans or by virtue of the authority that their office gives them or by the favor that they have with the king, they place so many of their adherents or servants in the most important towns and governments of which that they can be said to be masters. So the duchies, the counties, the marquisates, and the other grades of office and government for life have become hereditary.

The administration of justice ought to be indeed perpetual not in this or that person but in more persons in a senate or parliament. The administration of the military ought not to be committed for life nor to many persons. Not to many persons because a plurality of captains inhibits the management of the war, and the army led by one head will always conquer one led by more than one head; nor for life because military power makes men reckless, not merely bold, as that noble poet said of Achilles: *nihil non arrogat armis* (he thinks everything depends upon arms).[27] For

---

[27] Horace, *Art of Poetry*, 122.

this reason the Romans made all their magistracies for one year except the censors, and the dictators, whose authority was supreme, rarely served a year. Marius, Caesar, and Pompey by their continuation in the office and the government of the most extensive provinces and the largest provinces became masters in part or in full of the republic.

Finally, in the perpetuity of offices there are three disadvantages. The first is the one already discussed; the second is that the prince knowingly deprives himself of the ability to make use of a better subject that he will in time discover; the last is that it is possible that the one he has provided with this rank becomes incapable because of illness or unfit because of age or harmful because of passion rather than beneficial, so that the troops that he will have at hand will have little strength for the service of the king or will create more evil than good or will be completely useless. But if the prince ought not to bind his hands by making magistracies and offices permanent, so he ought not to harm himself by obligating himself by laws or statute always to change them. He should remain free to make use of them more or less and to confirm in or relieve of office according to the nature of the persons and the requirements that he seeks. So it was that Caesar Augustus when he received the news of the death of Quintilius Varus,[28] retained in office all the prefects of provinces so that in such an ominous and unusual situation and in such a dangerous occasion and time, the subjects were governed by practical persons of recognized prudence. Tiberius allowed many to grow old in the administration of the provinces and of the armies, and Antoninus Pius, as he sought always to have good and excellent ministers, so when he had them he loaded them with honors and riches. But because everything movable derives from a movable principle, the prince ought to have, besides the individual governors of the provinces, the generals of the armies, the captains of the fortresses, and similar officials whose charges are not permanent, his permanent council but without jurisdiction. Here will take place deliberations about important matters and about war and peace, here will be preserved knowledge of the past and of the practice of managing peoples, and all that which concerns good government both civil and military.

7 Of the Poor

Also dangerous for the public peace are those who have no interest in it, that is, those who find themselves in great misery and poverty.

---

[28] Varus was killed in battle in Germany in 9 BCE.

Having nothing to lose, they are easily roused at the appearance of novelty, and they willingly embrace all the means at hand to raise themselves through the ruin of others. So Livy wrote that in Greece, when war was rumored between King Perseus and the Romans, those who were oppressed by poverty desired that the world be turned upside down and favored Perseus while the good men who did not want any change took the side of the Romans.[29] And Catiline, aiming to shake up the Roman republic, made capital of those who were pitied because of their life or because of their fortune; as Sallust says, *homini potentiam quaerenti egentissimus, quisque opportunissimo, cui neque sua cara, et omnia cum pretio honesta videntur* (to a man in search of power the most needy are the most useful, for they have no possessions dear to them, and they think everything honest has a price).[30] Caesar when he aimed at the rule of his country paid off all those who because of debts or mismanagement or some other reason had fallen into great necessity and, because they had no reason to be content with their present state, he considered them useful for his own plan to subvert the republic. If there were some still whose extreme poverty he could not relieve, he said openly that they needed a civil war, and all those who had taken away the liberty of their country made use of these people because, as Sallust says, *semper in civitate, quibus opes nullae sunt, bonis invident, malos extollunt, vetera odere, nova exoptant, odio suarum rerum mutari omnia student* (always in cities those who have nothing envy the good, exalt the wicked, detest old institutions and want new ones, and try to alter everything because they hate their own condition).[31]

In France the great rumblings which we have heard even here have been born of the same sort of people. Caught up in the wars between the Most Christian [King] and the Most Catholic [King], and having acquired infinite debts, with many falling into poverty, and their soldiers not having the means to live and to spend as they were accustomed, the princes have determined to enrich themselves with the wealth of the church which in that kingdom amounts to more than six million scudi in income. So, using the opportunity of heresy, which they call new religion, they took up arms and have reduced that kingdom, otherwise so flourishing, to misery. The king then ought to secure himself against them, and this in two ways: by expelling them from the state or making peace in the

---

[29] Livy, *History of Rome*, 42.30.4–6.   [30] Sallust, *Jugurthine War*, 86.3.
[31] Sallust, *The War with Catiline*, 37. 3.

state to be in their interest. He can expel them either by sending them to colonies as did the Spartans with the Partheniae (because fearing that they might cause trouble, they sent them to Taranto)[32] or they can send them to war (as did the Venetians with many ruffians that filled the city, and they got rid of them on the occasion of the war with Cyprus),[33] or they can simply expel them as did Ferdinand, king of Spain, with the gypsies to whom he gave sixty days to leave the country.[34] They will acquire an interest if they are required to undertake something, that is, to attend to agriculture or to crafts or to some other activity which will provide them with an income to support themselves. Amasis, king of Egypt, issued a law that required every subject to appear and give an account of himself to the governors of the provinces of how he lived and with what means, and he imposed the death penalty on those who were not able to give an account.[35] In Athens the Areopagites severely punished those slackers who did not know any trade,[36] and Solon did not want a son to be required to support his father if through his negligence the son had not learned a trade.[37] The laws of the Chinese required that a son learn to exercise the trade of his father. From this there followed two benefits: the first, that the trades developed in this way toward greater excellence, and the second, that each man had the convenience of learning in his own household a trade with which to support himself. The unemployed and the lazy were not in any way tolerated, and even the blind and the cripples work to the extent that they can, and they are not admitted to the hospital unless they are completely helpless. Qinshi Huangdi, who gave to the Chinese the greater part of the discipline with which China maintains itself, wanted women to practice the trade of their father or at least attend to the distaff and the needle.[38] The kings of the Romans, in order to secure as much interest as possible from the people in the defense of the Republic, saw to it that each held landed property, so that the love of their possessions would compel them to love and defend the present state. Lycurgus, as Nabis[39] said to Quintus Flaminius, *fore credidit, ut per*

---

[32] According to the myth, the Partheniae were forced to leave Sparta after revolting because they were not granted civic rights, and went on to found the city of Taranto toward the end of the eighth century BCE; see Aristotle, *Politics*, 5.7 (1306b).

[33] 1570.   [34] 1499.

[35] Herodotus, *History*, 2.177. Amasis was pharaoh in the sixth century BCE.

[36] The Areopagus was the supreme tribunal of Athens.

[37] Plutarch, *Parallel Lives*, "Solon," 22.1.

[38] Qin Shi Huang was China's first emperor; he reigned from 259–210 BCE.

[39] Last tyrant of Sparta, 205–192 BCE.

aequitationem fortunae ac dignitatis multi essent, qui pro Republica arma fer-rent (believed that because of equality of fortune and dignity there were many who would bear arms for the Republic).[40]

But because not everyone is able to own land or to exercise a trade, and because for a human life they need others, the prince ought himself or through others to provide the poor with a means to gain their livelihood. To this end Caesar Augustus undertook much construction and encouraged leading figures of the city to do the same, and in this way he kept the poor people quiet. To an engineer who proposed a way to transport huge columns to the Campidoglio at a modest expense, Vespasian responded that the idea greatly pleased him, and he remunerated him for it, but it failed to provide a way to earn their living to the common people. So he inferred that he spent willingly in order to provide a livelihood for many which that plan would have left behind. Finally you will secure your position with these by entrusting the Republic only into the hands of those for whom peace and quiet count and disturbance and novelty are dangerous. So Quintus Flaminius, wishing to reorganize the cities of Thessaly, made that party more powerful for whom it was useful that the Republic be safe and tranquil.

---

[40] Livy, *History of Rome*, 34.31.18.

Book Five

1 Of Acquired Subjects, How they Ought to be Treated

We have discussed sufficiently, if I do not deceive myself, natural subjects; it remains that we think briefly, as is our custom, about acquired subjects. The prince ought to take great pains to see to it that acquired subjects have an interest in his dominion and government and that they become quasi natural subjects; otherwise, if the people have no affection for him, his principality will be as a plant without roots. Just as every little wind blows over a tree which is not well-rooted in the earth, so every light occasion alienates from their lord subjects who are ill-affected. They easily shift with fortune and follow the flag of the one who conquers. From this comes the changes and revolutions in states. The French lost Sicily in one evening[1] and in a little more time the Kingdom of Naples and the duchy of Milan[2] for no other reason than that there was no method to give the people an interest in their government and to give them a reason to embrace and defend it. Seeing that there was no advantage in living under the French rather than under the Spaniards or another people, they did not care to unsheathe the sword to their benefit. For the same reason the kings of France and the dukes of Milan have many

[1] This refers to the Sicilian Vespers of March 31, 1282. That evening at the time of Vespers a popular revolution broke out in Palermo and spread to the whole island. Thus the House of Anjou lost the island, which eventually was taken over by Peter III of Aragon.
[2] In the course of the Italian Wars the French lost the Kingdom of Naples in 1503 and the duchy of Milan in 1521.

times lost dominion over Genoa and, and in times somewhat more in the past, the Latins were despoiled of the Empire of Constantinople and the English of the extended territories that they had on the Continent because they did not know how to win over the souls and to satisfy the wishes of the subjects and to govern them in such a way that they had an interest in their government. In the war that Selim waged against the Mamelukes,[3] the peoples of Syria and Egypt, fed up and disaffected by the rule of those barbarians who were of a haughty nature and insolent customs, not only did not come to their assistance but with great promptitude opened the gates for the Turks. It is necessary then to win over the subjects and to do it in such a way that they benefit from our rule and from fighting for it. This will be carried out by the same means that secure benevolence and foster reputation about which we spoke above. In particular it will help toward this end to provide them with justice, peace, and abundance, and to foster religion, letters, and talent because the religious, the literati, and the talented are as it were the leaders of the others, and he who wins them over will easily win over the rest. The religious[4] hold in their hand the consciences of the people, the literati the understanding, and the judgments of the one and the other have the greatest authority with all, the former for their sanctity, the latter for their teaching, the former for the reverence they inspire, the latter for the reputation they have acquired, so that whatever they say or do is considered to have been well and prudently said or done, and so worthy of being embraced and followed. The artisans, then, excellent and skilled of every sort, serve to delight the others, so that the prince, if he has them on his side, will be easily loved and esteemed by all. So Charlemagne, beyond the respect that he showed toward religion and the favor that he always showed toward letters, displayed an incredible liberality and beneficence toward the poor than which there is nothing more gracious nor more effective for winning the gratitude and affection of the people nor more celebrated and magnified by all. It helps to be merciful, provided it does not appear to be laxity, and to show that to pardon and to grant grace comes naturally and by choice and punishment from necessity and concern for justice and the public peace. So Nero, at the beginning of his

---

[3] Botero refers here to the war waged successfully by the Ottoman sultan Selim I, starting in 1516, against the Mamelukes, former slaves who had ruled Egypt and Syria since the thirteenth century.

[4] 'Religious' here are members of religious orders.

rule, marvelously acquired the love and the gratitude of all with his pretense of mercy. When brought the sentence of the judges to be signed by him by which they condemned a man to death, he said, "How precious it would be for me not to know how to write."[5] The certain luster of excellent virtues helps not only to attach the subjects but even more to enchant enemies, as is demonstrated by the continence of Alexander and Scipio, the magnanimity of Camillus with the Faliscans, of Fabricius with King Pyrrhus, and of Emperor Conrad with Duke Miecyslaw. This Polish duke persecuted by Conrad sought refuge with Oderic, prince of Bohemia, from whom he hoped for aid and favor, but he found that he had been deceived by this thought. The Bohemian, out of thoughtlessness or avarice, negotiated with the emperor to hand him over into his hands; but he, possessed of a loyal soul, detesting such perfidy, warned Miecyslaw to beware of his host, so that admiring the goodness and virtue of his enemy, he surrendered to him freely.[6]

But above all it will be of great importance to respect the pacts and conventions made with them because there is nothing that more upsets the souls of vassals and acquired subjects than a change in the conditions under which they placed themselves under your rule. Nothing was of greater assistance to Nur ed-din, king of Damascus, who drove us out of Syria, than fidelity to his word; when the peoples saw that he did not burden immoderately those who had surrendered to him and that he did not fail to keep any promises that he had made to them, they gave themselves over to him voluntarily and obeyed him faithfully.[7] Important enough also is education; this is as it were a second nature, and through this means acquired subjects become as it were natural ones. To this end Alexander the Great selected thirty thousand Persian youths and saw to it that they were raised in the Macedonian style with regard to their dress, their arms, their writing, and their customs, with intent to make use of them in war as he did the Macedonians themselves. In the same way the Turk through education makes the Janissaries, who were acquired subjects born of Christian parents, into the most loyal soldiers that he has. They serve as the guard of his person; they are employed in all the matters of importance where fidelity and courage are required. In doing this

---

[5] Suetonius, *Twelve Caesars*, "Nero," 12.3.

[6] See *Wiponis Gesta Chuonradi II. Ceteraque quae supersunt opera*, ed. Harry Bresslau (Hanover, 1878), 36 (*BD*, 206, n. 4).

[7] Nur ed-Din (1118–74), a general of Turkish origin and emir of Aleppo from 1146, he conquered Damascus, unified Syria, and proved to be a determined foe of the Crusaders.

through education the Turk secures two great benefits. He deprives disaffected subjects of their strength and he increases his power with their sons. Also useful to this end are marriages of the prince himself and natural subjects with acquired subjects. Alexander the Great by taking as his wife Roxane, a Persian woman, conciliated those barbarians incredibly who in this way acquired a firm hope for a rule and government that was peaceful and benign. Of the Capuans Livy writes that wishing to rebel and throw in their lot with Hannibal, nothing held them back and caused them more unease than the relationships that they had contracted with the Romans.[8] A most noble way to win over acquired subjects was that employed by Tarquinius Priscus. Having conquered the Latins, a most powerful people, he did not make tributaries or subjects of them but joined them in a league and a fraternity. This was one of the principal foundations of Roman greatness; the Latins fought everywhere with no less courage than the Romans. Tarquin the Proud renewed this league in which he united all the Latin youth but without their own captains and insignia, and he mingled them with the Romans, and he made of the two fraternities one under Roman heads, and to give greater solemnity to this arrangement he had forty-seven cities of the league construct a temple to Jupiter Latialis on Mount Albano. Here they celebrated once a year the Latin Feasts with all the cities, where they shared a bull which the Romans sacrificed there; this showed that even though this was called a league and an alliance, nevertheless the Romans were in every way superior as we have stated elsewhere.

It helps also to introduce our language in acquired territories. So the Romans did in an excellent fashion, and so the Arabs have done in a large part of Africa and in Spain. Five hundred years ago William of Normandy did the same in England. To introduce our language, we should see that the laws are written in it, that the prince and officials conduct their audiences in it, and the same for business transactions, commissions, letters patent, and other such things. I will conclude with Charles the Great who, having expelled the Lombards, took over the exarchate and, having given it to the Roman Church, called it Romagna, so that the people, once they had forgotten the Greeks to whom they were formerly subject, would become attached to Rome and to the Roman pontiff.[9]

---

[8] *History of Rome*, 23.4, 7.

[9] Pepin handed over the exarchate of Ravenna to the pope in 754 in the Donation of Pepin; Charlemagne confirmed and expanded this gift in 774.

2 Of Infidels and Heretics

We have now two words to say about infidel and heretic subjects. It is necessary, first of all, to return them to their natural state,[10] and to win them over, because there is nothing that makes men more different and contrary one to the other than the difference or diversity of faith, and even if with them those means touched upon above are worthwhile, the principal basis for winning them over ought to be in their conversion. Now there are various ways to convert them. First it is necessary to have many, good men working together who with teaching and the example of an irreproachable life attract and lead these stray sheep to the truth. It helps more than can be said to have schools and to support teachers versed in the liberal arts and in every honorable exercise and entertainment for the sons of these infidels. In this way they win over the parents and the sons, the parents by the education and instruction that they give their sons. So one reads of Sertorius that by supporting good teachers and caring for the education of the youth, he won the deep affection of the Portuguese. The youth were won over because in school they also imbibed easily the faith and Christian virtues. To this end, the kings of Portugal, and especially John III,[11] founded in India colleges and seminaries in which a large number of youths from every nation were educated under the discipline of the Fathers of the Society of Jesus who have also in this way borne marvelous fruit in Germany and in the New World. In Germany the cities where they are found have been maintained in the Catholic faith, and they help the cities already infected with heresy. It is hard to estimate how large a multitude of the peoples of Brazil has converted, and in New Spain and Peru how much fruit has been gathered from those already converted. Many of the latter were in the beginning baptized by the first religious without much instruction; now with the schools and the instruction of the young they undergo renewal as it were in the faith and reform in their piety. But it is necessary that these teachers are persons from whom one is able to hope for edification and not to fear scandal and that beyond the necessary doctrine they have the gift of chastity and are far from any avarice or sordidness. There is nothing that more soils the good works and the spiritual assistance of the people than

---

[10] "Alla naturalezza" means to return them to the state of natural subjects as opposed to acquired subjects (*BD*, 209, n. 1).

[11] João III (r. 1521–57).

sensuality and the love of material things. So it will be necessary that the prince procure a supply of many good teachers for the instruction of the youth and, equally, many earnest preachers who know how, with teaching and with grace, to explain and make accessible the mysteries of our holy faith. In order to attract such people to the truth it will be profitable to concede every privilege that involves honor and comfort to those who will convert, such as to bear arms and serve in the military, to hold office, to be exempt from all or some taxes, and other such things that the conditions of time and place will suggest. Constantine of Braganza, viceroy of the Portuguese Indies,[12] promoted incredibly the faith in those lands by honoring and favoring the baptized and the new Christians in those lands. We ought not to overlook the zeal of Emperor Justinian who, as Evagrius writes,[13] drew the Heruli to the faith by offering them money; and in the same way, Emperor Leo VI[14] induced many Jews to the faith.

3 Of the Refractory

Of the infidels the most foreign to the Christian faith are the Muhammadans; the flesh, to which their sect is strongly inclined, is repugnant to the spirit of the Gospel. By the same reason, among the heretics the most distant from the truth are those who are disciples of a certain Calvin. Wherever they go they bear war in place of the peace announced to us by the angels and preached to us by Christ, and it is extreme madness to trust them in matters of state because, as experience has demonstrated to us, wherever they will come to power, they will cause an uproar, take up arms, and under the name of a religion covered with impiety and maliciousness, will carry out with fire and sword their evil intent. As they have no reasonable doctrine nor the authority of the saints, they will defend their sect with arms in the manner of the Turks. They have attempted to deprive the Most Christian King of his life, not only of his crown, and they have stirred up his patrimonial states against the Catholic King, and they have made war on Queen Mary, chased her out of her kingdom of Scotland, held her prisoner despite the word they had given her, and finally put her to death against every law of humanity.[15]

---

[12] Constantine of Braganza was viceroy of the Indies and governor of Goa from 1558–61.
[13] Evagrius the Scholastic (536–93 CE?), *Ecclesiastical History*, 4.20.
[14] Leo VI, the Wise, Eastern Roman emperor (r. 886–912).
[15] The lines from "They have attempted" to "every law of humanity" were suppressed in later editions.

With empty offerings they have enticed the Grand Turk against the princes. Gaining a foothold under the pretext of liberty of conscience, or of speech, or of action, or of life, they easily attract the people, who are for the most part of a sensual nature, and lead them wherever it pleases them more, because everywhere there are found evildoers and advocates of novelty and upheaval, either to cover up their crimes with the ruin of the republic or to improve their situation through a general disturbance. Heads and standard-bearers of these people are in all the states Calvin and his followers. Their business is to nourish sedition, foment rebellion, provide food for malice and hope for the ambitious, arm the desperate, sack churches and ecclesiastical properties for the benefit of the rapacious, and under the shadow of their gospel, which they proclaim with trumpets and tambourines, to incite the people against the nobles and subjects against their princes, and to shamelessly speak out every evil about the Catholics, and gradually to turn all public and private matters upside down. Meanwhile they seize cities, construct fortresses, send out privateers on the sea, and cast out from the world every manner of peace. The best possible remedy to be used with them is, as with every other evil, to resist beginnings, and then to employ the above-mentioned means to convert them. But if there is no hope of returning them to the truth and attaching them to our authority, it is necessary to make use of the counsel given by Terrentius Varro to Hostilius who placed all hope of keeping the Tuscans faithful and at peace in making it impossible for them to rebel if they had the mind to do so. This can be done in three ways: to discourage them, to weaken their forces, and to take away every means of their uniting, because uprisings are born either of generosity of spirit or a supply of resources or the unity of a multitude.

4 How they Have to be Discouraged

To this effect it helps to deprive them of everything that increases their spirit and their boldness, such as the splendor of nobility and the prerogative of blood, the use of horses, which is severely forbidden to Christians under the Turk, a militia and military exercises, which were prohibited to the Christians by Diocletian and other persecutors of the faith and by Theodoric, king of the Goths, to the Italians. No office should be allowed them, nor the wearing of a garment that has anything of the grave, the noble, or the magnificent about it but rather more of the mean, the vile, and the wretched; there is nothing that ordinarily depresses men more than to dress shabbily. For this reason the Ottomans do not allow the white turban to Christians. The Saracens took from the Persians even their name, so that in this way they would lose even the memory of their ancient valor and daring. William, duke of Normandy, after he acquired the kingdom of England, in order to humble that people changed all the officials and gave to the English new laws in the Norman language, so that they would realize that they were subjects of another nation and with new laws and a new language would also change their spirit and their thinking.

It will also be important to overwork these people, as Pharaoh did the Jews, or to assign them mean tasks, as did the Jews the Gibionites and the Romans the Calabrians, or to employ them in physical work such as agriculture or the manual arts because agriculture leads a man to an affection for the farm and the land so that he does not raise his thoughts to anything higher. So Cimon granted to the Greeks of other cities immunity and exemption from military service so that attending to the cultivation of their own holdings they would grow attached to them and so would not pay much attention to government or rule, which he assigned to his citizens along with regular military exercises on land and sea.[16] The mechanical arts bind a man to his shop on which his profit and sustenance depends, and because the welfare of the artisans consists in the sale of their products and their work, they are necessarily friends of peace, which benefits the flourishing of trade and the flow of commerce. Hence we see that those cities that are filled with artisans and merchants love peace and quiet above all. The ancient tyrants added to the above-mentioned methods an effeminate education for the boys as Dionysius of Halicarnassus relates of Aristodemus, tyrant of Cumae.[17] So that the sons of those whom he had murdered would never raise their heads but would have a totally vile and helpless spirit, he saw to it that until they were twenty they were raised in a womanly fashion. They wore long and loose tunics down to their feet, and their hair was similarly long and curly and their heads garlanded with flowers. Their faces were all spread with every tanning oil designed to make them appear more beautiful and delicate than they were naturally, and they associated indiscriminately with the ladies so that their feelings and manners had something of the feminine and the soft about them. With this procedure, just as Circe had

---

[16] Cimon (510–450 BCE) was an Athenian statesman and general who was a major figure in the creation of the Athenian maritime empire after the defeat of the Persians.

[17] *Roman Antiquities*, 7.9.3–5. Aristodemus (*c.* 550–490 BCE) was tyrant of Cumae.

turned men into beasts, so this tyrant aimed to turn boys into as many girls. But this was madness because wherever men are transformed into women, it is required that the women undertake the tasks of the men and leaving to them the needle and the distaff, they take to arms and take their revenge against the tyrants, as happened with Aristodemus himself. I will not omit saying that delicate and soft music makes men effeminate and vile so that, because the Arcadians due to the harshness of the site of their country were characterized by savage and severe habits, their elders, in order to tame and soften them as it were, introduced music and songs of which the softest and most delicate are those of the fifth and seventh tone which were often used in ancient times by the Lydians and Ionians, people given over to leisure and pleasure, so that Aristotle forbade in his republic similar songs and wanted them to make use of the Doric harmonies of the first tone.[18]

5 Whether Letters Are or Are Not an Aid to Render Men Brave under Arms

Because we have spoken of education, of which the most noble part is the study of letters, it will not be beyond our purpose to say two words about how they are an aid for war, so that the prince can judge whether it is wise to allow this or not to the above-mentioned refractory subjects. Let us suppose then that letters produce two effects very contrary to military *virtù*. The first is that they occupy the mind of a man who attends to them in such a manner that he takes pleasure in nothing else, as Archimedes demonstrates; while Syracuse was being put to the sack by the Romans, he stood immersed in his speculations as if nothing of this pertained to him. The second is that they make a man melancholic, as Aristotle and experience teach;[19] this is greatly contrary to what one seeks in a military person. Regarding the first effect, Cato was accustomed to say that the Romans would then lose their empire when they took up Greek letters, because when three Athenian orators came to Rome, he saw the youth run after them racing with one another so that he persuaded the Senate quickly to restrain them and turn them back lest the young Romans, so attracted by the sciences, be diverted from the military. And the Goths, thinking that letters made men unwarlike, resolved not to burn a great

---

[18] *Politics*, 8.7 (1342b).   [19] Aristotle (or Pseudo-Aristotle), *Problems*, 30.1 (953a).

quantity of Greek books as they had initially intended to do. With regard to the second effect, the French who are by nature merry and jolly (I speak of the nobility) take no account of letters or of the literati, and Louis XI, king of France, a prince of intelligence and of excellent judgment in matters of state, wished that his son Charles know nothing of letters other than those few words *qui nescit dissimulare, nescit regnare* (he who does not know how to dissimulate does not know how to rule).[20] More will be said of this opinion later.

On the other hand, the study of letters produces two effects of great importance for military valor. One is that it sharpens prudence and judgment and the other that it stimulates the desire for honor and glory. So, to decide the question, I would say that the study of letters is nearly necessary for a captain, and the reason is that they open his eyes as it were, perfect his judgment, and provide many aides for prudence and presence of mind. In particular, they excite and stir him with their stimuli for glory so that on the one hand he will be prudent and on the other ardent, and prudence joined with ardor produces an excellent captain. So we see that the premier captains that have ever existed, that is, Alexander the Great and Julius Caesar, were no less students of the sciences than courageous in arms. And there is no need for me to mention Hannibal, the Scipios, the Luculli, and so many other personages who were greatly dedicated to the study of the sciences and of the greatest valor in military enterprises.

I have said that it is nearly necessary and greatly useful rather than absolutely necessary, because there have been many excellent captains who, without knowledge or letters or any teaching, have arrived at the perfection of the military art, either through their outstanding intelligence or through long experience, such as were the Manlii, the Decii, the Marii, Diocletian, Severo, and other emperors. What sort of letters and studies they ought to embrace has been discussed above.

With regard to the soldiers, I confess that letters are not of use for them because the principal virtue of a soldier is prompt obedience to the commands of his officer. Now the study of letters increases prudence and caution, which pertain only to the captain, because he ought to have judgment and eyes for all the soldiers, and they ought to be blind

---

[20] This anecdote about Louis XI seems to have originated with Philippe de Commynes (1447–1551) in his *Mémoires*.

following his lead and under his command. So we see that the Swiss, because they are a rough nation far from any study, they are the best soldiers, and the Germans and the Hungarians, and the Janissaries. Emperor Julian,[21] who with incredible malice applied himself to the oppression of the church of God, perceiving that the Christians through their study of letters were becoming clever and prudent, prohibited for them schools or studies.

6 How to Weaken their Power

But because spirits, although vile, rise up every time they see at hand the power and means to manifest their resentment, it is necessary to deprive them of all power. Now their forces consist in a multitude of youth, in the instruments of war which are partly animate such as horses and elephants and partly inanimate which are defensive and offensive arms, military machines for land and sea, munitions, and strongholds fortified naturally or artificially, and the ability to obtain or make all these things which amounts to a supply of funds. It is necessary to deprive them of all these things, of the youth and of officers eminent for their counsel or authority by drawing them close to himself. When cities surrendered to him Caesar always wanted before anything else that their arms, their horses, and hostages be handed over, and as hostages he required all those of any merit, so in this way depriving the city of its vigor and its counsel. When he wanted to undertake his campaign in Britain, Caesar took with him the flower of the Gallic nobility; so he assured himself of their fidelity and made use of their vigor. Emperor Heraclius,[22] in order to control the Saracens and Arabia, took four thousand of their leading men under pretext of having hired them. But no one has ever more cleverly assured the loyalty of suspicious subjects than the Turk. As was mentioned above, he deprives his Christian subjects of the vigor of their youth. They are deprived of their arms not only by prohibiting their use but also the material and skill for making them. Wherever there is a large population and the material is not lacking, if there are artisans, they will make everything, as was seen in the siege of Carthage. As often as the Romans had wisely seized from the Carthaginians their arms and their warships, when

---

[21] Emperor Julian, called the Apostate by Christians, reigned from 361–63 CE and sought to reverse the christianization of the Roman Empire.
[22] Heraclius reigned as Byzantine emperor from 610–41; he was the first emperor to confront Muslim expansion out of Egypt.

necessity arose, going to work with the material they had at hand, all the many artisans made each day one hundred shields and three hundred swords besides arrows and machines to hurl rocks. Lacking hemp, they made use of women's hair to make ropes and timber from their houses to make ships. It does not promote security to leave them in fortified places or places easily fortified. The Romans, unable to dominate the Ligurian Apuani[23] with arms because of the harshness of the terrain which made them fierce and rebellious beyond measure, drove them from the mountains to the plains. The Romans wanted the Carthaginians, so often rebellious, to leave their fatherland and the sea and withdraw to some Mediterranean area. Pompey, in order to pacify the pirates, deported them from coastal lands to the country. Cato had all the cities of the Celtiberians[24] demolished and Aemilius Paulus those of the Albanians. Vitiges, king of the Goths,[25] fearing a rebellion, tore down the walls of all the cities of Spain except León and Toledo. Others have transported similar tribes into other lands. Emperor Probus,[26] having tamed Palfurio, a most powerful bandit in Pamphylia and Isauria, and purged those provinces of similar folk because it appeared that the land swarmed with such an evil breed of men, said "it was easier to expel the robbers than to make sure that there were none there," and to remedy the situation, he gave those sites to military veterans with the understanding that as soon as their sons reached their eighteenth year they had to send them to fight alongside the Romans so that they were introduced to the military life before they were to a life of robbery. Similarly, when it became clear to him that the Dacians on the far side of the Danube, who are now the Wallachians, the Moldavians, and the Transylvanians, could not easily be preserved in their devotion to the Roman Empire, Aurelian[27] made them move to the nearer side of the river. Charles the Great, weary of the frequent rebellions of the Saxons, moved ten thousand families into what are now the lands of the Flemings and the Brabantines, their descendants. Ordinary and extraordinary taxes now claim their money in which all human power now consists. Unfortunately, princes already know all about this, so there is no need for me to expand on it.

---

[23] The Apuani were a Ligurian tribe of ancient northwestern Italy.
[24] The Celtiberians were a Celtic-speaking people of the Iberian Peninsula in the late pre-Christian era.
[25] King of the Ostrogoths in Italy from 536–40 CE.
[26] Marcus Aurelius Probus reigned as Roman emperor from 276–82 CE.
[27] Emperor Aurelian reigned from 270–75 CE.

7 How to Weaken their Union

However great the diligence in discouraging them and weakening their power, subjects will lack neither courage nor power if they are allowed to unite. In this case *Furor arma ministrat, tamquam faces, et saxa volant* (Wrath supplies the arms when torches and rocks already fly).[28]

Now the way to prevent their unifying consists in two points: the first is to eliminate their mind and will to come to an understanding and reach an accord; the second is to frustrate their ability to do this. You destroy their intent by fomenting suspicions and differences among them, so that no one risks to reveal himself and trust in another; to secure this effect, secret and trustworthy spies are very useful. In this regard there occurs to me the method which Charles the Great used to restrain the people of Westphalia who although already baptized lived dissolutely and under grave suspicion of betraying the faith. He established a secret tribunal in addition to the ordinary officials; this tribunal[29] was entrusted to loyal and sincere persons of singular prudence and virtue to whom this most excellent prince gave the authority, without any other form of process and as it pleased them, to put to death expeditiously whomever they found to be a perjuror or bad Christian. And, so that these crimes could be discovered, there were besides the tribunals spies, persons themselves incorrupt, who moving about through the province without stirring any suspicions, took note of what each person did and said and reported to the tribunal which, whenever it found an accused person guilty, put him to death right away. One saw the person hanged and dead before one knew the crime that he had committed. This secret tribunal marvelously curbed the instability of those people because it proceeded with so much secrecy and severity that no one saw how it was possible to protect himself except with a good life, and no one dared to reveal or disclose himself to his companion.

There are various ways to prevent them from uniting, first by preventing family relationships among peoples and between one house with clients and another. The Romans did this with the Latin peoples, prohibiting them from intermarrying and forming any close relationships.

---

[28] Vergil, *Aeneid*, 1.150.

[29] This was the Judicium Occultum Westphalicum (Secret Tribunal of Westphalia) set up in 785, to condemn to death those Saxons who had not given up a number of pagan practices (*BD*, 223, n. 3).

After conquering Macedonia, the Romans divided it into four regions with capitals at Amphipolis, Salonica, Pella, and Pelagonia,[30] with the order that they could not establish any contacts nor contract marriages. Soon they had to remove their leaders with any reputation either by disinheriting them if they had given cause for this, because injustice never takes deep root, or by moving them elsewhere. In order to keep the peace in Macedonia Aemilius Paulus ordered the principal Macedonians to move to Italy with their sons. In order to end the tumult and disorder in Saxony, Charles the Great transported the nobility to France. Nor did he permit them any public council, nor magistracy, nor any means of forming an organized body. In this way the Romans completely weakened Capua. They wanted it to remain inhabited and frequented as a large area and as a congenial place for farmers but they did not want it to remain in the form of a city with a senate, a council, a commune, or public government, thinking that in this way a multitude would not be able to agitate or create a tumult. They prohibited their assemblies. If Abdullah, prince of the Saracens, prohibited the nocturnal vigils of the Christians, with how much more reason do we forbid assemblies of Lutherans, Calvinists, Turks, and Moors? Saladin, king of Damascus, after taking Jerusalem, removed our bells, so that they cannot come together at this sign, and the Turk did the same throughout. In truth, that is a sign, if the bells are hit by a hammer, of an incredible effectiveness and force to call the people to arms, as one saw in the city of Bordeaux when because of the salt tax they murdered the governor and rebelled against King Henry.[31] Because the bond of union is language, they should be compelled to speak our language, so that, if they speak, they will be understood, as the Catholic King has forced the Moriscos to do. But what will we say of the large cities which because of the least wind or rumor rage and run furiously to arms? The sultans of Egypt, wary of the innumerable multitude of inhabitants of Cairo, constructed across that city many wide and deep ditches so that it appeared to be a large district full of villages and municipalities rather than a city because they considered that the infinite population, restrained by the above-mentioned ditches, would not be able easily to unite. And of the many reasons for the peaceful quiet of Venice, I believe

---

[30] The Romans divided Macedonia into these four regions in 169 BCE. Pelagonia later became a region with its center at Heraclea. After a rebellion, the Roman province of Macedonia was established in 146 BCE (*BD*, 223, n. 4).

[31] Bordeaux rebelled against King Henry II in 1548.

that one of the principal ones is the canals which cross the city and divide it into many areas, so that the people are not able to assemble except slowly and with great difficulty, and so in the meantime a remedy is provided for troubles. To produce this effect it helps to have citadels and colonies close to trouble spots, and garrisons within and outside the city. For this reason the Grand Turk has such a large military of one hundred and fifty thousand cavalry divided between Asia and Europe into more than two hundred sanjuks[32] ready to move and get started quickly to put down any least uprising. But if none of these things helps against the refractory, then they ought to be dispersed and transported into other countries. So the Assyrians dispersed the Jews and forced them into Chaldea from where Alexander the Great drove them into Tartary (if what they say is true). Emperor Hadrian drove them into Spain where in the year of Our Lord 698 they rebelled against Christ because they had falsely become Christians, and against King Egica.[33] They were despoiled of all their goods, dispersed with their wives and children through all parts of Spain, and made slaves. In France King Dagobert did the same thing.[34] And if the Arabs called Almohads[35], who began to reign in Spain at the time of Alfonso VII, did not permit any Christian to live among them but forced them to become Muhammadans or put them to death cruelly, why are we not able to expel from our lands those of whose conversion and quiet we have despaired?

If they are heretics, let every incitement to heresy be taken from them, the preachers, the books, and printing presses. Antiochus forbade the Jews to read the Mosaic books publicly as they were accustomed to do on the Sabbath.[36] Diocletian commanded that all the sacred books of our law be burned.[37] How much more reasonably will we burn the books of Calvin and similar disseminators of impiety and dissension? Especially having the example of Constantine the Great who issued an edict that, under pain of death, everyone should burn the books of Arius.

[32] An Ottoman administrative term for a district.
[33] Evica was Visigothic king from 687–703. These events took place in 693.
[34] Dagobert I ruled the Franks from 629–34; He was the last of the Merovingian dynasty to wield real power.
[35] The Almohads began to enter Spain in 1146; Alfonso VII, king of Castile and León from 1126–57, allied with the Amorvides, devoted the last years of his reign to fighting against the Almohads in the south of the Peninsula.
[36] 1 Maccabees 1:56–57.   [37] 303–04 CE.

8 How to Take Away the Means of Uniting with Other Peoples

From what has been said in the preceding chapter one can easily understand what ought to be said in this one. Who takes from his subjects the ability to unite among themselves will much more easily take from them the means to unite with others because similar unions are formed by way of family relationships, friendships, hospitality, commerce, and secret agreements or dealings which it is necessary to prevent or cut off. This can be done by spies in our country or in the suspect one and guards at the ports and crossing points through which one enters or leaves our states; this is easily done on islands and in states enclosed by sea, by mountains, or by rivers. It will also help remove suspicious people from neighboring places, which is what the Grand Turk did the year after the day of Lepanto who making use of Ulug Ali[38] removed the Christians from marshy areas near the seashore of Greece, so that they could not unite with the Latins. The first and the last Philip of Macedon[39] took such liberty in this matter that not otherwise than shepherds with their sheep, they transported entire peoples from one place to another.[40]

---

[38] See above, 2.6 (p. 46, n. 34).   [39] Philip II (r. 359–336 BCE), Philip III (r. 323–317 BCE).
[40] Starting with *RS* 1596, Botero added another chapter here, "How to Pacify Disturbances Already Under Way." For this chapter, see Appendix A.

Book Six

1 Of Security from Foreign Enemies

So far we have discussed ways to maintain the subjects in peace and in obedience. Now we take up the way to protect ourselves from external causes of disturbances and of the ruin of states. We presuppose that security consists above all in keeping enemies and dangers far from our house because the nearness of the evil is a large part of the evil itself, than in taking up such a position that when he does advance he does not have the power to strike. Now he can be kept at a distance in many ways, the first of which is the fortification of the borders and the passes with fortresses suitably constructed.

2 Of Fortresses

Nature teaches us the art of fortification to protect ourselves; for no other reason does it surround the brain and the heart with so many bones and cartilages than to protect life by keeping dangers distant, and with a thousand types of shells, rinds, and hard, rough bark covers the fruits and with ears and bristles defends the wheat from the rapacity of birds. So I do not know why some doubt whether fortresses are useful to princes or not[1] because we see that nature itself uses them. There is no empire of such greatness or power that it does not fear or at least suspect the inclinations of its subjects or the mind of neighboring princes. In the one and the other case the fortresses give us security; there the engines and

---

[1] An allusion to Machiavelli, *Prince*, 20, and *Discourses*, 2.24.

munitions of war are kept, and you maintain as in a school and on exercises a certain number of soldiers and so from within a small enclosed area you defend a large territory and with little expense provide for many eventualities. The Greeks, who were of such intelligence, and the Romans, who demonstrated such good judgment in all their actions, made much of citadels as they relied on them in Corinth, Taranto, and Reggio; and the Romans defended their rule and their country with the help of the citadel of the Campidoglio even though it was not on the frontier but in the center of the state and the heart of the republic.

The events that can overtake a state are infinite, and the eventualities of war innumerable; for all of them provision is made by the fortification of the passes through which evils and troubles can enter. The Persians, who have always professed confidence in the great number and quality of their cavalry, have now experienced how useful and necessary is the use of fortresses, because the Turk, although defeated more than once, has gradually built fortifications in strategic locations, occupied large areas, and finally taken the great city of Tauris[2] and secured it with a large citadel. So the Persians, because they had no fortresses, have lost the campaign and the cities.

3 Of the Conditions of the Fortresses

But let us talk now about what fortresses ought to be. They ought to be in necessary or at least useful locations. Necessary are those which if not fortified leave your territory open and your state exposed to the violence of enemies, useful are those which defend populous or rich cities or will serve as a recourse or refuge for peoples. They ought likewise to be distant, so that they keep the enemy and the danger far from us because while the enemy strives to take the fortresses, our country will remain without disturbance or trouble and they can meanwhile make the necessary provisions. Of such a sort is Malta with respect to Sicily and the Kingdom,[3] and Corfu with respect to Venice. And if the fortresses will be not only far from us but in the territory itself of the enemy, they will provide greater security. Such are Oran, Melilla, Peñen de Velez, Ceuta, Tangier, Marzagam,[4] and Arzilla[5] (all strongholds of the Catholic King

---

[2] Today Tabriz in northwest Iran.   [3] The Kingdom of Naples.
[4] Mazagam, today El Jadida, south of Casablanca.
[5] Arzilla, today Asilah, south of Tangier in Morocco.

in Africa), with respect to Spain. Such were Rhodes, Naples, Malvoisie,[6] and Famagusta.[7] They ought to be few, so that they can be suitably provisioned and furnish men and munitions without dispersal or diminution of their forces. They ought to be strong, either because of their site or their construction. And they will be such of site either because of the roughness of the terrain or because of the benefit of water either running or stagnant. Such are Mantua and Ferrara but above all Venice, and in Germany Strasbourg, and in the Low Countries the infinite locations of Holland and Zeeland. These two provinces I consider to be the strongest by nature under heaven. Because of the incoming and outgoing tide of the sea which engulfs a thousand places and because of the greatest rivers which flow here and there and surround them on every side, they are incredibly secured, and because they are so low, by breaking through the levies and the dykes they can be flooded and covered by water from the sea and from the rivers. Well constructed will be those fortresses to whom the form will give more strength than the site or the material. They will have walls with well-conceived flanks, firm and solid terrepleins, and wide and deep ditches. One ought to consider the terreplein more than the wall, and the ditch more than the one or the other. But all these things are not enough if the fortress is not well provided with provisions, engines, munitions, soldiers, and chiefly with an excellent commander because a stronghold cannot make out of cowards and low types brave and bold defenders. On the contrary, a good number of excellent soldiers can fortify any place, as weak as it might be. So we see that fortresses deemed impregnable have been taken with ease because the princes, trusting in the site of the fortress, have not provided a suitable garrison. And it has happened ordinarily that the same fortresses have been taken through the steepest and most inaccessible approach as Mount Aornos[8] and the Stone of India[9] attest which were taken by the Macedonians, Carthage taken by Scipio from the lake side,[10] and Calais, taken from the sea by Francis, duke of Guise.[11] Antiochus the Great

---

[6] I have not been able to locate Malvoisie; the word usually designates a wine.

[7] This sentence was deleted in subsequent editions.

[8] The citadel of Mount Aornos or Aornis in Bactria was taken by Alexander the Great in 327 BCE. It has been identified as a summit in Pakistan, the Pir Sar.

[9] This is the rock of Sisiméthrès, a Bactrian leader, taken by Alexander the Great; it was in present day India (*BD*, 238, n. 6).

[10] Scipio Africanus took Carthage in 210 BCE.

[11] Francis, duke of Guise, took Calais from the English in 1558.

seized Sardis, when the famous warrior Achaeus[12] was there, from the side which was considered impregnable; when he saw birds flying safely over the high wall, he concluded that there were no sentries there.[13] On the other hand, places weak by nature and little helped by artifice have conducted the most glorious defenses because princes lacking confidence in their fortresses have furnished them with reliable soldiers and captains. In our day Eger in Hungary and the town of Malta attest to this.[14] Both, though weak due to their location because they could be easily shelled and due to their walls because they had been constructed with little skill, nevertheless were defended gloriously by the valor of the soldiers and the captains which constitutes in reality the vigor of defenses. So Agesilaus upon being asked why the city of Sparta did not have walls, pointing to his armed citizens said, "Behold these." Cities ought not to be fortified by wood and rock, he added, but by the force and valor of the inhabitants. But nothing helps if it is not in a location where it can be supplied because if the attack is vigorous and the siege persistent, every fortress will eventually fall into the hand of enemies. The fortresses that cannot be supplied are the cemeteries of soldiers, and such was Nicosia in Cyprus.[15] For this reason the best fortresses are those that are located by the sea because with a favorable wind they can be assisted.

4 Of Colonies

In order to hold in check enemies and warlike peoples, the Romans at the beginning of their Empire instead of fortresses established colonies within their borders. There, by settling a good number of Roman citizens or Latin associates on lands won by war and taken from their enemies, they protected themselves against unforeseen attacks. It can with merit be argued which provides greater security, the colony or the fortress, but without a doubt it is the colony because it includes a fortress and not the reverse. The Romans, who understood reason of state very well, made much greater use of colonies than of fortresses. But in our times fortresses are much more in use than colonies because they are much

---

[12] A Greek Macedonian nobleman and general who died in 213 BCE.

[13] Antiochus took Sardis, the capital of ancient Lydia, in 215 BCE.

[14] Botero refers to the siege of Eger in western Hungary by the Turks in 1552 and the Great Siege of Malta by the Turks in 1565. Both became symbols of heroic resistance.

[15] Nicosia fell quickly to the Ottomans in 1570 at the start of the Ottoman-Venetian War of 1570–73.

easier to establish and of greater utility at present. Colonies call for a great deal of industry and prudence in founding and organizing them, and the good that comes from them cannot be gathered so quickly because it only matures with time. But one sees that colonies are much more secure and of nearly perpetual utility, as Ceuta and Tangier, important Portuguese outposts on the coast of Mauritania,[16] attest; they developed into colonies and are maintained bravely against the forces of the Sharif and Barbary. Calais, an English colony established by Edward III in the year of our salvation 1347, has become the last place that that people has lost on the continent. But you ought not to found colonies far from your state because in this case, since you cannot easily supply them, they either remain as prey for enemies or, accommodating to situations or to the times, they govern themselves without respect to their origins. So acted the many colonies developed by the Greeks and the Phoenicians in all the lands bathed by the Mediterranean Sea. After judiciously considering this, the Romans founded more colonies in Italy than in all the rest of their Empire, and outside Italy they did not establish any until six hundred years after the foundation of Rome, and the first two were Carthage in Africa and Narbonne in France.

5 Of Garrisons

But after the Roman Empire, having grown marvelously, reached all three parts of the world, the Romans did not consider colonies suitable for their purposes because of the distance of the places and the ferocity of the peoples on their borders (they were on the one side the Alemanni and on the other the Parthians). So they kept on the banks of the Rhine, the Danube, and the Euphrates huge armies, so that under Caesar Augustus all the Roman garrisons amounted to the sum of forty-four legions which came to two hundred and twenty thousand infantry apart from the cavalry. There were then two fleets, one stationed in Ravenna and the other in Miseno, that dominated the whole Mediterranean Sea. That of Ravenna stood as it were ready for all that could happen in the Ionian Sea and on the seas of the Levant while that of Miseno[17] stood over as it were the seas to the west. But in this disposition of such large armies and garrisons

---

[16] Mauretania designates here the coast of North Africa.
[17] Miseno or Misenum on the Gulf of Naples was established as the principal Roman naval base in 27 BCE.

there was this shortcoming, that the soldiers collected in one place, easily, either due to the art of their captains or to their own ferocity, mutinied, greatly endangering the Empire. So it happened that when each army called out its own general as emperor, cruel civil wars necessarily followed. For it is not possible that a large number of soldiers united in one body remain in place for a long time without causing trouble or rebelling, either one against the other or all against the prince; and if the captains are factious and eager for change, it is an easy matter to hatch their plots and fan the fires. For this reason it is necessary either to direct them against the enemy or to distribute them over several locations because the division disperses their forces and lessens their spirit and ardor, and it reduces the ability of captains and people of malicious intent to win them over. This is perhaps the reason that the Turk, who has nearly sixty thousand cavalry in Europe and a little fewer in Asia, has never had any trouble. He keeps them apart, here and there, so that it never happens that they find themselves all together, except for some campaigns, and they do not realize their own strength and so do not rebel out of pride, nor are they able to be easily directed or won over by officers. Each of them resides on his timar,[18] or what we would call farm, assigned to him by the Great Lord in place of a salary, and the desire of and delight in their fruits and comforts keeps them quiet.

6 Of Keeping the Frontiers Deserted

Some peoples, in order to make it difficult for enemies to enter their territory (so imitating nature which has separated empires by mountains, seas, and rivers, but also by vast deserts such as Mauretania from Guinea, Numidia from Nubia, and Nubia from Egypt), have established desolate areas on their borders. The Suevi[19] did so in the ancient world as did Tahmasp, king of Persia, not many years ago who, in order to keep the Grand Turk at a distance from his state, allowed to go to ruin and left desolate the land within a four days' journey from his borders.

7 Of Prevention

A most noble way to keep the enemy at a distance from our house and to secure ourselves against his assaults is to anticipate them by carrying

---

[18] A timar was a small, temporary fief given by the sultan to soldiers.
[19] The Suevi were a Germanic tribe.

the war into his house because he who sees his own possessions in danger easily leaves others' in peace. And the Romans kept to this method in all their important campaigns except in the war with the Gauls and in the Second Punic War which they were not able to finish until they carried their arms across the sea and over the Alps. Hannibal when he advised Antiochus about how to conduct a war against the Romans said that it would not turn out well unless he attacked the Romans in Italy. So I do not understand why in our days some discuss whether it is better to await the Turk at home or attack him on his lands. The ancients never had any doubts about this. It was always the opinion of the great generals that it was better to attack than to be attacked because an attack that is not completely foolhardy upsets and throws the enemy into disorder, seizes part of his income and his lands, takes possession of his provisions or forces him to destroy them himself, and draws to the attacker's side those who are discontent or dissatisfied with their government. If he conquers, he gains much; if he loses, he risks little, especially if the campaign takes place far away. Finally, the fortunes of war, which are endless, favor the attacker rather than the attacked. Hannibal and Scipio, whom we can call lights of the military art, recalled with embarrassment their fighting the one against the Romans outside Italy and the other against the Carthaginians outside Africa. The Turk has warred against Christians not by awaiting us on his territory but by anticipating not only our intentions but our thoughts so that having attacked us now in one place now in another, without giving us time to attack him, he has seized unlimited territory from us. But one should also take note that to attack requires greater forces, or at least equal forces to those of the one whom you wish to attack, greater or at least equal in number or in ability or in strategic location. And he who does not feel himself secure, ought to anticipate by fortifying the passes and the important locations where the enemy will lose forces or time and give you an opportunity to gather your troops or to bring in foreigners as happened at Malta. When the Turks besieged Saint Elmo for the whole month of May, they lost the flower of their soldiers, and ours had time to unite and gather spirit to attack the enemy.[20]

But if you do not have the forces to forestall and do damage to your adversary, it remains to incite some powerful enemy against him, to do what you cannot do yourself. Genseric, king of the Vandals, having been broken in a terrible naval battle by the patrician Basil and fearing the

---

[20] The reference here is to the Great Siege of Malta in 1565.

worst, persuaded the Ostrogoths and the Visigoths to attack the Roman Empire. In this way he protected himself.[21] But in this it is necessary to handle oneself in such a way that you do not come out even worse, as happened to Ludovico il Moro, who, to defend himself against the Aragonese, became the prey of the French.[22]

8 Of Maintaining Factions and Plots

A certain form of prevention consists in exploiting factions that exist in the countries of enemies or neighbors and in understandings with councillors, barons, generals, and people of authority near the prince, so that they dissuade him from taking up arms against us, or divert them elsewhere and render them useless by slowing operations, or help us by warning us of his designs, because an evil foreseen harms much less.[23] But if the plots will be so bold that they arouse suspicion of rebellion or treachery or tumult, so much the better; they will keep us completely secure if they cause a disturbance in the country of our enemies. The pretended queen of England[24] used this method – which we should use with enemies of the faith – with the Catholic King in Flanders and with the Most Christian King in France. By fomenting with all her power the evil tempers and heresies born in those countries and assisting them with advice and money, she has kept the fire far from her house, and with the same skill by favoring in Scotland those who were dissatisfied with Queen Maria[25] or ill-affected toward the French faction or infected with heresies, she has not only insured herself against that kingdom but nearly become ruler of it. But she has taught us that *non est consilium contra Deum* (there is no counsel against the Lord).[26]

9 Of Leagues with Neighbors

Defensive leagues contracted with cities or princes near the enemy or jealous of his greatness are not of little moment because his fear and

---

[21] The facts here are misleading. Genseric, king of the Vandals from 427–77 CE, surprised and annihilated a Byzantine fleet under the command of Basiliscus (later emperor) off Cape Bon, on the northeastern coast of Tunisia, in 468 (*BD*, 245, n. 1).

[22] In 1494 Ludovico il Moro, duke of Milan, induced the French to attempt to drive the Aragonese out of Naples. This unleashed the Italian Wars that lasted until 1559.

[23] A loose translation of a dictum attributed to Cato and often cited in the Middle Ages, "Nam laevius laedit, quidquid praevidimus ante" (*BD*, 246, n. 2).

[24] Elizabeth I.   [25] Mary Stuart, executed in 1587.

[26] This last sentence was suppressed in most later editions.

suspicion that the league states unite brings it about that he has no desire to move against any of them. In this way the Swiss gain security because, given the defensive league among them, there is no one who has any desire to attack the least of their villages. And the Venetians have enjoyed a long peace under Suleiman, king of the Turks, only because that prince knew that if he attacked them, he provided an occasion for Christian princes, due to the common danger, to unite with one another. But we have spoken enough about leagues elsewhere.

10 Of Eloquence

This is very valuable, also, to convince an enemy to desist from a campaign. Lorenzo de' Medici, in the greatest trouble and danger because of the war of Sixtus IV and Ferrante of Naples against the Florentine Republic, traveled from Florence to Naples and, conferring with the king, knew how to speak so well and with such efficacy, that he dissolved the league and reconciled with the Florentines.[27] With the same skill Galeazzo Visconti made Philip of Valois turn around when with a great army he was approaching Milan.[28] Alfonso of Aragon, at war with René of Anjou over the claims that the one and the other had to the Kingdom of Naples, was taken prisoner at Gaeta and taken to Milan by the soldiers of Filippo Maria Visconti who was giving aid to René. There he accomplished with eloquence that which he probably would not have been able to do with arms. By showing to that prince how dangerous it would be for the state of Milan if the French acquired the kingdom and became powerful in Italy, he drew him over to his side and obtained such assistance and favor that when René was finally defeated, he remained lord of Naples.[29]

Another instrument useful to draw forces to us and take them from the enemy is to demonstrate to other princes that our danger is in any

---

[27] In December 1479, when Sixtus IV and Ferdinand I warred against Florence, Lorenzo de' Medici undertook a secret trip to Naples where he convinced the king to break with the pope. A peace was signed in February 1480. Botero draws his account of this incident from Machiavelli's *History of Florence*, 8.19 (*BD*, 248, n. 2).

[28] Philip, future Philip IV of France, having been summoned there by the pope, was on campaign in Italy in 1320. When he found his army encircled by the troops of the lord of Milan, Marco Visconti, and his son Galeazzo, he negotiated with them and then returned to France.

[29] This took place in 1435; see Machiavelli, *History of Florence*, 5.5 (*BD*, 249, n. 1).

event also theirs and that the greatness of the adversary will be dangerous for them no less than for us. The Romans used this a great deal in the Macedonian War, to unite the Aetolians with them in a league, and in the Aetolian War to unite with the Achaeans, and in Asia to join with diverse princes and peoples.

11 Of those Things that Have to be Done after the Enemy has Entered the Country

The treatment above applies to before the enemy has entered your states, but after he will have entered, some other provisions will help which we touched upon in the preceding books where it is discussed whether it is suitable for a prince to engage his subjects in military exercises or not. And in conclusion, everything possible helps that divides or weakens the enemy either by artifice or by force.

12 Of Depriving the Enemy of Food Supply

It will also help to deprive the enemy of every means of obtaining provisions, either by cutting off or tearing up the roads, as the Turks did before the troops of King Ferdinand in the campaign of Eszék,[30] or by destroying the crops as the French diligently did when Emperor Charles invaded Provence.[31] Duke Cosimo, seeing that his state was enclosed in such a way by nature that it was not possible to transport supplies there except through the part that bordered on papal territory, always kept the popes as friends and, on the other hand, so that no one entered there with the intent of seizing the products of the country, he ordered that once the grain had been harvested, each took his to the fortress which had been prescribed for each district; each then took out by hand as much as he needed, so that in the unforeseen case of war, for the enemy unable to bring his own food supply with him and not finding any in the country, there was only left starvation.[32]

---

[30] This refers to the attempt of Emperor Ferdinand I in a campaign of 1541–43 to take back from the Turks the city of Eszék, today Osijek in the Croatian region of Slavonia (*BD*, 250, n. 4).

[31] The army of Emperor Charles V invaded Provence in 1524 and besieged Marseilles but was unable to take it (*BD*, 250, n. 5).

[32] Starting with *RS* 1596, another paragraph was added here.

13 Of Diversion

Diversion differs from prevention in this, that prevention occurs before the enemy has come to attack us; diversion is employed after he has attacked us, by taking the war into his own territory, so that he leaves ours, as in prevention the war is taken into the territory of the enemy so that he does not take it into ours. An outstanding diversion was that of Agathocles when he was being stretched to the limit by a Carthaginian siege of Syracuse and was not able to hold out longer. Embarking with some of the soldiers, he passed over to Africa and from there made it so difficult for the enemy, that they were forced to recall the troops that they had in Sicily.[33] And no less noble and bold was the case of Boniface, count of Corsica, in the year of salvation 829. After the Saracens had attacked Sicily and put everything there to fire and sword, the count passed over to Africa with a good fleet, and confronting the enemy there, he was victorious, so that the Saracens, because of the danger to their own lands, were forced to leave Sicily in peace.[34]

14 Of Agreement with Enemies

But if the adversary is so powerful that there is no hope of defending ourselves, it will be the duty of a wise prince to escape imminent ruin with the least evil that is possible. In such a case one ought to consider useful any agreement or treaty that can be won by money. The Florentines have often helped themselves in this way who, by paying substantial sums of gold, have emerged from great trials. And the Genoese with nineteen thousand ducats made the army of Bernabo Visconti[35] turn around, and the Venetians did the same with Pippo,[36] general of King Sigismund, who put him to death forcing him to drink liquefied gold. In the same way the Venetians have always helped themselves with the Turk, giving presents to the vizier, paying large amounts to persons of importance close to the Grand Signior, and giving rich gifts to the same.

---

[33] Agathocles was tyrant of Syracuse from 316–288 BCE. This event took place in 310.
[34] Boniface II, marquis of Tuscany from 828–34, and prefect of Corsica, defended Corsica and Sicily against the Saracens, taking the war over to Africa (*BD*, 252, n. 3).
[35] Bernabò Visconti was lord of Milan from 1349–85.
[36] Filippo Buondelmonte degli Scolari, called Pippo Spano (1369–1426), was an Italian captain in the service of Sigismund of Luxembourg. Pippo was considered a traitor but the method of his death seems to have been a myth (*BD*, 253, n. 5).

15 Of Seeking Protection and Submitting to Others

But if you run the danger of losing not only your state but your liberty, then, yielding, you ought not to be ashamed to place yourself under the protection or even the rule of another, provided that he has sufficient power to defend you. So the Capuans submitted to the Romans in order to escape the cruelty of the Samnites; the Genoese submitted to the French, then to the duke of Milan; the Pisans also helped themselves briefly first by the patronage and then by the free rule of the Venetian Republic,[37] but unwisely, because the protectors, due to the distance between the two countries and the difficulties of the passes, were not able to defend them against their enemy, the Florentines, without much greater expense than utility. No prince will long protect a state when that results in more harm than utility.[38]

16 Of Standing Above the Fray while Neighbors are at War

But in order to assure the peace and security of your state, nothing is more necessary than to fortify yourself well when your neighbors are at war because it usually happens shortly after the peace and accord of those who were the first at war, that the storm of the war spills over to the neighbors. After the peace between Charles II, king of Naples, and Frederick of Aragon,[39] about twenty galleys departed from Sicily and Apulia, some Catalan, some Italian, which had served the two kings.[40] Having chosen a certain Brother Ruggiero[41] of the Knights Templar as their captain, they raided the coast of Macedonia and Greece and did unheard of damage everywhere. As their number increased, they boldly sacked the islands of the archipelago and assaulted the cities of the terra ferma, and they enriched themselves through the ruin of an infinite number of people; this lasted twelve years. Finally, they murdered the duke of Athens and took possession of his state. In the same way, after the peace

---

[37] From 1496–99.
[38] There follows here a brief chapter entitled "Of the Method of Julius II" in *RS* 1598.
[39] The Treaty of Caltabellota, in 1302.
[40] These were the Almogavars, soldiers from many Iberian kingdoms who originally fought in the early Reconquest in Spain and then later in Italy.
[41] Roger de Flor, corsair and mercenary captain.

between Filippo Maria and the Venetians,[42] the captains who had served these princes led their rival armies into the State of the church. Much later,[43] after the Venetians and Emperor Maximilian, the Spaniards and the Gascons, who had all fought in the war had put down their arms, they continued on with Francesco Maria[44] into the state of Urbino and tormented Pope Leo in such a way that in order to free himself, he paid out an unlimited sum.[45]

---

[42] Filippo Maria Visconti, duke of Milan, concluded peace with the Venetians at Ferrara in 1428, and it was renegotiated in 1433.

[43] These events took place in 1517. More than eighty years separated the two sets of events related here by Botero.

[44] Francesco Maria della Rovere (1490–1538), a condottiere and heir to the duchy of Urbino who had been dispossessed by Pope Leo X.

[45] Botero's discussion of the need for a prince to prepare for war in a time of peace seems to resemble Machiavelli's position in chap. 14 of *The Prince* (*BD*, 237, n. 1).

Book Seven

1 Of Forces [Resources]

Up till now we have discussed the means by which a prince can govern his people peacefully. Now we discuss the ways by which a prince can also expand his state. These are without a doubt the resources which I am accustomed to call the instruments of prudence and valor. It would take a long time to try to show in detail all those things that can be called the resources of a prince, so that I will content myself with the principal ones, which are people, many and of high quality, and money and food supplies and munitions and horses and offensive and defensive arms. And I will not delay to demonstrate how munitions and arms are to be made and assembled because the Arsenal of Venice, which is filled with every military instrument for sea and for land, can serve as a mirror and a book for every wise prince. Here, in the space of a mile and one half or a little more and surrounded by high walls, is gathered such a quantity of all the materials and all the instruments necessary for all the needs and necessities of naval and land warfare so that he who sees it scarcely believes his eyes. Here under large vaults are kept hundreds of galleys, some large, some slender, made with inexplicable mastery. And they are constructed continuously in such good order that one always sees in one day the start and completion of a galley in every detail. Here there are vast rooms, some filled with artillery of every sort, some with pikes, swords, and arquebuses, others with breastplates, helmets, and shields so well made and polished that the sight of them alone is sufficient to terrify the cowards and incite to war the spirited. Elsewhere you will see large rooms, some filled with iron and bronze, others with hemp, others with wood.

Elsewhere iron is purified and liquefied to make cannon balls, nails, and anchors. Elsewhere bronze is cast to make artillery. Elsewhere hemp is worked into rope and sails and shrouds. From wood are made oars, masts, planks and all that is needed for the navy. Finally, there you will get an idea of the foresight necessary for a prince who wants always to be armed; as Alfonso d'Avalos,[1] marquis of Vasto, deservedly said after seeing and considering the size and importance of a similar place, he would have wanted the Arsenal of Venice before four good cities of Lombardy.

About provisions and horses it occurs to me to say nothing that was not said in passing as it were about agriculture. There are then two types of resources to which the others can be reduced, people and money; and even if he who has people has money, we will say two words about this latter type of resource, so that we may speak more at length of the other.[2]

2 Is it Fitting for a Prince to Accumulate Treasure

Nothing is worse in a prince than to make profession of accumulating money without a worthy goal. The first reason for this is that it hinders all the works of charity and beneficence, from which it follows necessarily that the roots of subjects' love for the prince are torn up which are in large part the benefits that they receive from him. Also, he who has this stimulus to accumulate treasure is compelled to burden his subjects more than is customary and more than he ought. Unable to tolerate immoderate burdens, they then will desire a change in the state and in the government, and not willing to tolerate them, break out in some scandal. I add that those who give themselves over to avarice and money, trusting immoderately in riches and treasures, often disdain all the other means of good government with the result that they lose their states and their treasure goes into the hands of their enemies, as happened to Sardanapalus[3] who left forty million scudi to those who murdered him, and to Darius[4] who left eighty million to the great Alexander

---

[1] Alfonso d'Avalos (1502–46) was a general of Emperor Charles V who served as governor of Milan and commander of the imperial army.

[2] In *RS* 1598 Botero added a sentence here that is important to understand his thought: "But before going further, let us say that this expansion (*agrandissement*) of the state is of two types, intensive and extensive. With the first one improves dominion (*dominio*), with the second one extends it; but without the other, this is harmful instead of being useful."

[3] Sardanapalus is the name given by the Greeks to the last king of the Assyrians, Ashurbanipal (667–626 BCE).

[4] Darius III, king of Persia, who died in 331 BCE.

who defeated him and expelled him from his state, and to Perseus[5] who also left his money to those who deprived him of his kingdom. But what noble thought, what honorable purpose can a prince have who has given himself over completely to the art of avarice? Let Tiberius Caesar speak, or not to go so far back, Alfonso II, king of Naples,[6] who gave his pigs to his subjects to fatten them, and if they died, made them pay him. He purchased all the oil of Apulia and all the budding grain, and then he resold it at the highest price that he could while forbidding anyone else from being able to sell it until he had sold all of his. But what will we say of the selling of offices and magistracies? Is there anything more unworthy of a prince and more harmful to subjects? The greed for gold leads princes to every crime and unworthy action and takes out of their hands a means to virtue and to that which makes for their glory, and it happens then ordinarily that the ill-gotten wealth of princes is spent more wrongfully by their successors. David used all due care to accumulate a great supply of gold and silver which was the greatest that had ever been collected;[7] it amounted to one hundred and twenty million scudi. With all this Solomon, his son, apart from that which he spent for the construction of the temple, used the money so prodigally for the construction of palaces in the city and in the country, for summer and for winter, for gardens and splendid fish-ponds, for a multitude of horses and carts, for male and female singers, for display and delights of every sort, so that, because the treasure left him by his father was not enough, he burdened his people in such a way that unable to bear the infinite burdens, the great part of them rebelled under his son.[8] Now, what will they do with so much treasure unjustly acquired? Or what fruit can one hope for from it? Using every sort of extortion and injustice, Tiberius over many years gathered sixty-seven million scudi, which his successor, Caligula, wasted in one year, and this will happen ordinarily because a prince, especially a young one, who sees a great treasure in his hands, commonly takes to strange thoughts and passing fancies that have no end, and confident in

---

[5] Perseus, the last king of Macedonia, conquered by Roman armies in 168 BCE.

[6] Alfonso II of Aragon (1448–95), duke of Calabria and son of Ferdinand I of Aragon whom he succeeded as king of Naples from 1494–95. These lines about Alfonso are cited verbatim from Jean Bodin, *Les six livres de la république*, edn. of 1583, 6.2 (*BD*, 262, n. 8.); see also Jean Bodin, *The Six Bookes of a Common-weale. Out of the French and Latin Copies, done into English by Richard Knolles* (London, 1606), 6.2. In this Book Seven Botero frequently draws on Bodin's *République*, edn. of 1583, 6.2, "On Treasure."

[7] Botero takes this from Bodin, *République*, 6.2 (*BD*, 262, n. 1).

[8] Roboam, son of Solomon; see 1 Kings 12 and 2 Chronicles 10.

his wealth, undertakes great works with his resources, hates peace, disdains friendship with his neighbors, starts wars that are neither necessary nor useful and are often harmful for himself and his own. For this reason God does not will that the king has *argenti et auri immensa pondera* (immense amounts of silver and gold).[9]

3 That it is Necessary that the Prince have Treasure

Nevertheless, it is necessary[10] for the service of peace and for the necessity of war that the prince always have at hand a good sum of ready money because to wait to raise the money necessary in times of need, and especially of war, is a difficult and dangerous matter.[11] Difficult because the clamor of the army, which interrupts commerce and trade, the cultivation of the fields, and the gathering of the harvest, also necessarily ends the ordinary taxes and customs dues. Dangerous, because harmed and knocked about by the licence and cruelty of the soldiers, both friendly and hostile, and by the evils of the war, if beyond this they are harassed and assessed for further contributions by the prince, the people will make trouble. Therefore, it is necessary to have money ready for similar necessities with which the enemy is held at a distance and the people enjoy without disturbance the fruits of the earth and its revenues. Therefore, at a time when war confronts us, it will not be possible easily to raise money and to secure arms, two procedures of which I do not know which is more difficult. So it is necessary that the money be on hand, so that there is nothing else to do than to raise the troops. Otherwise, while consultations are under way about how to raise the money, the quickness of the enemy and the disruption of the war deprives us of the means to raise money and troops. The Turk displays a marvelous speed in his campaigns because in his preparation for them he makes use of the treasure and the money that he has on hand to recruit the soldiers and ready the arms and make every other provision for the campaign, and he then recovers the money spent with the taxes that he imposes on his people. But he who does not have funds available, while he thinks about and deliberates about the means to

---

[9] Deuteronomy 17:7.

[10] Starting with *RS* 1590, there is inserted here "for reputation, because the power of states is assessed today no less from the supply of money than from the size of the territory, and".

[11] Bodin underscored that financial reserves ought to be on hand so that the prince was not compelled to begin a war with loans and subsidies, *République*, 6.2, p. 906. (*BD*, 264, n. 1).

make provision for it, ordinarily loses the time needed for this business and often the opportunity for victory. And the most frequently used way to procure money is that which ruins kings and kingdoms, that is, the payment of interest, and in order to pay the interest ordinary revenues are pledged, so that it is necessary to impose extraordinary ones which commonly then become ordinary. So one evil is remedied by a greater one, one falls from one disorder into another, and finally the state collapses and is lost.

Since therefore it is not expedient to make profession of accumulating treasure, and it is necessary to have some treasure, what is to be done? Virtue resides in the middle; therefore they ought to accumulate money without making profession of it. This will be done in two ways, by keeping alive all the revenues of your state while abstaining from all superfluous revenues and from all unsuitable giving.

4 Of Revenues

The revenues of a prince are of two sorts: ordinary and extraordinary, because they are drawn either from the products of the land or the results of human labor. They are drawn from the earth in two ways because some lands belong directly to the prince, others to the subjects. To the prince belong patrimonial lands and those that have no other owner, to the cultivation of which he ought to attend not otherwise than the good father of a family and take from it all that the quality of the lands allows because some are good for grain, others for pasture, others provide woods, others other things like lakes, ponds, rivers. Furthermore, of the fruits of the earth some come from under the earth, others from above. From under the earth come metals and mines of gold, of silver, of tin, of iron, of mercury, of sulphur, of alum, of salt, and besides this jewels, precious stones, and marble of infinite sorts. From above the earth come hay, grains, beans, and beasts large and small, domestic and wild. The benefits of the waters are of many types; they generate many animate things to support human life, such as fish, oysters, and other such things, and inanimate such as coral and pearls, and of uncertain nature, such as sponges which Aristotle places in the middle between animate and inanimate things.[12] Muhammad II,[13] having acquired enough land, sent out colonies of slaves, to which he assigned each fifteen acres of land,

---

[12] *History of Animals*, 8.3.1 (588).   [13] Mehmed II.

two buffaloes, and seed for the first year. After twelve years he wanted one-half of the crops and a seventh of the other half in the years following. So he established a good perpetual income.[14] From the lands that belong directly to his subjects the prince draws money through taxes and imposts, which when they meet the needs of the republic are licit and just because according to reason particular goods serve the public good without which the latter could not be maintained.[15] But these taxes ought not to be personal but real, that is, not on heads but on property; otherwise all the burden of the taxes will fall on the poor as ordinarily happens because the nobility unload the burden on the people and the large cities on the countryside. But in the course of time it happens that the poor, unable to support the weight, fall beneath it, and in the end the nobility have to make war at their own expense and the cities pay huge subsidies as happened in France. In Rome the whole weight of the taxes and impositions was on the rich. But the goods of the subjects are certain or uncertain. I call certain the immovable goods and uncertain the movable goods. Only the stable goods ought to be taxed. The attempt to tax movable goods turned all Flanders against the duke of Alba.[16] And if you want, in case of extreme necessity, levy contributions also on movable goods; I would not disapprove what they do in some cities of Germany: leave it to the conscience and oath of persons. As to the products of industry, by which I understand every type of trade and commerce, they are taxed when entering or leaving the country. There is no sort of income more legitimate and just than this because it is reasonable that whoever makes a profit on what is ours or from what is ours make us some payment. But because those who carry on commerce are either our subjects or foreigners, it is just that the foreigners pay something more than the subjects. The Turk also has this policy. For the goods that are taken from Alexandria, the foreigners pay ten per cent and the subjects five per cent. In England foreigners pay quadruple what the natives pay. And because riches tend to find their way there where the things necessary for use in everyday life more abound, the prince ought to employ all

[14] Botero takes this example nearly verbatim from Bodin, *République*, 6.2 (*BD*, 266, n. 5).

[15] This principle follows Bodin, *République*, 6.2, with the significant difference that for Bodin these taxes may be collected in time of necessity; for Botero they may be collected on a regular basis (*BD*, 267, n. 3).

[16] Fernando Álvarez de Toledo (1507–82) was named governor of the Low Countries in 1568. After he introduced new taxes in 1572, a revolt broke out. He had to surrender to the insurgents the northern provinces, and he was recalled to Spain in 1573.

diligence to encourage his subjects to the cultivation of the land and to practice trades of every type, about which we will speak more fully in its place.

5 Of Loans

But if revenues are not adequate to the needs, the prince can borrow from wealthy subjects, either at interest, which he ought not to do except in extreme cases since interest is the ruin of states, or without interest which will not be difficult if the prince keeps his word and pays his debts on time without serious harm to his creditors.[17] Henry II, king of France, when he wanted to rebuild his army after its defeat by the imperials at San Quentin, summoned the three estates of his kingdom and, through the mouth of the cardinal of Lorraine asked them to find a thousand persons throughout the state who would each lend him a thousand scudi without interest.[18] This he easily obtained, and with the three million of gold which he accumulated he renewed the war and made important acquisitions. So without oppressing the people who were already worn out by previous contributions, he found a way to undertake glorious campaigns. He had learned earlier that to borrow money at interest gained nothing but the collapse of revenues and the loss of credit. He left in fact such great debts that the crown of France still feels their weight.

6 Of Aid from the Church

The goods of the church ought to be a last resort on which it is not right to lay hands without permission of the Supreme Pontiff and with necessity on the part of the republic. The authority of the pope justifies the prince before God and necessity justifies him also with the people, and if either one or the other is lacking, it is almost impossible that matters go well, of which I would be able to adduce many examples but I leave that behind in order not to offend anyone. However, I do not want to omit saying that King Manuel of Portugal[19] was a most fortunate prince in his

---

[17] Interestingly, Botero does not discuss interest from the perspective of the church's prohibition. See also "usury."

[18] After the defeat at San Quentin in August 1557, Henry II summoned the Estates-General to Paris the following winter, to obtain the subsidies necessary to continue the war.

[19] Manuel I, king of Portugal from 1495–1521, supported the voyages of Vasco da Gama and Pedro Alvarez Cabral.

undertakings in Africa and in India because in the one and in the other he made incredible acquisitions, and he increased, one can say, the gold and silver along with the expenses. There came to him then the desire, at the suggestion of others, to take a large sum of money from the ecclesiastical state, and he obtained the permission of Pope Leo. When this became known in Portugal, it caused infinite grumbling, so that the king, not under any necessity and seeing a change in spirit, agreed to cede the grace that he had obtained to the clergy, and they in turn, to show him their affection, made him a gift of one hundred and fifty thousand scudi. After this, from then on his enterprises and his reputation continually declined.

Now aid comes from the church in two ways, either from the sale of part of its lands or from part of the income of the lands. The sale of immovable goods, as has happened more than once in France,[20] is like taking a hatchet to one's legs and cutting one's muscles. Beyond that, the permission of the pope is carried out in such an ill fashion that twice that is alienated than was authorized by the bull, and it appears that a sacrifice is made to God through a diminishment of the income of the church.[21] Making use of a part of the income is more tolerable for the clergy and often necessary for the republic. This has been seen in the late wars in France of which the clergy has in great part paid the expenses with more than twenty million scudi contributed to the king, and in Spain where the clergy has for many years supported sixty armed galleys and paid out more than double this amount.[22]

7 Of Extraordinary Income

We have been talking about the ordinary income beyond which the princes have some other extraordinary sources of income, some from

---

[20] An allusion to the surrender of church lands during the reigns of Charles IX (1560–74) and Henry III (1574–89), in order to provide funds to meet foreign and domestic crises, especially campaigns against the Huguenots.

[21] Pius V, Gregory XIII, and Sixtus V all issued bulls authorizing and justifying the alienation of church lands in France. The sale of these lands then surpassed by a great deal what the papal bulls had anticipated (this was especially the case at the time of the coming to the throne of Henry III in 1574) (*BD*, 271, n. 4).

[22] Starting with *RS* 1590, Botero added here: "But I confess to never having seen nor read that anything of significance has ever been accomplished through the subsidies given by the church. In addition, it appears that campaigns undertaken with church funds have been regularly failing, and even if they have sometimes been successful, little fruit has been gathered from the victory."

their own people, others from foreigners. From their people they have regalian rights,[23] confiscations, condemnations, gifts. From foreigners they have tribute, pensions, honors, and other similar things, all of which they ought to spend and invest as if they were ordinary income.[24] Who will manage his income in this way will necessarily lay by a certain part which he ought to deposit in his treasury for cases of necessity.

8 Of Abstention from Inappropriate Expenses and from Giving out of Vanity

Inappropriate expenses are those which have no apparent purpose for the public good, bring no benefit nor security to the state, no grandeur nor reputation to the king. These are infinite because vanity has no limits. Because we have spoken about this elsewhere,[25] we will move on. But there is nothing more necessary than the regulation of gifts which ought not to be made except to people of merit and with moderation. If they are made without previous merit, those who do merit are offended, and this has overturned some states of Christendom. If moderation is not practiced, the font of this beneficence soon dries up so that the prince often passes over from profuse giving to extortion. Nero in the fourteen years that he reigned made gifts of fifty million scudi. Galba, his successor, issued an edict revoking all the gifts made by him and leaving to those who had received them only the tenth part. And Nero, after giving away such a great amount of gold and silver, lacking material for his prodigality, turned to assassinations, and Caligula did the same.[26]

9 How it is Necessary to Conserve the Surplus

But because it is difficult for a prince to protect himself from the importunities of flatterers, favorites, and other similar types of people if he has money on hand, it is necessary to find a way that makes it difficult to

---

[23] The temporary regale allowed the French king to collect the income of vacant bishoprics.

[24] Starting with *RS* 1598, Botero inserted here: "And the power of a prince ought not to be evaluated so much from his ordinary income as much as from the ease with which he can obtain money through extraordinary means. Of this the clearest sign is that most princes have sold or pledged or in another way alienated the ordinary revenues and support themselves with extraordinary aids."

[25] This probably refers to Botero's *Del dispregio del mondo libri cinque* (Milan, 1584) (*BD*, 273, n. 2).

[26] Botero treated this topic earlier in 1.22 (p. 33), using the same examples.

lay hands on the money, a precaution that the ancients also took in different ways. After the expenses of the government had been paid, Caesar Augustus lent the money that remained at interest and with security, and Antoninus Pius in a similar fashion at five per cent, and Alexander Severus did the same. But no prince ought to follow the example of lending at interest, not only because this is not a matter for a prince but because it contravenes reason and the precepts of the church. When lending freely[27] he obtains two good results. First, he secures safeguards for his money by taking security for it. Second, he puts the subject under obligation to him, and he gives him the opportunity to enrich himself which in the long run benefits the prince. The Romans, when they were free, accumulated the public treasure in large portions of gold similar to bricks. The kings of Morocco formed their treasure into a great ball of gold which they placed on the dome of their Great Mosque. Today princes wall up or bury or store in cases of iron their riches and their treasure which William, duke of Mantua, jokingly called great devils. And this suffices about money.[28]

10 Of People

We come now to true resources which consist in people because all other resources are reduced to them. Whoever has people in abundance, has also all other things in abundance to which man's intelligence and industry extends as will appear in the course of our treatise. So from here on we will use indiscriminately now the term people now the term resources. Now with regard to people, there are two types of resources to consider, the number and the valor.

11 Of a Numerous Population

First, it is necessary to have enough people because, as Servius Tullius[29] said, for a city that aspires to great undertakings nothing is of greater need than a numerous multitude of citizens with which it is able confidently to prevail in military contests, because the few, due to the fury of

---

[27] That is, without interest.

[28] In *RS* 1590 Botero inserted a long chapter here, "In the Accumulation of Wealth One Ought Not to Continue *ad Infinitum*." This chapter is found below in an appendix.

[29] Servius Tullius was, traditionally, the sixth king of Rome, who reigned roughly from 578–535 BCE.

an epidemic or due to some misfortune, are easily ruined, as happened to the Spartans who, broken once by the Thebans at Leutra[30] by the death of 1,700 citizens, lost their hegemony in Greece. The Thebans and Athenians, defeated in a battle with King Philip, collapsed altogether. On the other hand the Romans conquered the world with valor but no less with the infinite number of their troops. These were so many that at the same time they could carry on a war in many locations far from one another: in Italy, in Spain, in Sardinia, in Sicily, in Macedonia, and they did not lose their spirit because of one or of many defeats; they even increased with the defeats of the army and they multiplied with their losses. Cineas called them a Lernean Hydra.[31] And King Pyrrhus[32] after conquering the Romans in a great battle and seeing that they had swiftly rebuilt a new and powerful army, was so dismayed in such a way that, despairing of being able to conquer with arms, he set about to treat for peace but in vain. Without a doubt their numbers gave the Romans the victory over the Carthaginians because the number of the dead was undoubtedly greater on the part of the Romans than on their enemies; in the First Punic War the Romans lost seven hundred quinqueremes[33] and the Carthaginians five hundred. In the second more Romans died at the Battle of Cannae than Carthaginians in the whole war.[34] No one will deny that in the wars with Pyrrhus, with Numantia,[35] with Viriathus,[36] Athenion,[37] at the time of the social wars, with Sertorius, with Spartacus, and with many others, more Romans died than did their enemies, and yet they conquered because of their inexhaustible numbers. The Arabs, the Saracens, the Tartars, and in our time Mahmud, king of the Massagetae,[38] the scourge of India, and the Turks have always

---

[30] The Battle of Leuctra in Boeotia in 371 BCE.

[31] Cineas, a Thessalonian by origin, was a minister of King Pyrrhus. He was sent to Rome in 279 BCE after the Battle of Heraclea, to negotiate peace. The hydra of Lerna was a monster with many heads that reconstituted themselves as soon as they had been cut off.

[32] Pyrrhus, king of Epirus (r. 306–302, 297–272 BCE).

[33] The quinquereme, developed from the trireme, was an ancient galley with five rows of oars on each side; its precise structure is disputed.

[34] The most plausible figure for the number of Roman deaths at the Battle of Cannae is 50,000 (*BD*, 283, n. 1).

[35] Numantia was a village in northern Spain around which coalesced opposition to the Romans; the war lasted from 153–133 BCE.

[36] Viriathus was the leader of the Lusitanian resistance to Rome in the western part of the Iberian Peninsula. He died in 139 BCE.

[37] Athenion led a slave revolt in Sicily that was suppressed in 101 BCE.

[38] Mahmud of Ghazni (971–1030) was the most prominent ruler of the Ghaznavid Empire that included parts of today's Iran, Afghanistan, and Pakistan.

undertaken the greatest campaigns more with a great mass of men rather than with valor.

I add that whoever abounds in men also has plenty of money because with a multitude of people tributes increase and these enrich the sum in the treasury. Neither Italy nor France have gold or silver mines, and yet they abound in one and the other metal above every other province of Europe for no other reason than the inestimable number of their inhabitants who bring in money by commerce and trade from the ends of the earth. Where there are many people it is necessary that the land be well cultivated (so that *Suidae* writes that in his time France was cultivated more by the multitude of their men than by their skill)[39], and from the earth is drawn the foodstuffs necessary for life and the material of the artisans. Now the abundance of goods and variety of products enriches both individuals and the public. If Spain is considered a sterile province, this is not because of a lack of land but because of the scarcity of the inhabitants; the land is favorable and most suited to the production of all that belongs to civil life, and if it were cultivated, there would be enough to support an infinite number of people as was the case in ancient times when it supported the great armies of the Carthaginians and the Romans besides their own peoples. And there was no province that for a longer time and with greater energy tormented the Roman armies, and soon after they were defeated and torn to pieces, they reinvigorated themselves and assembled greater armies. But not to speak of ancient events any longer, it is held for certain that the king of Granada, in the war that he waged against King Ferdinand[40] had under his flag fifty thousand cavalry of which there are not so many today in all Spain and Portugal taken together not because the nature and quality of the land has changed or the air altered, but because the number of inhabitants has diminished and the cultivation of the land has declined. The inhabitants are less than in the ancient world, first, because of the wars in which the Moors took possession of Spain; in this, in addition to the captives sent to Barbary and the dispersal of the others, there died in the space of three months seven hundred thousand persons. There followed then the war in which

---

[39] *Suidas* indicates a Byzantine encyclopedia of the tenth century published in Milan in 1499 in Latin with the title *Suidae Lexicon Graecom*. Botero probably read there the passage cited here from the *Geography* of Strabo, the Greek geographer and historian (64 BCE to 24 CE) (*BD*, 283, n. 7). Starting in *RS* 1590, "Strabo" replaced "Suidae" in the text.

[40] Ferdinand I, the Great, king of León (r. 1037–65), who united León with Castile and Navarre.

for seven hundred years the Spaniards fought with the Moors and finally drove them out of Spain. During this period there died subsequently an infinite number from one side and then from the other, and so many cities and counties were deserted. As soon as they saw themselves free of this war, they turned their arms to campaigns in Africa, in Naples, in Milan, and in the New World, and ultimately to the recovery of the Low Countries, and in all these campaigns countless died by the sword and from privation, and an incredible number continually moved to these countries, to live, to do business, and to man garrisons.

I add to the things already mentioned the edicts of King Ferdinand, which were imitated afterwards by King Manuel of Portugal, which expelled from Spain 124,000 Jewish families; it is estimated that this came to eight hundred thousand persons.[41] This led Bajazet,[42] king of the Turks, considering the matter superficially, to say that he wondered about the prudence of King Ferdinand who deprived himself of that which enlarged and enriched his states so greatly, that is, people. So he gladly received the Jews expelled from Spain in Rhodes, in Salonika, in Constantinople, Santa Maura,[43] and elsewhere. Agriculture then declined in the same province because this nation, inclined by nature to the profession of arms and to haughtiness, took up voluntarily the military career and the profession of arms from which they drew honor and profit. Not only are the Spaniards negligent in the cultivation of the land but also in the manual arts so that there is no province more lacking in artisans and industries. Wool, silk and other materials are for the most part exported, and that which remains is processed for the most part by Italians as are the fields and vines worked by the French.

---

[41] In 1492 Ferdinand II, the Catholic, of Aragon and his wife, Isabella of Castile, signed the decree expelling the Jews from Spain. Manuel I of Portugal followed with a similar decree in 1496.

[42] Sultan Bajazet II (1447–1512) in 1492 took in the Jews expelled from Spain and even sent ships to transport them.

[43] Santa Maura is an island off the west coast of Greece, also called Lefkada.

Book Eight

1 Two Ways to Increase People and Resources

People and resources grow in two ways: by increasing one's own and drawing to oneself that of others. You increase your own through agriculture, the crafts, favoring the education of children, colonies. You draw to yourself by winning over your enemies, by ruining neighboring cities, by the granting of citizenship, with friendship, with alliances, by the hiring of soldiers, by ties of kinship, and by other similar methods which we will briefly discuss successively as we proceed.

2 Of Agriculture

Agriculture is the foundation of all growth, and we call agriculture every activity that has to do with the land and makes use of it in some way; the early kings of Rome were most astute and diligent in this, especially Ancus Martius.[1] Denis, king of Portugal,[2] called the farmers the sinews of the republic. Isabella, queen of Castile, was accustomed to say that in order for Spain to abound in everything, it would be necessary to give all to the Fathers of St. Benedict because they took marvelous care of their lands.

Therefore the prince ought to favor and promote agriculture and show that he takes account of those who understand how to improve and make fertile their lands and whose farms are extremely well cultivated. It is his duty to direct and get started all that pertains to the public good

---

[1] The legendary fourth king of Rome, who reigned from 642–617 BCE.
[2] King of Portugal (r. 1279–1325), called "the Farmer."

of the country: to drain swamps, to uproot and prepare for cultivation useless or excessively wooded areas, and to aid and support those who undertake similar works. So Masinissa, king of Africa,[3] brought it about that Numidia and the Mediterranean shores of Barbary, which had previously been uncultivated and deserted, became with diligence most fertile and productive of every good, and Tacitus writes of Tiberius Caesar that with every effort and care, not sparing any money or labor, he remedied the infertility of the land.[4] And because the causes of generation and abundance are humidity and heat, it is also the duty of the prince, aiding nature, to channel rivers or lakes through the countryside; in this sense one cannot sufficiently praise the ancient rulers of Milan who, by opening one canal from the Ticino and another from the Adda, enriched beyond belief that most fortunate territory.[5] The poets relate that Hercules in a duel with the River Achelous[6] broke off one of its horns. With this they wanted to hide the historical truth, namely, that Hercules altered the bed and diverted the course of the river because it greatly damaged the fields, and the poets called the mouths of the rivers horns. So it is the responsibility of the prince to take measures against such problems and, finally, to keep alive all the ways to make his land abundant and fruitful in all that for which he knows it to be suitable. And if neither plants nor seeds are found in his state, it will be his responsibility to bring them in from elsewhere. So the Romans brought cherries and peaches from the furthest parts of Asia, and gradually other fruits too. One sees that in Portugal ginger brought from India does very well, and I remember having eaten ginger grown in Paris. And what I have said of trees and fruits should also be understood of animals.

And it ought not to be permitted that lands be uselessly employed either for parks, of which England is full to the great laments of the people who as a result endure not minor shortages of grain, or for other such things. Nor should one be frightened off by the expense that the greater part of the aforementioned works require because either they can be performed in the winter by slaves or by galley-slaves if there are any; or if there are none, those can be employed in such works who otherwise would merit the galleys or death, just as the Romans assigned similar men to extract metal or cut marble. If these are not found, there will never be

---

[3] Masinissa (238–148 BCE) was the first king of Numidia.   [4] Tacitus, *Annals*, 4.6.

[5] Ticino is an Italian-speaking area of southern Switzerland dotted with lakes, and the Adda is a river in north Italy, a tributary of the Po.

[6] Achelous, a river in western Greece, and also the river god.

lacking gypsies and vagabonds without any purpose whom it would be better to employ in the service of public utility than to allow them to go about begging. In China, an excellently regulated province, begging is not permitted. All are employed to the extent that their ability allows: the blind, if they have of themselves no means to live, are employed turning mills by hand; the maimed, as much as they are able, to do something else. Only those are allowed to enter the public hospitals who are altogether helpless. The Romans were accustomed to have similar works undertaken by soldiers when they had nothing else to do as is seen in the Marian canals in Provence[7] and the Drusine canals in Guelders,[8] and the Via Emilia and Cassia. Caesar Augustus, seeing how the canals that carried the waters of the Nile into the fields were obstructed and plugged up, had them dredged and redirected by his army. The Swiss facing similar needs made use of the work of the communes, employing it to dam up a river or to level a mountain or to divert a torrent or to fortify a road so that the communities themselves carried out great projects in a short time. Besides this, the prince also ought to have the goal that money not leave his country without necessity. If in his state there are cases of necessity, even if they require expenditures, it is an expenditure that remains in the country or over time returns to the fisc through taxes or customs. This is not the case once the money has left, because it is lost as well as the gain that might have been earned from it. Many places in Italy that were earlier deserted have now been under cultivation for some years, such as the Pontine marshes which not only covered a large stretch of land without use, from which are now drawn unlimited benefits, but also infected the air in such a way that Rome became unhealthy. Outstanding also are the improvements made by the Venetians in the Polasina near Rovigo[9] and by the duke of Ferrara in the valleys of Comacchio[10] which produce grain sufficient for a great city. And it would be possible to do the same in many parts if the princes would attend to it and would not be such lovers of the present benefit that they neglect the future.

---

[7] At the mouth of the Rhône River, south of Arles, the Romans under Caius Marius (157–86 BCE) dug a canal, called the Marian ditches (le fosse Mariane) to facilitate the provisioning of troops by sea.

[8] Drusus (38–9 BCE) built canals in Guelders in the Netherlands to facilitate the passage between the sea and the Rhine River.

[9] This is a region south of the Venetian territory on the Terra Ferma and north of Ferrara.

[10] Southeast of Ferrara.

3 Of Industry[11]

There is nothing more important to make a city grow and to fill it with inhabitants and an abundance of wealth than the industry of its people and the number of its crafts, some of which are necessary, others congenial for civic life, others desirable for display and decoration, others for refinement and the entertainment of indolent persons. From this comes an influx of money and of people who work, who trade the products of the work, or who supply material to the workers, who buy, sell, transport from one place to another the artful products of man's intelligence and skill. Selim I, emperor of the Turks, in order to populate and ennoble Constantinople, transported several thousand excellent craftsmen from the royal city of Tauris and then from great Cairo. Nor did the Poles wrongly understand this point, when they elected Henry, duke of Anjou,[12] their king; among the things that they wanted from him was that he bring to Poland one hundred families of artisans.

And because art competes with nature someone will ask me which of the two contributes more to enlarge and populate a place, the fertility of the land or the industry of man. The industry, without a doubt, first because the things produced by the artful hand of man are much more and of much greater value than the things produced by nature because nature provides the material and the subject but the subtlety and art of man provides the unspeakable variety of the forms. Wool is a simple and raw fruit of nature. How many beautiful things and what a great variety and multiformity does art make of it? How many and how great the profits does his industry reap who cards, warps, weaves, dyes, cuts, sews, and forms it in a thousand ways and transports it from one place to another? Silk is a simple product of nature; what a variety of beautiful cloth does art make of it? It makes the excrement of a vile worm to be esteemed by princes, valued by queens, and finally everyone wants to be held in honor because of it. Furthermore, a much greater number of people live from industry than from rents as is attested by many cities in Italy, especially Florence, Genoa, Venice of whose grandeur and magnificence there is not space to speak. Perhaps two-thirds of the inhabitants here support themselves by their work with wool and silk. But who does not see this

---

[11] This chapter was initially a part of *Magnificence of Cities*; Botero moved it here and left only a reference to it in the earlier work.

[12] Henry was elected king of Poland in 1571; he gave up this office in 1573 to return to France to become king there as Henry III.

with every material? The revenues that are drawn from the iron mines are not very large but from the profits that derive from the processing and the trade of this iron an infinite number of people live, those who excavate it, those who purify it, those who cast it, those who sell it retail or wholesale, those who manufacture from it engines of war, defensive and offensive arms, innumerable tools for use in agriculture, architecture, and every craft, for daily needs and the innumerable necessities of life which require iron no less than bread. He who would compare the revenues that the owner draws from the iron mines with the benefits that the artisans and merchants take from it through their industry, and which also incredibly enrich princes through taxes, would find that industry surpasses nature by far. Compare marble with the statues, the colossi, the columns, the friezes, and the infinite works that are made from it; compare the timbers with the galleys, the galleons, the ships, and the vessels of infinite types for war, for merchandise, for pleasure, with the statues, with the furniture of the house, and with other things without number that are made with the plane, the chisel, and the lathe; compare the coloring matter with the painting and the price of the former with the value of the latter and you will understand how much more valuable is the work than the material (Zeuxis,[13] a most excellent painter, considered his works nothing because, he said generously, they could not be bought for any price), and how many more people live by means of the crafts than from the immediate benefit of nature. And so great is the resource of industry that there is not a silver mine nor a gold mine in New Spain or in Peru that ought to be put on the same level with it, and the tax from the commerce of Milan is of greater value to the Catholic King than the mines of Potosì[14] or Jalisco. Italy is a province where there is no mine of importance, neither of gold or silver, just as France also has none; nevertheless, both the one and the other abound magnificently in money and in treasure, thanks to industry. Flanders also has no veins of metal, and nevertheless, so long as it was at peace, because of the many, varied, and marvelous objects that were fashioned there with skill and inestimable ingenuity it did not envy the mines of Hungary or Transylvania, and there was no country in Europe more splendid, more abundant, or more populated, nor an area of Europe or in the world

---

[13] Zeuxis of Heraclea (464–398 BCE).
[14] Starting with *RS* 1596, the mines of Zacatecas in Mexico replaced Potosí in Bolivia.

where there were so many cities, so great, and so often visited by foreigners so that, rightly, because of the incomparable treasures that Emperor Charles took from there, some people called those lands the Indies of His Majesty. Nature imposes its forms on prime matter, and human industry creates on the natural composite an infinite variety of artificial forms because nature is to the craftsman what prime matter is to the natural agent.[15]

Therefore the prince who wants to populate his city[16] ought to introduce there every sort of industry and craft by bringing in outstanding craftsmen from other countries, providing them with accommodations and suitable comfort while taking account of their attractive talents, encouraging creativity and works that have something singular or rare about them, and rewarding perfection and excellence. But above all it is necessary not to allow raw materials to be taken out of your state, not wool, nor silk, nor wood, nor metals, nor any other such thing because with the materials the craftsmen will also depart. A much greater number of people live from the sale of finished materials than from raw materials, and the income of princes is by far richer from the export of finished products than of raw materials, for example, of velvet more than silk, of serge more than wool, of linen cloth rather than flax, of ropes rather than hemp. Having understood this in recent years, the kings of France and England have prohibited the export of wool from their states, and the Catholic King has done the same. But these ordinances have not been able to be fully carried out so fast because these provinces, abounding as they do in the most delicate wool, do not have an adequate number of workmen to process it all; and although the aforementioned princes without a doubt would have done this because the profit and the tax for the finished wool is much more than that from the raw wool, nevertheless it also helps to populate the country because many more people live from the finished wool than from the raw wool, and from this comes the wealth and greatness of the king because the great number of people is that which makes the land fertile and which, by hand and by skill, gives a thousand forms to the natural material.

---

[15] Here Botero uses the language of Aristotle and Thomas Aquinas to describe the relationship between human activity and nature.

[16] In *RS* 1590 alone Botero replaced "city" here with "state."

4 Of Matrimony and the Education of Children

The ancient legislators, unaware of a higher virtue,[17] attempted to multiply their citizens by favoring marriage in an extraordinary fashion. Lycurgus ordered that he who had not taken a wife be expelled from public spectacles and in the middle of the winter be led naked through the squares. And if he was old, he did not want the young people to honor him as they did the others of that age. To encourage this matrimony, he ordained that wives be taken without a dowry and that more account be taken of their virtue than of their property. Solon also determined likewise; he did not want dowries to be given in money, so that it did not appear as if the women were bought, but with clothing and vases of little value as takes place today in Hungary and in nearly all Africa and Asia. And to encourage men to generate offspring legitimately, he did not want bastards to have any obligations to their fathers. Philip II, king of Macedon,[18] when preparing for war against Rome, ordered that all males take wives and procreate sons, so that he would have enough soldiers. The Romans also attended greatly to the same as is attested by the celebrated speech of Q. Metellus when he was censor;[19] in it he exhorted all those who were able to take wives and beget children. Caesar Augustus enthusiastically recommended this speech in an edict. So that every man would readily place his neck under the yoke of matrimony, they provided the poor with farms because those who have no property and live from day to day either do not want to have children or consider them less desirable. So that even if without the union of man and woman the human race is not able to multiply, yet the multitude of conjugal unions is not the only cause of its multiplication. Beyond this the care to raise them and the resources to support them are necessary without which they either die prematurely or survive useless and of little benefit to the country.

France has always been heavily populated and filled with people. Strabo gives the reason when he says that French women were the best for natural fecundity and for the care that they gave to raising children.[20] Do we not see that the care of man in multiplying lettuces and cabbages

---

[17] The phrase "unaware of a higher virtue (non avendo cognizione di più alta virtù)" was deleted in *RS* 1598. It may have originally been inserted to affirm the value of virginity and celibacy.

[18] This should be Philip V of Macedon (r. 221–179 BCE).

[19] In 102 BCE.   [20] Strabo, *Geography*, 4.1.2.

can do more than the fecundity of nature can with nettles and other weeds? And that although wolves and bears generate more offspring in one birth than sheep and that comparatively more lambs are killed than young wolves or bear cubs, nevertheless there are more lambs than wolves for no other reason than that man takes care to raise and pasture the lambs but persecutes and wages war on wolves? The Turks and the Moors have each many wives, and the Christians, apart from the infinite multitude who make a pleasing sacrifice to God of their chastity, do not take more than one, and yet Christendom is proportionately much more inhabited than Turkey. The north has always been more populous than the southern regions; from there came so many peoples that trampled upon the Roman Empire, and while the men were without a doubt more chaste there than here, the southerners took more women and the northerners scarcely one. From what does this result if not from the difficulty of rearing children that follows from numerous marriages and wives, and the comfort that follows from one wife and fewer marriages? The love of a husband for many women is not so fixed nor ardent as toward one alone, and as a result the affection for the children is never so great and intense; it dissipates and disperses in many directions, nor does it take care or give thought to the education of the children, and if care is taken, there is not the means to raise so many. How does it help Cairo to be a city so populous if every seventh year the plague carries away so many thousands? Or how does its concourse of people benefit Constantinople if every third year the contagion depopulates it and, as it were, turns it into a desert? From where come the plague and the disease if not from the small and uncomfortable dwellings, from the uncleanliness and dirt of the living conditions, from the little order and government in keeping the city clean and the air purified and from other similar causes? Given these difficulties to rear children, even if an infinite number are born, there are few, relatively, who survive or become men worth something. For no other reason did the human race, which, propagated from one man and one woman, arrive three thousand years ago at no less a multitude than that which one sees today and has not continued multiplying proportionately, and the cities, begun with few inhabitants and then grown up to a certain number, do not pass beyond that. Rome began with three thousand, arrived then at four hundred and fifty thousand of military age and did not pass beyond this even though one might have reasonably expected that as it had increased from three thousand to four hundred and fifty thousand, it would still gradually increase infinitely. So Venice, Naples, and Milan do not exceed two hundred thousand persons, nor do other cities pass a certain number; this results from the difficulty of raising and nurturing a greater multitude of people in one place either because the land about it is unable to provide such a large supply of provisions, nor are the neighboring countries able to supply it, either because of the sterility of the land or the difficulty of transportation. So that if two things are required for the propagation of peoples, generation and education, even if the number of marriages perhaps helps the first, it prevents certainly the second. Thus I think that even if all the male and female religious were married, there would not be a greater number of Christians than there now is; and the dissolution and license introduced by Luther in Germany and by Calvin has not in any way helped to increase the number of people because, beyond the fact that impiety does not ever take root and grow, even if the number of conjugal unions has increased, the resources for raising and feeding the children have not.

It is not enough therefore that the prince encourage marriage and child-bearing if he does not provide assistance for the education and support of the offspring with beneficence toward the poor, aiding the needy, relieving those who do not have the means to marry off their daughters or to establish their sons or to maintain themselves and their family, giving something to do to those who are able to work, supporting with kindness those who are not able to do so. In this Emperor Alexander Severus was so loving that, raising at his own expense some poor young men and women, he called them Mamei and Mamaei after his mother, Mamaea.

5 Of Colonies

The Romans also increased their numbers with colonies, and rightly so because, as plants flourish beyond the nurseries where they were sown more than if they remained within them and as bees propagate when in swarms they leave the hives where if they remained they would die either of want or contagion, so many who if they remained in their country, would perish or would not establish a household nor leave children because of poverty or some other reason, would do both the one and the other if sent into colonies and provided with a dwelling and land. So Alba[21] sent out in many directions thirty colonies that called themselves

---

[21] Alba Longa was an ancient mythical kingdom located in Latium in central Italy that antedated the founding of Rome.

Latins; the Romans called on them many times and with their forces fought major wars. The Portuguese and the Castilians, following their example, have also founded diverse colonies, the former in Madeira, the Cape Verde Islands, Brazil, and India, the latter in the islands of the New World, in New Spain and in Peru, and ultimately in the Philippines. It is true that in this enterprise the one and the other followed rather the necessity of their own campaigns rather than the plan and example of the Romans because colonies are of little use to the country if they are established in very remote lands and from which assistance is not to be expected nor significant support. The Romans did not found any colonies outside Italy for the space of seven hundred years; they then established one in Africa, Carthage, and another in France, Narbonne, which could be said to be near because they were maritime colonies, and the Romans had dominion of the sea. In addition, they sent to the colonies the most base and vile people who were as it were the waste and the most troubled people of the city. But the Portuguese and the Spaniards have not sent and do not send him who is superfluous in his country but he who would aid his country and, perhaps, be necessary for it, and they take no excessive or corrupt blood but part of the most sound and genuine, so that the provinces grow weak and quite feeble. They could imitate the Romans by making use in their colonies not only of those of the Spanish nation but also of conquered subjects, naturalized, because the Romans besides the Roman colonies also established the Latins in the less important places.

6 Of Ways to Grow Rich at the Expense of Others

It requires no less judgment and prudence to draw to yourself and make your own what belongs to another, justly, than to increase your own; in this as in every other matter, the Romans demonstrated an inestimable wisdom. It would take a long time to explain their methods one by one, so that we will be content to point them out briefly.

7 Of the Means Taken by the Romans

The Romans increased their own possessions at the expense of others, first, by attaching to themselves their conquered enemies, the Albans, the Sabines, and many other peoples, then, by destroying neighboring cities and so compelling their inhabitants to make their way to Rome. Besides this, they granted Roman citizenship especially to innumerable persons of valor and of excellent qualities and in common to entire cities. Servius Tullius and Sempronius Gracchus granted it also to manumitted slaves. They also grew by joining to them many peoples and kings, some with the title of associates,[22] as with the Latin peoples, some with that of friends, as with the kings of Egypt and Asia, the Massilians,[23] and others, and this name of friend or associate the Roman people gave to well-deserving cities and princes. They also took advantage of protection; so they took possession of Capua by defending it against the Samnites and of the people of Messina by defending them against Hiero[24] and the Carthaginians. In this way the Turk has grown incredibly; having made himself protector of the Kurds, of the Tartars of Precop,[25] and sometimes also of the Georgians, he has made use of their forces no less than of his own. This type of protection of others is well enough known to the princes of our time. Henry II of France made use of it cunningly when after assuming the protection of the Empire against Emperor Charles V, he made himself cunningly lord of the three great cities, Metz, Toul, and Verdun. The kings of Poland have acquired Livonia in the same manner. The Romans also grew rich from the benefits and favors they made to princes; Attalus, king of Asia,[26] and then later Nicomedes, king of Bithynia,[27] moved by their marks of affection and by the benefits that they had received, made them their heirs when they died as did other kings. In this way the Genoese received Pera from the Emperor Michael Paleologus,[28] and Francesco Gattilusio[29] Mytilene from the Emperor John, the Venetians Veglia from Giovanni Bano,[30] Francesco Sforza Savona from

---

[22] *Compagni.*   [23] Citizens of Massilia (Marseilles).

[24] Hiero II, tyrant of Syracuse (r. *c.* 270–215 BCE).

[25] This was a name given to the Tartars of the Crimea.

[26] Attalus I, king of Pergamon, today Bergama in Turkey (r. 241–197 BCE). Asia here is Asia Minor.

[27] Nicomedes IV, king of Bithynia (r. 94–74 BCE).

[28] This took place in 1267 after the Genoese assisted him in the reconquest of Constantinople. The city of Pera rests on the peninsula of the same name that reaches out into the Bosporus from the European area of Istanbul.

[29] Francesco Gattilusio II, an aristocrat of Genoa and a corsair, received the island of Mytilene from Emperor John V Palaeologus in 1355 in gratitude for the aid that he gave him for the recovery of his throne (*BD*, 304, n. 7).

[30] Veglia is an island off the coast of Dalmatia. The Venetians took it from the Hungarian captain Giovanni Bano (Jan Horváth), count of Zara, who died in 1391 (*BD*, 304, nn. 8–9).

Louis XI for assistance that he had given him.[31] Emperor Frederick III gave Modena and Reggio to Borso d'Este for the courtesies that he had shown him in Ferrara,[32] and Alexander Farnese, duke of Parma, in the end received the most important citadel of Piacenza from the Catholic King for the infinite services that he had performed for His Majesty in the war and government of the Low Countries.

8 Of the Purchase of States

There is no way to enrich yourself at the expense of another that is more advantageous than this because you purchase that which cannot be paid for with money, and there is no commerce more worthy of a prince. So Clement VI purchased Avignon from Giovanna I, queen of Naples, with that which she owed to the church for back taxes.[33] Attendolo Sforza bought Cotignola from Pope John XXIII for forty thousand ducats.[34] Philip of Valois purchased Dauphiné from Prince Humbert for forty thousand florins (and what a state is that?[35]), and the duchy of Berry for sixty thousand.[36] Charles V acquired the county of Auxerre for thirty-one thousand golden francs.[37] But no people has enriched itself more by way of purchase than the Florentines just as there has never been a republic with more ready cash. They purchased the city of Arezzo from the lord of Cosse for forty thousand golden florins,[38] Livorno from Tomaso

---

[31] Louis XI, king of France (r. 1461–83), ceded Savona to Francesco Sforza, duke of Milan, in 1464.

[32] Emperor Frederick III bestowed on Borso d'Este, marquis of Ferrara, the title of duke of Modena and Reggio in 1452 (*BD*, 305, n. 1).

[33] The Kingdom of Naples was a fief of the church, and this is why it owed the church taxes. Giovanna I, queen of Naples from 1343–82, was also countess of Provence, and it was under this title that she sold the lordship of Avignon to Pope Clement VI in 1348 (*BD*, 305, n. 5).

[34] Muzio Attendolo, called Sforza (1369–1424), was a condottiere. He obtained as a fief from the anti-pope John XXIII the village of his birthplace, Cotignola, between Imola and Ravenna, for 14,000 ducats. His son, Francesco Sforza, married the daughter of Filippo Maria Visconti, and so acquired the duchy of Milan (*BD*, 305, n. 6).

[35] According to *BD*, 306, n. 1, this should be an exclamation point rather than a question mark; so there is a printing error in the text.

[36] Humbert II of Savoy sold Dauphiné, a territory of the Empire, to Philip VI, king of France, in 1349 (*BD*, 305, n. 7).

[37] Charles V, king of France, purchased the county of Auxerre from John IV of Chalons in 1371.

[38] Enguerrand de Coucy, a condottiere in the service of the Angevins, sold the town to the Florentines in 1384 (*BD*, 306, n. 4).

Fregoso for one hundred and twenty thousand ducats,[39] Cortona from Ladislaus, king of Naples,[40] and Pisa from Gabriel Maria Visconti.[41]

9 Of Enlistment[42]

Giovanni Galeazzo Visconti[43] was accustomed to say that there was no more noble commerce in the world than to acquire and to attract to one's service outstanding men, so that he did not spare money to attract outstanding men of every nation to his employment. Now this takes place in many ways. The most ordinary is to recruit foreign soldiers to serve in war. But besides this men are also brought into a country to populate it (as Leo IV induced Corsicans to live in the Borgo, named by him the Leonine City),[44] or to cultivate it (as John II of Portugal[45] brought in some German farmers), or to enrich it with their art and labors (as has been done most skillfully by Cosimo and Francesco, grand dukes of Tuscany)[46] or to earn money from the raw materials that exceed our needs. But so that we are able to have sufficient raw materials and finished products, the prince ought to see to it that raw material does not leave the state, not wool, not silk, not iron, not tin, nor any other such thing, because if the material leaves the kingdom, so also do the skills that work with it, and as a result the support of many thousands of men who would live from it. So therefore he ought to make every effort that the material that originates in his country is finished and artificially transformed in various ways by his subjects and so sold to foreigners because many more people will be supported and more benefits will result, both public and private, as I have demonstrated at greater length above.[47]

[39] Tommaso Fregoso was doge of Genoa for many years between 1415 and 1442 (*BD*, 306, n. 5).

[40] Ladislaus of Naples sold Arezzo to Florence in 1411 for 60,000 golden florins (*BD*, 306, n. 6).

[41] The Florentines made the purchase in 1411 for 60,000 golden florins but were only able to take possession the following year (*BD*, 306, n. 7).

[42] The word here is "condotta." Starting with *RS* 1596, the words "des Gens" were added to this title. The first meaning of "condotta" here is the contract by which a prince or a city hires a mercenary captain and his troops, but the meaning here is extended to take in other types of foreigners (*BD*, 306, n. 8).

[43] Duke of Milan (r. 1385–1402).

[44] Leo IV, pope from 847–55, fortified a quarter next to the Vatican which came to be called the Leonine city.

[45] Reigned 1477–95.   [46] Cosimo I reigned 1537–74, and Francesco 1574–87.

[47] The passage here from "But so that we are able" to the end of the chapter was deleted from subsequent editions, presumably because it was redundant after what was said in chap. 3, "On Industry."

10 Of States Taken as Pledges

States are also acquired when they are taken as pledges for money that has been loaned; such pledges, because it rarely happens that they are paid off, are considered by princes to be their property. The imperial electors sold to Emperor Charles IV[48] their votes to make his son Wenceslaus king of the Romans[49] for one hundred thousand florins apiece; and because he did not have so much money at hand, they took as a pledge sixteen cities of the Empire which they held permanently and their successors retained. Louis X,[50] king of France, received the county of Roussillon from King John of Aragon for four hundred thousand scudi which Charles VIII returned to the Catholic King for nothing; similarly, the Florentines received in pledge from Eugene IV[51] Borgo San Sepolcro for twenty-five thousand scudi, and John III, king of Portugal, received the Molucca Islands from Emperor Charles V for three hundred and fifty thousand scudi.[52]

11 Of Alliances of Kinship

Kinship and marriages also help greatly to grow rich at the expense of others; through them princes draw upon us and acquire for themselves rights and claims of importance. So Tarquin the Proud notably increased his resources when he gave his daughter to Octavius Mamilius, a man of great authority among the Latins. And we read that Pyrrhus took many wives in order to become powerful. The Carthaginians, in order to detach Syphax[53] from his friendship with the Romans, gave him as wife Sophonisba, daughter of their citizen Hasdrubal. The Venetians in a similar way set foot on the island of Cyprus.[54] Filippo Maria Visconti recovered the state, which three captains of his father had divided among

---

[48] Charles of Luxembourg, emperor from 1355–78.

[49] Wenceslaus, king of Bohemia, was king of the Romans from 1378–1400.

[50] In reality it was Louis XI who in 1462 received Roussillon as a pledge from John II of Aragon.

[51] Pope from 1431–47.

[52] This transaction took place at the Treaty of Zaragoza of 1529. The funds that he obtained enabled Charles V to finance his war against France and the League of Cognac (*BD*, 308, n. 3).

[53] King of an ancient Numidian tribe of the later third century BCE.

[54] This is an allusion to Caterina Cornaro, whom the Venetian authorities selected as wife of the king of Cyprus in 1468; upon the death of her husband she became queen of Cyprus and in 1489 abdicated in favor of the Venetian Republic (*BD*, 309, n. 6).

themselves, with the four hundred thousand scudi that came to him as the dowry from Beatrice da Tenda.[55] In this way the crown of England had already acquired Aquitaine and that of France Brittany. But no house has ever arrived at such greatness and power by way of women as the House of Austria. By a continuous chain of felicitous events Maximilian acquired the Low Countries through Maria, the daughter of Charles, the last duke of Burgundy; Philip, his son, received Spain and its dependencies as dowry with his marriage to Juana, daughter of Ferdinand and Isabella, to which states Charles, his son, succeeded; and in our times Philip, the most worthy son of Charles, has inherited Portugal and its dependencies, which are greatly extensive, through Isabella, his mother. And because this way to increase is most just and most peaceful, it ought also to be considered above all the other ways durable and secure.

12 Of Adoption

Another category of kinship is adoption, of which Joanna II, queen of Naples, made use against her enemies, and the Angevins and the Aragonese acquired rights over that most noble and most rich kingdom. Only with the French, through the Salic Law (which excludes from the crown of France all women) whose origin has never been known, does this manner of increase by way of kinship have no place.

13 Of the Method Used by the Poles[56]

The Poles have greatly increased their rule and their power by electing lords of other countries whose lands have been incorporated into the crown of Poland. So, to leave aside other examples, after electing the Grand Duke of Lithuania of the house of Jagiellon their king, they finally made that province a member of their imperium.[57]

14 Of Alliances

Power is also increased by the resources of others through alliances which usually make a prince stronger and more courageous because there are

[55] Beatrice was a wealthy Italian noblewoman, a widow. She was executed by Filippo Maria for alleged adultery in 1418.

[56] In the following editions this chapter was placed at the end of this book.

[57] Casimir IV Jagiellon became Grand Duke of Lithuania in 1440 and was elected king of Poland in 1447 where he reigned until 1492.

many things that he is not able and does not dare to do that he will undertake in concert with others because the alliance increases the satisfaction in success and diminishes the harm in failure. Now alliances are of different types: perpetual and temporary, offensive and defensive, and both offensive and defensive. In some alliances the allies are of an equal condition, in others one is superior to the others. The Romans were superior in their alliances with the Latins; they made the plans and the decisions for the campaigns, they appointed the generals and all the other officials of importance, and finally they managed the wars and enjoyed the fruit of the victories, so that the Latins were nothing but the servants of the Romans, and if they were also companions, they were so only in the labors and the danger of the war, without sharing at all in the glory or the acquisitions or the rule. In this, truly, the Romans showed admirable judgment because under the name of league and association they acquired with common resources the rule of the world for themselves alone; when the Latins wanted to reverse this, they had against them the forces of the Romans, the peoples subject to them, and the princes who were their friends and colleagues. Alliances including a dominant ally are those in which one contributes more to the common undertaking and participates more in the fruits of the victory than the other, and in these and in similar alliances one need not place much confidence because princes ordinarily are not moved by anything other than interest, and they do not recognize either a friend or an enemy apart from the benefit for which they hope or from the evil that they fear, and alliances only last as long as the benefits to the allies last. Now because the interest of many princes in one enterprise cannot be equal, it is not credible that the allies will move forward with equal spirit and readiness, without which equality the alliance will not venture anything of moment. And if as in a clock one hand or one counter-weight malfunctions it upsets the harmony of its operation, so also in alliances one partner who fails upsets the whole body of the alliance. This can be seen in the alliances contracted under Paul III and Pius V between the Catholic King and the Venetians against the Turk which although entered into with great enthusiasm and with a still greater victory, nevertheless yielded no progress because the interests of the princes were not equal;[58] Spain did not consider the

---

[58] The reference here is to the Holy League, at the initiative of Pius V, among Spain, Venice, and other states in early 1571. They defeated the Turks at the great Battle of Lepanto on October 7, 1571, but there was no effective follow-up to this victory. Early in the 1530s Pope Paul III had encouraged alliances against the Turks.

campaigns to the east of much importance, while they were of great benefit to the Venetians, and the campaigns in Africa did not count for much with the Venetians, while they were necessary for Spain. Hence since the Venetians feared the forces that the Turk had in the Levant and the Spaniards the nearness of Algiers, they were not able to move forward together with equal enthusiasm because of the diversity of their interests, and the pope remained in the middle having provided funds without obtaining any benefit. It follows that only in two ways can an alliance be formed against the Turks with some hope of success: one would be for all the princes that border on the Turk to move against him at the same time and that each attack him, for his part, not with limited forces but with all his power; in this case the interest of all would be equal; the other would be more noble: if more princes together, without any other interest than the honor of God and the exaltation of the church, attacked as one more places, as happened in those heroic times when many princes of Germany, of Flanders, of France, and of Italy, some selling, some pledging their states, brought together more than four hundred thousand persons and after defeating the Turks at Nicaea, the Persians at Antioch, and the Saracens in Jerusalem,[59] conquered the whole East and recovered the whole Holy Land. It is notable that in such a great campaign no king or emperor took part, and even if the kings of France and England and the emperors Conrad and Frederick[60] later went there not to acquire but to retain what had been acquired, they nevertheless did not accomplish anything worthwhile.

But returning to our topic, we conclude that alliances will then add to power whenever the interests of the parties are equal but whenever there is no equality of interests, we ought to hold it for certain that assistance from the alliance will fail. And so universally alliances are so much the better the greater is their stability and firmness, and so perpetual alliances are better than temporary ones, the offensive and the defensive together better than the offensive or defensive alone, and equality of the allies better than inequality. It is true that these (I speak of the equal ones), such as are found among the Swiss, are useful enough for defense but of no efficacy for offense, because in defense the danger for one easily stirs the others because of proximity, and fear of evil stirs more than the

---

[59] The conquest of Jerusalem took place on July 15, 1099.
[60] Conrad III Hohenstaufen, emperor from 1138–52, took part in the Second Crusade. Frederick II led the Sixth Crusade and was crowned king of Jerusalem in 1229.

hope of benefits. But on the offensive the fruit of victory has to be shared with all and so is not able to stir each partner so effectively, and is of little value. So although the Swiss have noteworthy opportunities to acquire rich states, they nevertheless have never done anything worthy of note and are content with a mercenary militia, at the service of this or that prince, which well rewards individuals with spoils obtained in war and with pensions which they draw in peace, but the public becomes weaker in this way because of the innumerable multitude of soldiers who die as a result of wars and because of the interests and dependencies with which the colonels and captains remain obligated to foreign princes.

15 Of Commerce, and Whether it is Suitable for a King to Engage in it

The most common way to grow rich from that which belongs to others is commerce, but because it is suitable for private men instead of princes, it will not be beyond our purpose to see in what case it is good for the prince to engage in it. We say, then, that in three cases trade is not unsuitable for a prince, even a great one. The first is when the means of private persons are not sufficient to maintain the trade, either because of excessive expense or the opposition of enemies or for some other cause. So the kings of Portugal have with great fleets acquired and with glorious victories have maintained commerce and trade with Ethiopia and India, and no campaign is unsuitable for a king in which resources are sought for the king. The second case is when the trade is of such importance that a private person would acquire with it excessive riches. As the Venetians send out great galleys of the republic for trade in spices which are purchased in Alexandria and sold then in England, in Flanders, and in other such places, through which the public grows rich beyond measure, it is not unfitting to acquire justly the riches worthy of a king. The third case is when the commerce is undertaken for the public welfare and well-being. So great princes at the time of extreme shortages and needs of their subjects buy foreign grain and resell it to the great benefit of their subjects.

16 Of the Method Employed by the Sultans of Egypt and by the Portuguese

The sultans of Egypt, for the conservation of their state, were accustomed to purchase young men of military age and appearance especially of the Circassian nation[61] and then after making them practice with arms and with the handling of horses made use of them in the army, after giving them their liberty, and with these troops they ruled for more than three hundred years Egypt, Syria, Arabia, and Cyrenaica, a usage, as far as I can conjecture, employed much earlier by the Parthians because we read that in their army of fifty thousand men sent against Mark Antony there were only four hundred and fifty free men.[62] Cleomenes, king of Sparta, when he needed soldiers offered liberty to slaves at fifty scudi per head and so he acquired two benefits, men and money. Omar, a follower of Muhammad, by promising liberty to slaves drew an infinite number to himself.[63] The Portuguese, because of the need that they had for men, every year send their caravels filled with goods to the ports of Guinea; there in exchange for their merchandise they take many thousands of slaves whom they transport to work on the sugar plantations and to cultivate the lands on the islands of St. Thomas and Cape Verde, and in Brazil, and they sell them to the Castilians who make use of them in the same way on the island of Hispaniola and in other places. The same shortage of men is the reason why men worthy of death are condemned to the galleys, to the quarrying of marble, to the extraction of metals, and to other similar labors.

17 Of the Method Used by the Chinese

The Greeks and the Romans, in order to draw some benefit from enemies captured in war, enslaved them and employed them to work the land and for other activities. But the Chinese do not kill them, nor hold them for ransom, nor chain them, nor determine them finally for anything other than to serve in war on distant frontiers far from their homeland, and in Chinese garb except that, in order to differentiate them from others, they wear red birettas which in China are worn only by infamous persons as it were or as a sign of ignorance.

18 Of the Method Used by the Turks

The Grand Turk multiplies troops and resources, among other ways, by the reception and shelter that he gives to men of every sect, provided

---

[61] Circassia is a region of the North Caucasus along the shore of the Black Sea, the homeland of the Circassian nation. These were the Mamelukes.

[62] Mark Antony led campaigns against the Parthians from 36–33 BCE.

[63] Omar I, 581–c. 644, caliph, second successor of the Prophet.

that they serve him faithfully in war. These constitute that brave band of cavalry called the Mutiferiaghi[64] among which there usually are not a few Christians drawn there by the desperation of their situation, by anger, by foolish ambition, or by some other diabolical cause.

[64] It is not clear who these are.

Book Nine

1 Of the Ways to Increase Resources

Up to now we have demonstrated the ways to increase resources extensively. We now speak of the ways which ought to be employed to increase them intensively, which are all those which increase valor. It is not adequate to have many soldiers; it is necessary beyond this to reinforce their valor because a few troops of valor are worth more than a multitude of cowardly and base men, as the victories of the Greeks and Romans attest who ordinarily with a smaller number of troops have bested enemy armies; the multitude has everywhere yielded to valor.

2 Whether a Prince Ought to Train his Own Subjects for War or Not

Before we go further it is necessary to decide this question much debated especially among the French: whether it is good for a prince to train and make use of his own subjects or foreigners in military campaigns.

Some princes by birth have made use not of all the people indifferently but only of the nobility; so in great part do the Poles, the Persians, and the French proceed. But because the nobles do not serve as foot soldiers, these nations always have had formidable cavalry but weak infantry. Because they hold suspect the *virtù* and valor which usually prevail among the nobility, tyrants who in order to stabilize the state have put to death and banished the nobility while giving their authority to the people, have sometimes trusted the latter. The Turk has placed his forces in the hands of acquired subjects who have been naturalized by education. He has selected more muscular and agile youths whom they call Azamoglioni[1] and having taken them from the homes and bosoms of their parents in their adolescence, he distributes them throughout Turkey where, raised in the laws and customs of the Muslims, they become Turks without being aware of it, and they know no other father than the great lord at whose expense they live nor any other country than that from which their wages and their benefits come.

In order to decide this controversy we presuppose that the principal foundation of a dominion is its independence and its standing on its own. Now independence is of two sorts. The one excludes all supremacy and superiority, and in this sense the pope, the emperor, the kings of France, of England, and of Poland are independent princes. The other independence excludes the need of help and support from others; in this sense those are independent who have resources either superior or equal to their enemies or rivals. Of these two forms of independence, the second is the more important because the former is as it were accidental and external, the latter substantial and intrinsic; the former makes me an absolute and supreme lord, the latter that I am powerful and have sufficient resources for the preservation of my state, and that I am truly a great prince and not a king.[2] Now I will not be able to be independent in this second sense without my own troops because a foreign militia, no matter that it is obligated to me, will depend more upon its own interests than upon yours and so abandon you in your need, corrupted by enemies (as the Celtiberi,[3] first suborned by the Romans abandoned the Carthaginians, and then suborned by the Carthaginians abandoned the Romans), now delayed (as were the Swiss in great times of necessity for the French, as happened more than once), now called home because of the dangers to their own country (as the Grisons threatened by Gian Giacomo de' Medici abandoned the service of King Francis in his great need).[4] It is not beyond our intention to consider that these mercenary

---

[1] This word is made up of two Turkish words, *adjiam* "stranger" and *oglou* "child" (*BD*, 318, n. 2).

[2] The phrase "and not a king" was changed to "and not a king of Yvetot" in *RS* 1590 and *RS* 1596, and in *RS* 1598 the whole phrase was suppressed. Yvetot was a small lordship in central France whose lord bore the title of "king" from the early fifteenth to the mid-sixteenth century (*BD*, 318, n. 4).

[3] An ancient Celtic people of northern Spain.

[4] In order to defend the Valtelline against the incursions of the condottiere Gian Giacomo de' Medici, the Grison troops abandoned the siege of Pavia in 1525, thus weakening Francis I (*BD*, 319, nn. 1–2).

troops, like merchants or shopkeepers of little credit, sell their services full of infinite defects, a thousand wages paid for dead or non-existent soldiers and troops hired at a favorable price because they are of so little value and poorly conditioned. Mutinies are an ordinary occurrence when they are not paid on time, and these endanger the states and stir disorder among the princes. This happened to the Carthaginians after the First Punic War, and the same befell Monsignor Lautrec at the Battle of Bicocca.[5] You do well if they do not assassinate you or betray you to your enemies (as they did Ludovico Sforza to the French near Novara),[6] or if, seeing themselves the stronger, they do not turn their arms against you (as did the Angles, when summoned by the Britons against the Scots and Picts, after they had chased these away, turn their arms at the end against those who had hired them). What will we say of the fall of the Roman Empire? Did it not come from foreign militias? The emperors made use of various nations in their wars, both civil and foreign (as Hadrian of the Alani,[7] Alexander of the Osrohenians,[8] Probus of the Bastarnae,[9] Spaniards, and Gauls, and Valerian of the Goths and others of other tribes). So these peoples having learned the practices of the Roman army and of other countries, became tyrants of the emperors and of the Empire so that its principal captains were barbarians: Stilicho, Uldin, Sarus, Rufinus, Castinus, Boniface, and Aetius,[10] and a good number of them were made emperors, entered into the heart of the Empire, trampled down Italy, took Rome, and transformed the provinces into kingdoms. The Franks occupied Gaul, the Burgundians the lands of the Sequani,[11] the Vandals Aquitaine, Spain, and Africa, the Suevi[12] and Alani Brittany, the Ostrogoths Macedonia and Thrace, the Slavs

---

[5] Odet de Foix, lord of Lautrec and Marshal of France, was defeated at Bicocca in 1522.
[6] In 1500.
[7] The Alani were a nomadic, pastoral people who inhabited the steppe plains northeast of the Black Sea.
[8] The Osrohenians inhabited an area of Mesopotamia whose capital was Edessa.
[9] The Basternae were a Germanic tribe that originated in present-day Poland and then migrated to the northern Balkans.
[10] These were all generals of the late Roman Empire.
[11] The Sequani, a Celtic people, occupied the lands between the Saône, the Rhône, and the Rhine rivers in the first century BCE. Their capital was at modern Besançon.
[12] The Suevi consisted of a number of Germanic tribes that came down from the area of the Baltic Sea and the Elbe River and threatened the Roman borders on the Rhine and the Danube.

Dalmatia, the Saracens Asia, Africa, and Spain. Radagaisus,[13] Alaric,[14] Attila,[15] Genseric,[16] Beorgor,[17] Theodoric,[18] one after the other sacked and oppressed Italy. For what reason was the empire of the East lost if not because the Emperor Caloyannis[19] recruited twelve thousand Turks against his enemies, and then retained six thousand at his side and let the others go. These, having become familiar with the area, seduced by the fertility of the country, excited by the ease of the enterprise, the incapacity of the princes, the discord of the barons, and the weakness of the forces, induced their lord Amurat[20] to cross the strait with sixty thousand soldiers. So, occupying gradually this or that city, finally Muhammad[21] with the conquest of Constantinople overthrew the Empire of the East.

These troubles following upon the use of foreign troops were the reason why Charles VIII, king of France, after liberating his kingdom from the English, in order to better defend it, put together an army of five thousand infantry. But Louis XI dismissed whoever had committed a number of murders or robberies, and he made use of Swiss in their place; Francis I, then, having seen the danger to France because of the need that it had for foreign help which in various ways was delayed, weakened, rendered useless, or entirely held up because of the tricks of the enemy, established in 1534 an army of fifty thousand infantry divided into seven legions; but after nearly disintegrating, it was revived by King Henry in 1556, but with little fruit because of the little order and poor administration.

But someone will say that whoever makes use of his own subjects in war and exercises them in arms will never be a peaceful lord of his state because the use of arms makes a man haughty, impudent, confident, who

---

[13] Radagaisus, an Ostrogoth chief, invaded Italy in 405, devastating Emilia and Tuscany. He was defeated by Stilicon in 406 at Fiesole.

[14] Alaric, Visigothic king from 395–410, sacked Rome in 410.

[15] Attila, king of the Huns, after marching through Gaul threatened Rome in 452 but was convinced by Pope Leo I to spare the city.

[16] Genseric, a Vandal king, created a Vandal kingdom in North Africa with its capital at Carthage. From there he pillaged Rome in 455.

[17] Beorgor, a king of the Alani, invaded Italy and was killed near modern Bergamo in 464.

[18] Theodoric the Great (454–526), an Ostrogothic king and an ally of the Eastern Emperor Zeno, founded a kingdom in Italy whose capital was Ravenna.

[19] Caloyannis was a name given to John V, Byzantine emperor from 1341–91.

[20] Sultan Murad II who besieged Constantinople in 1422.

[21] Mehmed II, the Conqueror, took Constantinople in 1453.

promises himself everything from the sword: *jura negat sibi nata, nihil non arrogat armis* (he denies that the laws were made for him; there is nothing that he does not take for himself by force of arms).[22] This is what we see to have happened in Flanders and in France where the people inured to war and bloodied by the long conflict, after peace was made with the foreigners, turned their arms against their country, against their natural king, against religion, against God. But in human affairs and especially in the handling and governing of the people, we are not able to avoid all the pitfalls; it is the duty of the wise king to avoid the greatest and most dangerous. Now of all the evils to which a state can be subjected, the greatest is dependence on the troops of others, and the state that makes use of foreign military as its principal strength finds itself in this situation. And with this evil come all those disorders that we have mentioned above that are so great and of such importance that those which can be adduced in comparison with them by the contrary party are little more than nothing.[23] But let us say also that the lack of confidence in his subjects follows from weakness of spirit and of judgment, so that all prudent kings with great diligence trained their peoples in the use of arms. Romulus left to foreigners the other crafts as vile and unworthy of a courageous and well-born man; he did not allow the Romans anything other than agriculture and the military; nor do we read that they revolted for a space of two hundred and forty years nor did they ever riot. Rather, they fought at their own expense with obedience and incredible readiness because their orders were good and the administration was in the hands of those who understood and attended to it. Alexander the Great exempted the Macedonians from every imposition except military service. Hiero, king of Syracuse, celebrated in Roman history, wanting to stabilize his rule in the state, acting quickly got rid of foreign soldiers by having them torn to pieces, and having chosen his own he formed them

---

[22] Horace, *Art of Poetry*, 122.

[23] *RS* 1598 adds the following here: "But let us add another argument greater still. There is nothing more prejudicial to states than the introduction of foreign customs because they bring with them changes in the state and the ruin of the republic; now there is no way by which these enter with greater impetus than through foreign armies. The Roman Empire attests to this but still more intensely does France because the heresy, which has ruined such a flourishing and powerful state, was introduced by the Swiss and German legions brought in first by Francis and then by his son Henry. This is shown by the multitude of lords, captains, and French soldiers who suddenly after the death of Henry showed themselves to be supporters of impiety, having drunk it in from the conversation and example of the foreigners."

into a brave and faithful army with which he maintained himself honorably in the state as long as he lived. But what of the lords of Venice, His Most Serene Majesty of Savoy, the grand duke of Tuscany; does each not have a good army which he keeps alive and in continual exercises? But it is agreed that they have never rebelled nor caused an uproar or sacked the countryside, or blocked the roads, or attacked lands, or disturbed the public peace or engaged in any other bad conduct. These are not defects of our militia but of discipline and administration.

We conclude therefore that it is necessary for a prince to train his own subjects in the use of arms so that his own troops are the substance of his forces and foreigners accessories. Livy teaches this when he recounts the fall of the two Scipios: *Cavendum semper romanis ducibus erit, exemplaque haec vere pro documentis habenda, ne ita externis credant auxiliis, ut non plus sui roboris suarum proprie virium in castris habeant* (The Roman generals ought always be on their guard, while keeping in mind this exemplary warning, not to trust foreign auxiliary forces to the point that they accept in their encampment a number greater than their own forces). But to maintain subjects prepared for war in time of peace, severity of discipline will help as well as prompt payment of those who serve. There will never lack Turks and Moors and Saracens against whom it is always possible to take up arms justly. But a matter to be clearly understood is to have a number of galleys on which those who do not know how to remain at peace would be able to ship out and give vent to their youth and bravery against true enemies. This will serve as a remedy and a diversion for their peccant humors.

3 Of the Selection of Soldiers

Now the first way to make your soldiers bold and courageous will be recruitment, that is to say, in their selection. Because not all are suitable in spirit nor physically prepared to endure the labors and the hardship of military service, to endure cold and heat, sun and moon, hunger and thirst, nor to spend entire days without rest and nights without sleep, to wade across rapid torrents, to jump over ditches, to climb walls, to accept duels as did the young David, to face up to unforeseen attacks, to stand up to the fury of fire, the storm of a cannonade, volleys of shot, clouds of lime, of burning oil, of Greek fire, nor to risk one's life nor to challenge death in a thousand ways. So you ought not to trust in every one, because the cowards, in the manner of scabrous sheep, will also depress the bold, and on the other hand the brave when united together grow in spirit and in force. To this end God ordered the captains of the Jews that before leading the army into battle they stand before it and address those under arms: *Quis est homo formidolosus et corde pavido? Vadat et revertatus in domum suam ne pavere faciat corda fratrum suorum, sicut ipse timore perterritus est* (Is there a man here fearful and of a timid heart? Let him go and return to his home, lest he make the hearts of his brothers to tremble as he himself is terrified by fear).[24] And because the love of spouses, of the houses they have built, of the vines planted anew, and of other similar delights and comforts is accustomed to hold men back from the dangers of war and to make them friends more of life than of honor, do not ever wish that these men be placed on the military rolls. Taking this into consideration Judas Maccabeus, although he faced an army of an infinite number of idolaters with a very small force, nonetheless *dixit qui aedificabant domos, et sponsabant uxores, et plantabat vineas, et formidolosis, ut rediret unusquisque in domum suam* (told those who had built homes, and married spouses, and planted vineyards, and were fearful, each to return to his own home).[25] The great captains have always counted more on the quality rather than the numbers of the soldiers. Alexander the Great subjected the whole East with thirty thousand infantry and four thousand cavalry. Hannibal setting out on the campaign of Italy and Rome, sent home seven thousand Spaniards in whom he had perceived signs of timidity, thinking that these troops would harm rather than help. Count Alberico da Cunio[26] restored to a degree the reputation of Italian troops, hitherto considered nearly infamous, when with an army of select soldiers that he called the League of Saint George he drove the English, the Bretons, and other ultramontane barbarians out of Italy which they had for a long time torn up and knocked about. It is known that George Castriotes[27] in so many battles with the Turks never had under his flag more than six thousand cavalry and three thousand ready infantry. With these he recovered and defended his small state and achieved glorious victories over Murad II and Mehmed II, Turkish princes. In our own

---

[24] Deuteronomy 20:8.   [25] 1 Maccabees 3:56.

[26] Alberico da Barbiano (1344–1409), count of Barbiano, Cunio, Lugo, and Zagonarra, a condottiere in the service of the Visconti, of Pope Urban VI, and the Angevins of Naples, created in 1378 an Italian mercenary force that defeated the Breton mercenary force of the anti-pope Clement VII on April 30, 1379.

[27] George Castriotes, called Skanderbeg (1405–68), head of the Albanian Janissaries, turned against his Muslim masters and held off the Ottoman forces. He became a hero of Albanian independence (*BD*, 326, n. 2).

times we know how much light and glory Giovanni de' Medici[28] brought
to the Italian military with the extremely accurate selection he made of
his soldiers. In the selection it would be desirable that all the soldiers
were ambidextrous, as Plato wanted,[29] that is, that they make use of the
left hand no less than the right, which he thought could be achieved by
long exercise. But let us leave the consideration of this to others as well
as of what nation and stature, of what practice and physiognomy soldiers
ought to be chosen, because these matters are treated differently by different authors.

4 Of Arms

Valor increases with the quality of the arms, defensive as well as offensive. So the poets have made up tales that the gods fashioned the arms
for the great personages celebrated by them; and our authors of romances
imagine enchanted and magic shields and breastplates in order to show
that forces grow with the value of the instruments that they use; and
because the horse is one of these instruments, they attribute also to their
heroes miraculous steeds. It helps in the first place to have defensive arms
because it is necessary to presuppose that the soldier who does not feel
himself equipped and protected by a breastplate and a coat of mail will
place hope for survival more in his legs than in his arms and will think
more of flight than of combat; it is also true of horses that those who
are caparisoned are more spirited than those who are led to war naked.
The Roman infantry fought fully armed when the military art flourished;
but setting aside gradually the exercises which with daily practice less-
ened the weight, the arms began to seem to be too heavy, so that they
asked permission from Emperor Gratian to set aside their breastplates
and then their helmets, so that when it came to fighting hand-to-hand
with the Goths they were easily overcome. Defensive weapons ought to
be well-tempered because this provides greater security, and besides this
light and flexible, light so that they are not too heavy and so an encum-
brance for the soldiers. As Tacitus recounts, in the war with Sacrovir the
enemy carried such heavy arms that they were as it were immobile so that
the Romans employed axes and hatchets to break them up as if they were

---

[28] Giovanni of the Black Bands (1498–1526), of a cadet branch of the Medici, served first as
head of a papal army for Pope Leo X (Medici) and then for the French and the emperor
in the Italian Wars.

[29] *Laws*, 7 (794e–795d).

knocking down a wall;[30] others used pitchforks and other instruments to throw these so clumsily armed men to the ground. These arms also have to be flexible, so that they can be easily handled and turned and are not an impediment or entanglement. For this reason David refused the arms offered him by Saul because they appeared to place him in a sack where he would have lost his agility and dexterity;[31] and in this respect the much longer German corselets are better than the Italian so that the German arms himself more quickly than the Italian and without the aid of others. [Defensive arms] finally ought to be of good form and proportionate to persons, so that Livy wrote that their long but narrow shields did not cover well the large and broad bodies of the Gauls, and so they remained exposed to the blows of the Romans.[32] But it is not my intention to describe here what form the helmets, corselets and other forms of defensive weapons ought to have; it is enough to point out and take into consideration the qualities that suit them. It is the prince's business to see which are those that his people use and, if necessary, to heed men who understand how to improve them; the Romans, for example, although of spirit and of singular judgment, did not refuse out of pride to take over the form of arms of the Samnites.

The offensive [weapons] are better the lighter and more finished they are and the more effective that they are at long range. They ought to be light so that they tire the soldier less and can be fired or thrown more often; well finished so that they can be used for a longer time; effective from long range so that they do so much the more harm to the enemy before he attacks us because, firing from afar, you can fire the arquebus three times, for example, in the same time that the enemy, who is not so far away, will only fire twice. So you will be ahead by a third, so that it will seem that you have three thousand arquebusiers and he two thousand even if there be two thousand on each side. So Vegetius wrote that the Martiobarbuli, soldiers whom Diocletian and Maximian called Jovian and Herculean, brought many glorious victories to the Roman emperors because with accurate darts they struck men and horses *priusquam non modo ad manum, sed ad jactum potuerit perveniri* (not only before they were hand-to-hand but before they were even in range of missiles).[33]

---

[30] Tacitus, *Annals*, 4:18; Sacrovir was a barbarian chief who led a revolt against Tiberius in 21 CE.

[31] 1 Samuel 17:38–39.   [32] *History of Rome*, 38.21.

[33] Vegetius, *Concerning Military Affairs*, 1.17. The reference is to balls or darts of iron (*BD*, 329, nn. 3–4).

Awareness of this led to the large arquebuses which without a doubt have brought an infinite number of victories to the Catholic King in the Low Countries. And the Reiter[34] who each carried four or six short arquebuses were never an important factor because of the shortness of the range of their weapons, and they were struck and killed by longer arquebuses with greater range; moreover, Francis, duke of Guise, routed and put to flight many of them with lances at Renty.[35] But enough of this.

5 Of the Ornaments of Arms

At this point we can discuss whether it is good to concede to the soldiers the use of gilded arms or of arms adorned with silver or in another way richly adorned, and there are examples and reasons that render each option probable. Sertorius and Caesar wanted their soldiers to bear arms with gold and silver decoration and wear coats stately and remarkable for the variety and beauty of the colors. On the other hand Hannibal disdained the richness of the arms and the uniforms in the army of Antiochus, considering them to be more apt to stimulate the avarice and cupidity of the enemy rather than to fight and injure them. Mithridates, having experienced that his armies with the gilded and adorned arms had been routed by the Romans, set aside then, belatedly, the display and adornments and reduced his army to steel and iron. But we conclude that all those things should be permitted the soldiers that make them spirited and brave and more fearsome and terrible to the enemy, which without a doubt includes the beauty and magnificence of their arms. For this there have always been in use helmets, crests, and diverse inventions to wear on the head, to make taller and to make persons larger than ordinary, both the infantry and the cavalry. And if Hannibal said that the adornments and richness of the arms incite the avarice and cupidity of the enemy, Caesar, no less a captain than Hannibal, thought that the beauty and splendor of arms made his soldiers more tenacious and proud. *Milites*, says Suetonius, *habebat tam cultos, ut argento et auro politis armis ornaret, simul et ad speciem et quo tenaciores in proelio essent, metu damni* (He had his soldiers so well equipped that he endowed them with arms shining with gold and silver, both as ornament and to make them

---

[34] The Reiter were German mercenary cavalry; in fact, they carried pistols rather than arquebuses (*BD*, 330, n. 1).

[35] Francis (1519–63), the second duke of Guise, defeated the imperialists at Renty on August 13, 1554.

more tenacious of their arms in battle, for fear of losing them).[36] But perhaps it would be good not to allow gold and silver indifferently in the armaments of all but only to veterans or to those who had been present in many battles or singled out by some memorable deed. So we read that Alexander the Great did not give silvered arms to his most valorous soldiers, who were thus called "Argyrispides,"[37] until they had conquered the Persians and dominated the East. Nevertheless I would not want a general to stand on display, so as not to give an example of it to the others, and with this to lead the captains and all the army into debt and misery, something that happened in one place that I do not want to name, because the general ought to allow but not introduce display.

6 Of Order

As the value of a fortress consists more in its form than in its material, so the fortress of an army is found first in its order rather than in its number or in anything else; hence the church is called terrible in the manner of a well-ordered army. I call order the way that soldiers line up and are situated in battle, which is of such importance that victory depends in great part on it because as long as the order stands firm the army cannot be routed, and it is said to be a rout every time that the order breaks down and is shattered. Two peoples have been most glorious because of the greatness of their campaigns and the victories that they have won: the Macedonians and the Romans. The Macedonians dominated the East with the phalanx, the Romans the whole world with the legion. These were two forms of military order nearly insuperable but the legion was much better conceived and ordered than the phalanx because the phalanx, all of one piece and of an entire body that consisted of a great number of soldiers who with their lances (or sarissae as they called them) intertwined like a thick hedge, did not have agility in their movement; when locked together they were not able to move, when not locked together they were worth nothing. So it was good only on flat terrain because in areas that were not level it necessarily came apart and broke up as in the battle between Aemilius Paulus and King Perseus.[38] But the legion as one body of many members (because there were three types

---

[36] *The Twelve Caesars*, "Julius," 67.3.   [37] From the Greek, "having a silver shield."
[38] The Battle of Pydna in Greece in 168 BCE. Perseus was the king of Macedonia.

of soldiers: princes, *hastati*, and *triarii*,[39] divided into cohorts, and the cohorts into centuries, and the centuries into *contubernia* or maniples[40]) was more flexible and more agile and as a result more suitable for every situation in war and so produced the known effects. Livy writes of the Celtiberians that in critical points of battle they formed a type of wedge *quo tantum valent genere pugnae, ut quacumque parte perculere impetu suo, sustineri nequaeunt* (which is so effective that it is impossible to resist its shock wherever they charge the enemy).[41] Syphax, a powerful king of Numidia, equal to the Carthaginians in wealth and in size of population, was vastly inferior to them in the ordering of his infantry because he had no skill nor any formation to draw up and arrange his troops. For this reason he asked the Romans, with whom he was on a friendly basis, that they give him several centurions who would instruct his people how to follow the standards, to march, to keep formation, and so on. Having obtained this, he was conscious right away of the result of the order of battle. In a clash of arms with the Carthaginians he emerged the victor in a great battle. Experience has shown that the Italian military does not have a good reputation because of a lack of order, and there is no wise captain to whom to entrust Italian soldiers in a campaign against the Germans and the Swiss. And the Venetians can testify to this; because they have no other infantry but Italians, they have been defeated as many times as they have confronted ultramontane armies, at Rovereto,[42] at Caravaggio,[43] and at Vialà.[44] The Germans and the Swiss uphold their reputation as good soldiers only by virtue of their battle formations because when it comes to shrewdness, to vigor of soul, to diligence, to agility they yield by a large margin to the Italians, as do the French and the Spaniards as is seen in all the individual combat between Italian soldiers and those of the abovementioned nations, on foot as well as on horseback, at Trani, Quarata, Asti, Siena, and elsewhere. Nevertheless, they lose in the large-scale battles only because in them the ultramontanes conquer through their battle formation which has no place in individual combat.

---

[39] Soldiers of the first line, soldiers armed with javelins, veteran soldiers who made up the third line, respectively.

[40] Groups who shared the same tent.   [41] *History of Rome*, 40.40.3.

[42] The Venetians were defeated at Rovereto south of Trent in 1487 by the troops of Count Sigismund of Tyrol.

[43] In 1448 by the troops of the short-lived Ambrosian Republic of Milan led by the condottiere Francesco Forza (Sforza), later duke of Milan.

[44] More commonly known as the Battle of Agnadello where the French defeated the Venetians in 1509.

7 Of the Justice of the Cause

The justice of a cause greatly animates courage because a firm hope always accompanies him who is in the right and strengthens his spirit because *spes addita suscitat iras* (hope added awakens angers),[45] and anger sharpens courage. He whom justice accompanies prosecutes his cause with spirit and exposes himself with greater security to dangers; in addition, subjects serve their prince promptly and support him with their property. I add that he who combats an injustice acts with greater indignation and vehemence than he who commits one; on the other hand, he who acts unjustly is not able not to know for certain that God opposes him, and this opinion is enough to unnerve the soldiers and deprive them of spirit and force. Therefore, the prince and the captain ought to see to it that their soldiers consider the war to be just. This they will do by making just demands of the enemy by way of ambassadors or *fetiales*[46] (which the Romans used with solemnity) and rejecting unjust ones, by calling upon God to witness that they did not make war lightly, nor out of ambition, nor to misuse the life and blood of their own without reason but for the defense of religion, the preservation of the state, and for their honor. Caesar observed this in an outstanding fashion during the civil wars; in the midst of the din of arms he never abandoned negotiations for peace, sent various ambassadors, proposed diverse agreements, and finally used every artifice to demonstrate that he was a lover of peace even if he was desirous of war, so that when Pompey and the others rejected every accord, anger and the desire for vengeance increased in his soldiers.

8 Of Recourse to God

But there is nothing that so reanimates the soldiers and stimulates their hope and ardor in a more lively fashion than recourse to His Divine Majesty. Plato advises us to implore heavenly favor not only at the start of major and difficult enterprises but also of easy and light ones, so that the best end follows upon a good start.[47] So much the more does this

---

[45] Vergil, *Aeneid*, 10.263.
[46] These were priests whose function was to declare war and preside over the negotiation of treaties and agreements.
[47] *Timaeus*, 27c.

hold in military campaigns, which are the most dangerous and the most important beyond all the others, the defense of fortresses, the siege of enemy cities, and battles in the open field, and in all other military operations. Onasander, following the doctrine of his master Plato, did not want the army to leave the country without cleansing itself with a solemn sacrifice.[48] The Romans did not undertake any enterprise without first attending to the auspices. David did not go to war nor take up any matter of importance without first inquiring religiously for the divine will. Constantine the Great in the war against the Persians always carried with him a tabernacle in the form of a church where Mass was celebrated, and each legion had its own mobile temple where the deacons and priests resided so that they were called "field Masses." He also made use of the Cross as a standard and pledge of victory. All the histories affirm that the victories of the two Constantines resulted more from their prayer than from their armed forces.

This recourse to God produces many good effects. One is that it acquires divine protection, and *si Deus pro nobis, quis contra nos?* (if God is with us, who can be against us?).[49] The second is that it gives us confidence and near certainty of victory which revives and reanimates the spirits wonderfully. Thirdly it nearly assures the happiness of the next life which also renders the armies incredibly bold because there is nothing that more comforts and more rouses man's spirit in danger of life and in every military action where death has such a large part than the hope of a heavenly life. Now so that this recourse is made as is suitable and with the result that is desired, it is necessary that the general provide the army with religious persons who by preaching, by exhorting, by confessing, and by helping the soldiers in every manner, individually and in common, keep them continually alert and intent, free them from their sins, and fill them with the grace of God. If so many young virgins conquered in this way the madness of tyrants, the monstrosity of executioners, the violence of torments, and the opposition of the Roman Empire, what will be difficult for soldiers under the protection of God and in the grace of His Divine Majesty? Certainly for no other reason have the Catholics completely conquered the Huguenots in France and in Flanders in so

---

[48] Onasander Platonico was a Greek philosopher of the first century BCE; Botero cites here the Italian translation of his *Strategikos, Dell'ottimo capitano e del suo officio* (Venice, 1546), fols. 24–25ᵛ (*BD*, 335, n. 3).

[49] Romans 8:31.

many battles and at such a disadvantage if not because they have fought for the truth, the others for a lie, they with the hope of God's protection, the others with a desperate spirit, they armed with the holy sacraments of the church and of Christ, the others charmed by Calvin and other ministers of impiety. And among the Catholics those have fought with greater courage in the aforementioned provinces against the Huguenots and at Malta and Lepanto against the Turks who have gone with a better disposed spirit and more united with God.

9 Of Keeping Soldiers Far from their Home

Next, it increases the courage of soldiers to lead them far from their homeland, and the reason is that distance removes the ease of flight to which the nearness of home often leads, and the affections for parents, children, wives, friends are not so strong from a distance as from nearby. From this it follows that in the defense of cities it is necessary not to trust landowners because respect for parents, love of children, jealous attachment to their wives, concern for their property, and similar passions bind their hands as it were and confuse their judgment. But when they find themselves in foreign lands where they do not have parents nor wealth and see enemies all about them, they are forced to take heart and to fight. Hannibal well understood this because, when intending to pass over into Italy and so first to secure Spain and Africa, he stationed Africans for the defense of Spain and Spaniards for the defense of Africa. He considered that the one and the other would do better away from home than at home, and this is the reason why the Italian soldier is of little use in Italy and is highly regarded outside Italy. The Portuguese have shown little excellence in their own country and in neighboring places but they have performed outstandingly in India, where they have a small number of soldiers, despite the Mamelukes, the Turks, the Persians who are known to be excellent at arms, and the most powerful kings of India, and have seized rule over the ocean and the very rich states of Ormuz, Diu, Goa, Malacca, and Molucca,[50] because when they found themselves so far from home and from any assistance, they fought desperately. And the feats of the Spaniards in the New World ought to be attributed to the same cause (after God).

[50] The Portuguese established control over Ormuz in 1514, founded a factory in Diu in 1535, occupied Goa in 1510 and Malacca from 1511–1641, and began to trade with the Moluccas (not Molucca) in 1511.

10 Of Discipline

Discipline is the nerve of an army, and I call discipline the art of making a good soldier, and I call a soldier good who obeys with valor. One inculcates this in them first by removing the occasions and enticements of corruption and luxury. Forms of corruption are wine, baths, women, boys, sleep, delights, and excessive ease, which as Livy writes enervated the army of Hannibal at Capua.[51] And to quarter his soldiers in such an opulent city filled with delights was considered a greater mistake of such a great captain than not to have led his army immediately on to Rome after his great victory at Cannae because the latter was to postpone victory whereas the former was to deprive himself of the forces necessary to conquer.

But let us talk more in detail of the various forms of military corruption. Types of corruption then are precious objects and delicate furniture; Pescennius Niger[52] learning that some of his soldiers were drinking from silver cups, prohibited in the camp every use of similar vessels. Another form of corruption is the use of beasts of burden by individual soldiers; for this reason Scipio Minor[53] in the campaign of Carthage made his soldiers sell them all so that they had either to get rid of so much baggage or carry the weight themselves, and Metellus in the Jugurthine War prohibited that any soldier who had a charge in the army have a servant or a horse to carry anything. Corruptions are also the delicacies and sweets that Metellus also banned so that all those who were in the camp to sell anything other than necessary foods had to leave. And in the campaign of Numantia, Scipio also ordered under grave penalty that all those who were not soldiers clear out of the camp, along with their charms, without delay and not return for any other business except to sell provisions. When a young man completely perfumed came before him to thank him for the grant of a prefecture, Vespasian gave him a brusque look and said, "I would have wanted you rather not to have stunk with oil," and revoked his patent. A similar account is given of Andreas Gritti when he was a commander of Venetian forces.[54] A young man came before him

---

[51] *History of Rome*, 7.38.

[52] Pescennius Niger (140–94 CE) was a pretender to the imperial office who was defeated by Septimius Severus at Issus in 194.

[53] 185–129 BCE, called the Second Scipio; he was the adopted grandson of Scipio Africanus.

[54] Andrea Gritti served as commander of the Venetian forces in the war of the League of Cambrai and was then doge of Venice from 1523 until his death in 1538.

dressed up and smelling of amber and musk who asked for a position in the war that was in progress at the time. He responded that he choose one of two things if he wanted to serve: the oar or the hoe, so implying that he considered him good for nothing other than a rower or a sapper. Corruption is to plunder and to commit evil deeds in the homes of friends, a matter in which Emperor Aurelian was extremely severe. When a foot-soldier was found with the wife of his host, he was tied by his feet to the peak of two trees forcefully bound together the one to the other. When the bonds were relaxed, he was torn into two pieces. He also wrote to a military tribune that if he valued his life, he would watch the hands of his soldiers that they did not touch the hair of another and that they thought to become rich with booty from their enemies not from the tears of their friends. But most dangerous for soldiers is leisure because if they have nothing else to do, they mutiny and do much evil, as the soldiers of Scipio in Spain attest where after finishing the war against the Carthaginians, they began to live licentiously, to plunder the territory of friends, to scorn the authority of the captains, and finally having put to flight their own tribunes, created new officers. So it is necessary to prescribe exercises for them, to lead them from one place to another, to have them dig trenches and ditches, to channel rivers, and to undertake similar tasks. M. Aemilius,[55] in order to take away their leisure, had the soldiers pave the road from Piacenza to Rimini, Caius Flaminius,[56] from Bologna to Arezzo. Mario had them build the ditches that were named after him, the Marian and Drusine dykes in the Low Countries. Augustus Caesar after creating Egypt a province, in order to make the land more fertile and suitable for agriculture, had his soldiers clean out the ditches into which the Nile flowed which had been blocked with age.[57] Hadrian kept his soldiers in continual exercises, and so that they felt the work to be less a burden, he always went first walking fully armed up to twenty miles a day and contenting himself with the same minimal rest and eating the same as the privates. Emperor Probus, making use of the work of his soldiers, built many bridges and colonnades and temples and other public buildings of importance. Because he wanted the Romans to be separated

---

[55] Marcus Aemilius Lepidus, a consul of the second century BCE, oversaw the completion of the Via Aemilia in 187 BCE (*BD*, 341, n. 1).

[56] Caius Flaminius Nepos, a tribune of the people in 232 BCE and later a censor, lengthened the military road toward Rimini named after him, the Via Flaminia (*BD*, 341, n. 2).

[57] Here Botero repeats what he had written above in 8.2 (p. 136); it was deleted here in subsequent editions.

from the Britons, Severus employed the army to raise a wall from one sea to the other precisely in that area where the River Tweed and the Cheviot Hills divide England from Scotland.[58]

But because our nature desires pleasure and is not able to tolerate labor without the seasoning of enjoyment, and so soldiers commonly engage in gambling which often results in serious incidents, it is necessary sometimes to provide them with pleasant exercises. Sforza da Cotignola[59] did not allow his soldiers to play at dice or cards or in other such ways, and to steer them away from these he engaged them in contests useful for war, wrestling, pole-vaulting, running, jumping, and so imitating Valerius Corvinu[60] and Papirius Cursor[61] who also used these methods to exercise and entertain the soldiers. No less was this the case with Emperor Aurelian who did not allow a day to pass without some physical exercise because in this way he acquired strength and agility. These games were most useful in that they taught a man something that he could turn to his advantage in military actions of which it will not be irrelevant to provide an example. Among their games the Romans were accustomed to play this one. Fifty or more young men after having with various scuffling staged a certain mock battle came together in a square formation with shields over their heads closely united in such way that two of them, who remained outside the formation, climbed lightly on top of it (because this roof of shields declined a little, the first standing on their feet, the next bending over from hand to hand and the last kneeling on the ground) as if they walked over a solid roof, now all threatening and coming to blows, now running from one side to the other, others playing military games.[62]

The usefulness of this exercise was recognized in the Second Macedonian War. The Roman soldiers when they besieged Heraclea approached the city on a roof formed in this way. Then at an equal height with the

---

[58] It was Hadrian who built Hadrian's Wall, starting in 122 CE in the north of England near the border with the Scots; Severus had it repaired after attacks at the end of the century. It is the River Tyne, not the Tweed.

[59] Sforza (1369–1424), a condottiere, was born at Cotignola near Ravenna. His son Francesco later inherited through marriage the duchy of Milan.

[60] A Roman politician and military leader of the third century BCE who took Sicily during the First Punic War.

[61] 360–305 BCE, many times consul, dictator in 324 BCE, and reputed to be the finest warrior of his generation.

[62] This passage is a free translation of Livy, *History of Rome*, 44.9, where it is associated with his description of the siege of Heraclea. The last clause does not seem to make sense (*BD*, 343, n. 1).

enemy they easily drove them from the walls, jumped over them, and seized that place. To this effect it will help to exercise them in various types of mock battle, of the attack and defense of bridges, of ports, of fords, of the shores of rivers, of narrows, of barriers, of ditches, of trenches, in skirmishes, in individual combat (but without danger of death) or of more soldiers, on foot or on horseback, in wading across rivers, in breaking lances, in sword play, in firing the arquebus, in transport of artillery from one place to another, in ascent or descent, through flat country or over mountains. It goes without saying what a profitable exercise it is to have them practice following the standard, turning without disorder to the right or to the left or wherever the occasion and the need can require, beginning or meeting a charge or other similar movements which soldiers execute, all the while enjoying themselves, with a view to anticipating the actions and true instances of war, and they will grow in valor of soul through the boldness which they will acquire and in valor of body through the agility which they will gain. As Vegetius says, *Sciendum est, in pugna usum amplius prodesse quam vires* (It should be known that in battle practice is of more benefit than strength).[63] And besides this, they will remain healthy, cheerful, and quiet.

11 Of Reward

But the two principal pillars of discipline are reward and punishment. The former serves to impel to the good, the latter to punish the bad; the former works for noble and generous spirits, the latter for the low and rebellious; the former serves as a prod, the latter as a brake. Now rewards are either honors or benefits, and honors are of two types because some are given to the dead and others to the living. Statues and tombs are erected for the dead and funeral orations are given in their praise. Alexander the Great had the most magnificent marble statues erected for the soldiers who lost their lives in the battle fought at the River Granicus.[64] The first person among the Romans to be honored with a funeral oration was Brutus who died in the war against the Tarquins, and the same custom was introduced in the city of Athens where those were praised from the tribune who died in the Battle of Marathon and later in the battles of Artemisium and Salamis. But the most worthy speech was that given by Pericles in praise of the citizens who died in the war of

---

[63] *Concerning Military Matters*, 2.23.   [64] His great victory over the Persians in 334 BCE.

Samos.[65] The Romans differed from the Greeks in this: in Athens those only were publicly praised who lost their lives in war; in Rome citizens were also honored in this fashion, and women, not only men. Lycurgus did not want his citizens to practice otherwise in their study of eloquence than in the praise of those who died courageously for their country and in the blame of those who fled battle because of cowardice. Besides this the Romans bore the bodies of illustrious personages with great pomp to the rostrum where the nearest relative celebrated their virtues with a magnificent oration; once the funeral services were over they placed a wax effigy of the deceased in the most dignified part of the house in a small, richly adorned room. Afterwards these effigies were carried in the funerals of the deceased members of the House; they were covered with a *toga praetexta*[66] if they were consuls, of purple if censors, of gold if they had received a triumph, and they were carried on a superbly adorned cart with hatchets, fasces, and other standards of offices and magistracies that they had held; they were then set on the rostrum in seats of ivory, than which, according to Polybius,[67] one could not present to the youth a spectacle more beautiful and more efficacious to incite them to every honorable enterprise. The dead were also honored with public sepulchers; the first one to receive this type of honor was Valerius Publicola.[68] The Spartans did not allow a title to be placed on any sepulcher except for those who died in combat. Don John of Austria after the glorious Battle of Lepanto had erected in Messina a monument filled with the arms of those who had died with great nobility, and he had a generous eulogy inscribed at its bottom. In addition, he had a magnificent Mass sung for their souls, and he had performed other offices of Christian piety in which he and the flower of his captains participated.

Even if every honor that is shown to the dead is an incitement to the living, nevertheless the same rewards of praise and statues are also given to the living. With regard to praise, the kings of Sparta before attacking in battle sacrificed to the Muses to signify the glorious memory that their own would acquire if they bore themselves courageously. Nor was this held in any less esteem by the Romans; after the battle was over and the victory won, the consuls and other captains were accustomed to praise in

---

[65] This war was fought between Athens and Samos in 440–439 BCE.

[66] A *toga praetexta* was off-white in color with a purple border that indicated that the wearer was a senator or other magistrate such as an aedile or consul ("The Roman Toga," *Ancient History Encyclopedia*, www.ancient.eu/article/48, accessed October 31, 2015).

[67] *Histories*, 6.53.10.   [68] He was a consul several times between 514 and 509 BCE.

the presence of the whole army those who had carried themselves with great courage. So Scipio after the conquest of Cartagena[69] praised the courage and ardor of his soldiers whom neither the furious sorties of the enemy nor the height of the wall nor the depth of the moat nor the incline of the citadel could frighten but who with an indomitable spirit overcame every difficulty and broke down every obstacle. And the same Scipio, in the battles of Africa, more than once commended publicly Laelius and Masinissa[70] for their gallantry against the Carthaginians and Syphax. Also honored with statues were the noble actions of the living which among the ancients were made of marble or bronze, on horseback or on foot, armed or unarmed; the Romans erected a bronze statue to Clelia[71] (not to mention others)who fled the camp of King Porsenna by swimming the Tiber to return to Rome. A great honor were the crowns that were given for saving the life of a citizen, which were called civil crowns, as well as the mural and flowered crowns which were given to the first man who jumped onto the walls of a city or into the trenches of a camp under attack; these were considered the highest honors that could be obtained in war even if, because they were made of couch-grass or oak leaves, they were of no monetary value. Hence Caesar Augustus, a most judicious prince, in order to preserve their credit and reputation, bestowed them very rarely and with much greater difficulty than the necklaces and other items of gold and silver that were usually given to those who had shown great courage in battle. At the time of the taking of Cartagena when Scipio wanted to give the mural crown to the first soldier on the wall of the city, a controversy arose between the soldiers on land and the sailors that resulted from so much competition and ambition, that the captain, in order to cut short the dangerous strife and scandal, had to bestow two crowns, one to Q. Trebellius, an infantryman, and another to Digitius, a marine. Similar strife broke out between Spaniards and Italians in the taking of Düren[72] when two soldiers, one a Spaniard and the other an

---

[69] This refers not to Carthage in North Africa but to the city on the Mediterranean coast of Spain, Cartegena, later named by the Romans New Carthage (*BD*, 346, n. 1).

[70] Gaius Laelius (235–160 BCE) was a Roman general and politician, and a friend of Scipio, who fought in the Second Punic War; Masinissa (238–148 BCE) was king of Numidia who in the same war fought first on the side of the Carthaginians and then on that of the Romans.

[71] Clelia was a legendary young girl who was handed over to the Etruscan king Porsenna and swam the Tiber to return to Rome.

[72] A town in the Rhineland which Charles V took from William of Cleves, an ally of Francis I of France, in 1543.

Italian, each claimed that the reward was his. Truly this most beautiful type of reward, which is purely honorary without any utility, is worth being restored, to the glory of the army and of courageous soldiers. And even if sometimes after a great battle some are created knights, a purely honorary reward, knights are also created in time of peace who have never seen a naked sword and who are made only gentlemen; hence soldiers who are not of noble blood remain deprived of this sort of incentive to *virtù*. It was also a great honor to bear the rich spoils [*spolia opima*] to the temple of Jupiter, and such spoils were those that the captain of the Romans took from the captain of the enemy, and in the whole period of the Roman republic not more than three men had this honor; they were Romulus, Cornelius Cossus,[73] and Marcus Marcellus.[74] Caesar Augustus honored the military with many creations; he wanted thirty captains to receive triumphs, and he awarded the decorations of a triumph to a much greater number.

Much to our point would be that the prince take care to have written down accurately the wars and campaigns prosecuted by him or under his auspices, because in this way not only would his own *virtù* come to be celebrated but that of all his captains and also of individual soldiers who with some memorable gallantry distinguished themselves. This would be a great incitement to the others because, if so much is made of a tomb with a brief script in a chapel, how much greater recognition would anyone receive in being celebrated in an excellently written history which would be circulated throughout the world and read by all? In this respect truly have the Castilians greatly failed because having accomplished so many things most worthy of memory, crossed so many seas, discovered so many islands and continents, subjected so many countries, acquired finally a New World, they have not seen to it that their undertakings, which surpass by far those of the Greeks and Alexander the Great, have been chronicled by persons who know how to do so. In this as in some other matters the Portuguese have ventured much more than the Castilians because they have had a good number who, in Portuguese and in Latin, have shone light on their great deeds. Recently Father Giovanni Pietro Maffei[75] of the Company of Jesus has recounted them with such

---

[73] A Roman politician and general of the fifth century BCE.

[74] Marcus Claudius Marcellus (268–208 BCE) was consul five times and an important military leader.

[75] Giovanni Pietro Maffei, SJ (1536–1603), long a professor of rhetoric at the Roman College, wrote a number of books on early Jesuit history, including *Historiarum indicarum*

elegance of phrase, greatness of concepts, and gracefulness of style that he is not able to be worthily praised by any person less eloquent than himself. But this intent to recount the undertakings of his own in order to spur them on to *virtù* characterizes no prince more than the Grand Masters of the military orders of Saint Lazarus, Saint John, and Saint Stephen because the knights of each order, because they are not many, can each expect to merit this reward for their efforts, and because they are all nobles they will value this award at its proper worth.[76] But to write histories is an affair of the prince (because others are not able to know fully the causes and successes of campaigns and their circumstances) and of those supported by him and with his authority, his favor, and his money; otherwise nothing of value results. Understanding this well, Charlemagne provided every advantage to the persons he chose to compose histories, and he gave orders that they should recount all the memorable deeds of those nations subject to him.

But to return to our topic, the ancients used also some other rewards that joined the honorable with the useful, such as crowns of gold, necklaces, equestrian trappings, possessions, cattle, slaves, the doubling of wages or of the ration of wheat, the promotion from a lower grade to a higher grade than which nothing can be more effective to stir valor; and the Romans used this remarkably well because in the legions all the military ranks in which honor and great utility were joined were given to those who merited them more, so that Vegetius wrote that the military spirit of the legions declined when ambition determined the rewards of *virtù* and favor the promotions owed to courage.[77] Christian princes have an excellent means to reward in this way with the multitude of commendams[78] and priories of the military religious orders, and especially the Catholic King who, besides the properties of the Order of St. John, possesses in Spain all the income of the Orders of Saint James, of Alcantara, of Calatrava, and of Montera of which he is, by apostolic

---

libri XVI (Florence, 1588) which recounted the Portuguese conquests and the Jesuit missions in Asia.

[76] The Knights of St. John (or Hospitallers) and the Knights of St. Lazarus of Jerusalem both dated from the Crusades. The Knights of St. Stephen were founded by Cosimo de' Medici, Grand Duke of Tuscany, in 1561 to fight the Ottoman Turks.

[77] *Concerning Military Affairs*, 2.3.

[78] The tenure of a benefice held initially until the appointment of a regular incumbent but later held permanently by the incumbent.

concession, the Grand Master.[79] All these properties that were distributed as awards for *virtù* and in remuneration for services performed in the wars against the infidels have been the chief cause of the many brave deeds of the Spaniards against the Moors, and as now they have chased the Moors out of Spain so they would be adequate to subject those in Africa if they were employed for this purpose. Truly the Knights of Saint John merit the highest praise because they have never abandoned their campaign against the infidels but have always given the greatest example of their courage and have greatly served the Christian republic. They follow in the footsteps of the Knights of Saint Stephen so that their name strikes greater horror in the Turks and the Moors than entire armies, and they are every day either blessed by so many Christians who have been liberated from the most cruel servitude of the Turks and the Moors or they are awaited by so many thousands of poor Christians who find themselves in such miserable servitude, with their feet chained, in Algiers or Tunis. And what work is more pious, what campaign more Christian than the liberation of captives? Or what captivity can be imagined to be more unhappy or hard than that in which bodies are most cruelly tormented and souls so dangerously tempted?

But of the greatest importance is that the soldier be confident that even if in war he is maimed or disabled, the prince will not abandon him but will provide him with proper treatment and a livelihood. Most soldiers avoid the dangers of war not so much because of the fear of death (which generally causes little pain and no hardship) but because of the disabilities and casualties that are likely to happen because of wounds and other mishaps. This fear disappears with the assurance of the good will of the prince who will provide for him, care for him, and show him respect; this not only helps to inspire those who at present serve in the war but it also encourages and inspires others to endure the same troubles and to run the same risks. Without a doubt, when he sees his fellow citizens and companions returned from war, though wounded and bruised, to be favored and settled by the prince, who of a proud and brave spirit does not feel himself moved by a certain desire to do something himself?[80]

---

[79] The first three of these orders all dated from the twelfth century and were founded to aid in the Reconquest; the last named dated from 1317.

[80] In later texts this sentence reads "Who is there of such a cowardly and vile spirit (*codardo e vile* instead of *fiero e bravo*) who seeing his fellow citizens and companions return from the war, although wounded and bruised, to be favored and settled by the prince does not feel his spirit moved by a certain desire also to do something himself?"

But if, on the other hand, those returned from war, beyond their wounds and weaknesses will also have been abandoned by the king, afflicted by poverty, and consumed by misery, who will ever be either so foolish or so bold that he does not feel his heart frozen over and his spirit lacking? The Romans well understood this; they assigned to the soldiers who had served the republic well excellent properties as well as other things and, not to add other examples, it suffices to mention the decree in favor of the soldiers of the first Scipio to whom were given two days[81] of land for each year of military service. But if the prince is liberal not only with the soldiers in their misfortunes but also assures them that should they die in his service, he will take care of their wives, children, sisters, and other relatives, there is nothing more effective to make them run through fire and face missiles and death itself.

12 Of Punishment

In governing reward is useful but punishment is necessary because virtue is its own reward and has no need of external stimulus, but vice and wickedness if they are not restrained by the fear of punishment turn everything upside down. For this reason among others legislators and the founders of republics have always attended more to punish and to repress crimes than to reward virtuous actions. In war then if you do not reward those who carry themselves well, you will not be loved; but if you do not punish the guilty, you will not be obeyed, and nothing can be worse than this when it comes to military matters. For this reason all well-known captains have been severe and with various penalties and punishments have partly maintained, partly reformed military discipline. Not to mention the Manlii, the Cursori, and others, Caesar Augustus, a great lover of peace, was so severe with the soldiers that not only did he sometimes decimate the companies that had turned their backs to the enemy and given up their position, but he also fed them with barley rather than grain, and Tiberius, wanting to get the army back on its feet, renewed all the types of ancient penalties and punishments that were in use at the time of the old Romans. Now, military punishments were of two sorts: some brought shame and dishonor, others also pain and loss. Public rebukes and reproaches of cowardice resulted in shame, and these were directed

---

[81] A "day" (*giornata*) of land was land that could be covered in one day's journey.

at individuals and also to a whole army. Livy writes that M. Marcellus[82] after the flight of his soldiers directed such an acerbic and terrible address to his soldiers that with the vehemence of his words and the harshness of his rebuke he did not afflict them less than did the enemies with their wounds and their attack; and to increase their shame he commanded that to those who in the battle had lost their standards barley was to be given instead of grain, and he made their captains stand without their belts and with a bare sword in their hand. Sempronius Gracchus[83] made those soldiers eat standing who had shown little courage. In Sparta those who by fleeing had saved themselves were not able to give or to take wives; they were forced to wear certain multi-colored cloaks, their beards partly shaven and partly long, and it was allowed to everyone to strike or abuse them. The Romans were very severe toward those who fled a skirmish and let themselves be taken prisoner out of cowardice. Those who fled the Battle of Cannae were condemned to serve outside of Italy until the war ended, and they were not able, whatever act of courage that they performed, to receive any military honor. It was a great shame and infamy to be banned from camp (which Caesar did with some insolent centurions in the war of Africa) and to deprive standard-bearers and captains of their office and rank; but of no less loss than of great shame was the prohibition that those who had fallen into the hands of the enemy because of cowardice be redeemed or rescued; this the Romans applied to those who were captured by the Carthaginians because of ineptitude. Nor was there ever any people that less esteemed captured citizens than the Romans, so that they never considered recovering through exchange those who remained in the hands of the Carthaginians. But a terrible thing was the decimation by which they put to death one out of every ten who had behaved badly because in this case even if only one suffered harm, fear and danger made the blood of all freeze. Because some Spaniards had surrendered in a cowardly fashion to the French, the Great Captain permitted that the other soldiers tear them to pieces, so that, with this example, no one would think to escape but to fight, and so would despair of finding safety through cowardice with friends, not only with the enemy. On this point it does not seem good to omit the dictum of the Lacedaemonian

---

[82] Marcus Claudius Marcellus (268–208 BCE), general, hero of the Second Punic War, and five times consul. See Livy, *History of Rome*, 27.13.

[83] Tiberius Sempronius Gracchus was the father of the Gracchi brothers and twice consul, in 177 and 163 BCE.

Clearchus[84] that a soldier ought to have a greater fear of his captain than of the enemy.

13 Of Emulation

Valor also increases through methods that nourish emulation and competition. Lycurgus introduced emulation in his republic as an incitement to virtue, because a man, naturally jealous of his own excellence, cannot bear that others surpass and put their foot down before his, especially in honorable ventures; and this effect is most vehement in soldiers, as in those who are governed more by passion than by reason. So the Romans nourished emulation, both with the diversity of nations (because in their armies they made use not only of their citizens but of the Latin peoples also and of auxiliaries, all of which competed), and with the difference of the soldiers in the legions (because there were the *principes*, the *hastati*, and the *trarii*), and if the first two yielded, the weight of the battle remained with the *trarii* who to outdo the others and to have all the honor of the victory, surpassed themselves. The captains then using their skill, arranged emulation and competition between nation and nation, between cavalry and infantry, between one wing and another, between one legion and another. After scaring his whole army with the fame of the strength and the courage of the Germans, Caesar said that if the others did not want to follow, he would go into the battle alone with the tenth legion; so he stirred such emulation and such ardor in the others that they offered to compete with him. In our time experience has shown that the perfect army is not the one that is not made up of diverse nations, because the contest is that which makes each nation employ all its strength and more than that in order to have the honor of the victory, so that if there is only one nation in the field, it languishes and does not perform worthy deeds.

14 Of the License Given to the Janissaries

The Turks make the Janissaries ferocious and brave, allowing them an extreme liberty, even license, which they grant to them, because it is permitted them to raise their hand and to strike, to affront and to displease anyone without ever being punished; from this there arises a boldness, as

---

[84] Spartan general of the fifth century BCE.

they think, and a great heart. But they deceive themselves because boldness comes only from a knowledge of one's own strength, and strength is not known where there is no opposition because to overcome one who does not fight back is no great matter. Also, artillery does not have as great an effect on the sea as it does on land because the ships and the galleys are never as stable and solid as the walls, and they resist less. Now the Janissaries who are used to striking this man or that without any opposition would become much more rapidly cowards than courageous in military campaigns where they encountered resistance and opposition, unless something other than the license of which we have spoken helped them. Because if their boldness increases when they assault and strike whoever it seems good to them without him being able to show resentment or to return the blows nor even to oppose or avenge himself, without a doubt that will fail them wherever they meet with adversity or resistance, so that the license given them makes them more quickly overbearing and impertinent rather than spirited and brave.

15 Of Labor

To wear out the soldiers has two good effects: first, it hardens and strengthens them, accustoms and inures them to the hardships of war, so that some valiant captains have been in this regard nearly inflexible with the soldiers. Papirius Cursor worked his infantry and cavalry incredibly hard and, once asked by his knights that by virtue of past services he spare them a part of their effort: "I am content," he said, "that when you dismount you do not caress the backs of your horses as you are accustomed to do." The other effect of tiring them out is to make them desire battle in order to end the labor. In the Cimbrian War[85] Marius spent a great part of his time putting his soldiers through various exercises; he led them now to one place now to another, and he made them among other things dig a wide and deep ditch where a branch of the Rhône River flowed. Finally, he kept them so fatigued that to get relief from it they wanted to come to hand-to-hand fighting with the barbarians. Similarly Sulla, so that his soldiers would want a battle, kept them three days in continual and hard exercises, making the River Cephissus[86] change its course and

---

[85] This war was fought between the Roman Republic and the Cimbrian and Teutonic Germanic tribes migrating down from the Jutland Peninsula, 113–101 BCE.

[86] A river in Boeotia in Greece.

digging large ditches, so that, exhausted, they cried out in a loud voice for battle.

16 Of Determination

A certain deliberate determination is of no little moment because it removes and cuts off every other plan or thought in the captains and soldiers apart from fighting, and it directs and disposes all equally to the campaign. Francis I, king of France, having determined absolutely to pass over into Italy, turning to his barons, said, "I have determined to cross the mountains personally without delay. Whoever will persuade me to the contrary, not only will not be listened to by me but he will annoy me greatly. Let each one of you attend to carrying out what is committed to you and what pertains to your office."[87] With these words he enflamed and determined for each one that the deliberation of the king was the deliberation of all. We read of Aratus, general of the Sicyonians,[88] that although a good captain in other respects, he had this one shortcoming, that every time that he ought to have entered into battle he was not able to make a decision and so held back; there is not anything worse than this in the commander of an army, not only because he himself was prevented from acting but his soldiers languished and lost their spirit and their bravado. It is not beyond our intention here to mention what Aemilius Paulus said to his soldiers at the start of the Macedonian War because with this he cut short every other thought than to conduct themselves well in the campaign. So he told them not to try to understand nor to intervene in the councils of war but to leave in the breast of their general all that they ought to do, and as good soldiers to attend only to three things: to keep their body strong and agile, to have their arms polished and sharp, and to eat in an orderly way, so that they could respond to every sign of the captain.

17 Of Placing the Soldiers before the Necessity of Fighting

Grand and incomparable is the force of necessity and when it is joined with *virtù*, it increases courage infinitely, so that some captains have

---

[87] It is a question here not of Francis's first invasion of Italy in 1515 but his return in 1524 (*BD*, 356, n. 3).

[88] Aratus (271–213 BCE) was a statesman and general of the ancient Greek city-state of Sicyon and a leader in the Achaean League.

sought every means to place their soldiers under the necessity to conduct themselves well. Hannibal led his soldiers into the middle of Italy so that they would not hope in anything other than courage, so that exhorting them to fight, he said *Nihil nobis relictum est, nisi quod armis vindicaverimus. Illis timidis et ignavis licet esse, qui receptum habent, quos suus ager, sua terra per tuta ac pacata itinera fugientes accipient; vobis necesse est fortibus viris esse et omnibus inter victoriam mortemque certa desperatione abruptis, aut vincere aut, si fortuna dubitabit, in praelio potius quam in fuga mortem oppetere* (Nothing is left to us now but what we can conquer by force of arms. Those who have a place of refuge or a farm or property of their own as a retreat to receive them after a safe and peaceful journey, they can afford to be frightened and cowardly. But you must bear yourselves bravely and, since there is no possible middle way between victory and death, you must either conquer or – if fortune is unfavorable – perish, in battle rather than in flight).[89] Cato the Elder, wanting to confront the army of the Spaniards, led his army far from the sea and from the armada that had transported them and placed them in the middle of the enemy: *Nusquam nisi in virtute spes est*, he said, *et ego sedulo, ne esset, feci; inter castra nostra et nos medii hostes, ab tergo hostium ager est; quod pulcherrimum, idem tutissimum est, in virtute spem positam habere* (Your only hope now is in your courage, and I have brought this about on purpose; the enemy is between us and our camp, and to our rear the territory is hostile. Nothing is more beautiful and at the same time safer than to have to put all your trust in your own courage).[90] When he was deliberating about attacking the Cimbrians near the city of Aix, Mario pitched camp in an elevated and comfortable location but without a drop of water and seeing his soldiers complaining that they would die of thirst, a situation which he had purposely brought about in order to incite them more to feats of arms, he showed them a river in the distance which ran near the camp of the enemy, and he said: "Whoever has thirst will have to purchase that water with blood." In a situation no less evocative of courage, William, duke of Normandy, having crossed over to England in order to acquire that kingdom, burned the fleet that had brought them there. Hernán Cortés did the same thing after he arrived at Vera Cruz for the campaign of New Spain. Attilius Regulus and Metellus Celiber placed their soldiers in situations of violent necessity. In the Samnite War when the Romans turned their backs to the enemy and fled toward their encampment,

---

[89] Livy, *History of Rome*, 21.44.7–8.   [90] Ibid., 34.14.3–4.

Attilius flew there with a section of the cavalry, took a position before the gates with a drawn sword in his hand, reproached them with cowardice and flight, bitterly abused them, and at the end said that he did not intend to allow anyone to enter unless he was victorious, and so they had to choose between fighting him or the enemy, with the result that they recovered their spirit because of their shame, turned back against the enemy, and conquered them. During the siege of Contrebia when five companies had abandoned their position,[91] Metellus immediately commanded that they recover it, and he commanded that those who had fled be put to death. The fear of their own accomplished more than did the fear of the enemy, and shame won out over the fear of danger so that they returned to the battle and recovered their position. It was with regard to this situation that the Roman senate issued the magnanimous decree that prisoners ought not to be redeemed. With such a law the senators compelled the soldiers to fight and conquer or to die honorably because if they lost, there remained for them no hope of rescue. We will add here an order of Aemilius Paulus to make the sentries more vigilant and alert. When he arrived at the head of the army, he ordered that soldiers serve as sentries without a shield so that they would be lighter and be more on alert because they had no hope to defend themselves in case of an assault.

18 Of Binding Soldiers by Oath or Execration

Some captains who have been unable to compel themselves and their soldiers to fight by burning fleets and other such measures have sought to bind themselves and armies through oaths or terrible incantations. This the Acarnanians did when they saw the very powerful and fierce Aetolians attacking them.[92] They sent their wives, their children, and all those over sixty to secure places of refuge. All the others then swore and bound themselves, in the most strict way possible, to die first before returning home if they were not victorious. When the enemy realized this, they abandoned their campaign. When soldiers insistently asked the consul Marcus Fabius to lead them out against the Etruscans who had abused

---

[91] Contrebia was a Celtiberian city in the valley of the Ebro River in Spain; the Romans with Metellus as consul conquered it in 143 BCE.

[92] Aetolia was a region in central Greece that organized the Aetolian League of city-states. These events took place in the early Hellenistic period.

them, he made them swear that they would not return if they did not come back as victors, as they did. But it should be noted that in these cases one should see to it that oaths and other forms of obligation be undertaken voluntarily, cheerfully, and readily by the soldiers; if they are forced and violent, they encumber the spirit and confuse and perplex it so that there results an effect contrary to that which was desired. This happened with the Samnites who were constrained by their captain to swear on an altar one by one (and centurions were there with a naked sword) to die before fleeing and to consider as an enemy any of their own who might flee. They remained so dumbfounded and confused that they enabled Lucius Papirius to gain a most glorious victory. From the beginning Roman soldiers gathered together in tens or hundreds and swore that they would not flee nor abandon their post except to capture arms or to wound an enemy or to save a comrade; this most beautiful custom, which was purely voluntary, was changed to a legal obligation during the consulate of Lucius Paulus and Marcus Varrone, whose soldiers however fought ineffectively. It is of great importance that the obligation be spontaneous, not compelled, and that it proceed from a cheerful heart, not from a rigid commandment. In a stranger way Hasdrubal, captain of the Carthaginians, wanted to compel his own soldiers to fight. He cruelly tore out the eyes of some of the Romans whom he had taken captive and cut off the nose, the ears, and other members of others; afterward he nailed all these mutilated parts to a wall in order to persuade the Carthaginians that they ought to be resolved to die fighting rather than to remain prisoners of the Romans. But he greatly deceived himself in that they became fearful rather than bold, and they sought not to expose themselves to the danger of such torments by fighting but to save themselves by flight. But if the soldiers cheerfully and of their own will swear or in another way commit themselves to stand firm and courageously, they will undoubtedly increase their courage, as happened in the city of Eger. It can serve as an example of incomparable courage for all those who find themselves in similar situations, and so it will not extend beyond our purpose to commemorate here what happened. Eger is a city of Hungary where neither the location nor the walls are strong because the site is overseen by several high places and the walls were constructed in an old style. Mohamet Pasha besieged the city in 1562[93] with an army of sixty

---

[93] This Ottoman siege of Eger took place in 1552, not 1562 (*BD*, 361, n. 2).

thousand Turks and shelled it heavily with fifty cannons. Inside were two thousand Hungarians who with inestimable courage defended it against thirteen vigorous assaults of the enemy, and to increase their courage still more, it is said that while awaiting an assault, they swore under pain of death that no one among them would speak of an accord nor of surrender under conditions nor of any response to the enemy other than with arquebuses and cannons and, should it come to a long siege, rather to die of hunger than to place themselves in the hands of such a cruel and impious enemy. They ordered furthermore that the troops unfit to fight continually reinforce the shelters and trenches, fortify the walls, construct new bastions and earthworks, rebuild collapsed and other weak sections. To prevent treachery they prohibited that more than three people gather together in the city, and finally ordered that no one think about anything else than to defend the homeland or to die. In addition they ordained that all provisions, public or private, should be distributed equally to each one and that the more delicate foods be set aside for those wounded in battle. Finally, if the Lord God had supported their just cause, that all the spoils of the enemy would be placed in one space, so that after the victory they would be shared equally by each. It is also said that after the Pasha had made them many offers if they surrendered, they only responded by setting on the walls a funeral coffin covered in black between two lances showing by this sign that they would come out only if they were dead.

19 Of Familiarity with the Enemy

Soldiers disheartened sometimes by a misfortune that they have undergone or by a useless rumor of the strength of the enemy are reinvigorated and refreshed by the experience that they have had of their own strength either in skirmishes or in some other way. Julius Caesar perceived this perceptively but more notable was the foresight of Marius. The Romans were terrified by the routs that they had received from the Cimbrians, a most ferocious people, so that it seemed to them that they had to fight with giants and with an insuperable tribe. In order to undeceive them and to show them that the Cimbrians were men like others, Marius engaged the soldiers for several days before confronting them with the enemy. During these days he accustomed their ears to the language of the barbarians and their eyes to their features so that finally the fear disappeared from their breasts.

20 Of Exploiting your Advantage

It is of great importance to know and to exploit that in which you have an advantage over your enemy. The Carthaginians were many times defeated in Africa by Marcus Regulus because they did not know where their forces were superior to the enemy. Meanwhile there came from Greece with some mercenary soldiers Xanthippus the Lacedaemonian, a very brave knight and of great intelligence. When he understood how and where the Carthaginians had been conquered, he began to say openly that the defeats they had suffered were due not to the ability of the Romans but to their own unwise tactics because although they were superior in cavalry and elephants, they had fought not in level areas where the cavalry have a great advantage but over hills and slopes where the infantry and so the Romans had the advantage; so having changed the type of war and transferred it from hills to level areas, he won a complete victory for the Carthaginians. In the Second Punic War Hannibal, realizing that he was superior to the Romans in cavalry, sought to confront them in the open field and there he remained the victor as many times as the Romans boldly engaged him. But Fabius Maximus, aware of the disadvantage, never left the mountains and rough terrain. The Turks have been victorious in so many battles with the Christians for no other reason than their advantage (common to them and to nearly all the barbarians) in cavalry; as they abounded in an almost infinite multitude of horses, they never doubted their victory when they fought on open land. In addition, without fighting us apart from cutting off the roads, seizing and hindering our provisions, upsetting our order with improvised attacks, wearying us with constant raids and skirmishes, and finally encircling us on every side, they have opposed and conquered us. Now there is nothing that adds greater boldness than to see oneself superior to the enemy in some way, and so a good captain ought to seek the advantage and exploit it.

21 Of Forestalling the Enemy

To attack rather than to wait to be attacked increases the ardor of the soldiers. This is true in every case but it is necessary when you are clearly inferior in numbers and you are forced to fight, because to attack not only heartens your own troops but frightens and confounds the enemy, leads them to fear ambushes and a greater force, and causes disorder among them. I would be able to give many examples of this but one of Julius

Caesar will suffice. Crossing the Hellespont on a small galley, he met Cassius, captain of the contrary faction, with ten galleys; not only did he not flee, which would have been in vain, but by heading directly toward him he frightened him in such a manner that he yielded.

22 Of Stratagems

Astuteness[94] and artifice add notably to courage because military stratagems are not only licit but bring great praise to a captain. Lysander the Lacedaemonian was a person of great sagacity who made use of artifice no less than force. When he was reproached for this, he was accustomed to say that when one was not able to put on the skin of a lion, he ought to wear that of the fox.[95] E. Carbone said that when he had to deal with the lion and the fox that nested in the soul of Sulla, he feared the fox much more than the lion. But the deceit ought to be only military. In this Lysander greatly sinned because he claimed to be no less deceitful with the pacts that he entered than cunning with the war parties. But with regard to stratagems the Carthaginian Hannibal was outstanding. He never attacked, one can say, nor did he engage in a skirmish without assisting force with artifice and arms with intelligence. So he exploited marvelously the quality of the country and the nature of the site, the valleys, the woods, the forests, the sun and the wind, and every opportunity of time and place or other circumstance. And there is nothing that wins more credit and reputation for a captain and that renders the soldiers more well-disposed and confident. Without a doubt it is necessary that the captain be perspicacious in these matters and quick-minded so that, even if he himself does not want to prevail by virtue of a licit and commendable deceit, he is able to foresee and avoid one.

23 Of the Particular Way that Caesar Increased the Spirit of his Soldiers

Caesar, in order to increase the spirit of his soldiers, made use of a singular and wonderful method. He not only did not diminish the reputation of the enemy forces but increased and magnified them as much as

---

94 The word here, *astuzia* (and its adjective *astuto*), was used frequently in the political literature of the time. It was morally ambivalent, often depending on the writer; it could mean acceptable astuteness or artfulness or on the other hand unacceptable cunning and deceit.
95 See Machiavelli, *Prince*, chap. 18.

possible. Realizing that the news of the coming of King Juba[96] with a large army created great terror among his soldiers, he summoned them together and told them to know for certain that the king came to them all at once with one hundred thousand cavalry, three hundred elephants, and a huge number of infantry. He did this so that his men, disposed not to be terrified by such a great multitude of the enemy, would consider their true number to be negligible and scorn them.[97]

[96] King of the Numidians.
[97] Several paragraphs were added to this chapter in subsequent editions.

Book Ten

1 Of the Captain

In this part I will be even more brief than I am accustomed to be because Alexander Farnese, duke of Parma, represents today to the world such a clear and living example of the perfect commander of an army that he is able to serve better than many precepts and even books. Managing the army under a most merciful and most just king[1] in the service of the church and of God he has conquered and dominated, in the manner of Fabius or Marcellus,[2] rebellion and heresy, overcome the difficulties of the sites and nature of locations, conquered unconquerable places, vanquished invincible peoples; and not to speak of another, there is no virtue of a captain, no military skill, no gallantry, no courage that he did not demonstrate in the siege of the incomparable city of Antwerp.[3]

To stir up the courage of the soldiers then depends in great part on the prudence and leadership of the captain who makes use of the above-mentioned means and of others which will be addressed in due time. It is a common opinion that it is much better to have a good captain with a poor army than a good army with a poor captain. The reason is that a good captain can also make a poor army into a good one with discipline and other means, but how can a good army make a general without judgment and experience into a perceptive and excellent one? So Homer said that an army of stags led by a lion was better than an army of lions led by

---

[1] Philip II of Spain.

[2] These two consuls in the Second Punic War were called, respectively, "the shield" and "the sword" of Rome, the defense and the offense.

[3] This famous siege took place from July 1584 to August 1585.

a stag.[4] When Alexander the Great learned that forty thousand persons were to be found on an inaccessible mountain in an impregnable location but that the captain was cowardly and base, he assured himself of victory because, as he quickly confided, the worthlessness of the commander would open the road and the door, as happened. The Numantines had many times routed the Romans who were led by various officers but after the campaign was entrusted to Scipio, the contrary happened so that the Numantines[5] when asked by their elders how they had lost courage so quickly that they turned their backs toward those whom they had so often put to flight, they responded that the sheep remained the same but the shepherd had been changed. Proceeding to the war in Spain and wishing to highlight the certainty that he had of victory, Caesar said that he went against an army without a captain. And to be sure many campaigns are brought to an end, many difficulties overcome, many wars ended, many victories gained more by the art and courage of the head than of the rest of the army. And it would be superfluous to mention Themistocles who saved Athens with his remarkable counsel, Epaminondas[6] who with his gallantry lit up Thebes which had previously been of little account, Xanthippus who with his singular shrewdness reanimated the Carthaginians who had so many times been torn to pieces by the Romans, Fabius Maximus who with his delaying tactics secured Rome, and others.

2 Of the Ways that the Captain can Make his Soldiers Spirited

Even if all these above-mentioned means to increase courage depend, in whole or in part, on the captain, yet we consider now some that consist not in management but in his person itself.

3 Of Good Fortune

The first thing with which a captain inspires his soldiers is his good fortune, and this is nothing other than the concurrence of the divine power

---

[4] This saying is not found in Homer; it is usually attributed to Iphicrates, an Athenian general of the fourth century BCE, or to Plutarch (*BD*, 372, n. 1).

[5] The inhabitants of Numantia in Spain resisted the Romans for twenty years before the city was taken and destroyed in 133 BCE after a long and brutal siege.

[6] Theban general and statesman (*c.* 410–362 BCE) who broke the dominance of Sparta among the Greek city-states.

with which His Majesty accompanies those who have been elected as ministers of his justice or as executors of his divine will. Such was Joshua at whose prayer he stopped the sun and lengthened the day,[7] and Cyrus, whom he called his servant even though he was a gentile,[8] and Alexander the Great to whom he gave the passage of the Pamphylian Sea,[9] and Genghis, king of the Tartars, the passage of the Indian Sea, and Attila and Tamburlane who were called the scourges of God, and many others whom it pleased him to favor with many and varied victories. But here we ought to note that the good fortune in wars is not always given to the captain but to the prince whom God favors by means of his members. *Dux fortis in armis Caesareis Labienus erat, nunc transfuga vilis* (Labienus was a brave leader in the army of Caesar but now he is a base fugitive).[10]

Renzo da Ceri was a most fortunate captain while he served the Venetians but most unfortunate under King Francis and Pope Clement.[11] Andrea Doria did nothing memorable under the auspices of the same King Francis and in the campaign of Sardinia experienced such an adverse fate (if it behooves a Christian to use such a term). Under Charles V he accomplished great things. And so with others God shows sometimes that he favors not the captain but the prince. Sometimes, however, the intention of the captain is so good that God rewards him even if the prince does not please him and is afflicted and punished in another way. So His Majesty prospered the campaigns of Narses[12] against the Goths but did not permit that Emperor Justinian I, whose minister he was, enjoy a peaceful dominion over Italy because he raised up the Lombards who occupied most of it. Sometimes God denied success to the prince and to the captain because of the sins of the people; so he permitted the bitter death of King Josiah.[13] But if God is pleased with the prince and the captain, and the sins of the people do not hinder good fortune, then one cannot doubt victories and triumphs, and if this happy outcome is not always the companion of virtue because God also prospers Gentiles, Turks, and Moors against bad Christians, nevertheless it

---

[7] Joshua 10:12–14.   [8] Isaiah 44:28.

[9] Now the Gulf of Antalya, in southern Turkey. Alexander passed through it on his way to conquer Persia.

[10] Quoted from memory from Lucan, *On the Civil War*, 5.345–46 (*BD*, 374, n. 3). Labienus was a leading officer under Julius Caesar who later went over to Pompey.

[11] Renzo degli Anguillara (*c.* 1475–1536), a condottiere in the service of the pope, was lent to the Venetians in 1510 early in his career (*BD*, 374, n. 4).

[12] Lived 478–573 CE, one of the generals of the Byzantine Emperor Justinian I.

[13] 2 Kings 23:25–29.

ordinarily happens so. So we see Charles V in Germany, Francis, duke of Guise, and Henry and Charles, his sons, and Alexander, duke of Parma, with few troops obtain glorious victories in wars undertaken by them for the faith. On the other hand, Louis de Condé, Gaspard de Coligny, Casimir, count palatine of the Rhine,[14] and William of Nassau and the others who have led armies in favor of impiety and rebellion have been beaten and defeated and killed, conforming to what is written, *impii de terra perdentur* (the impious will be lost from the earth).[15]

But let us return to our proposition. When therefore the soldier sees good fortune in the campaigns and designs of a captain, he follows his banners without fear and does great things; he promises himself certain victory and considers every difficulty to be negligible.

4 Of Courage and Example

The courage and example of the captain is also effective because it extends and spreads to the whole army, so that we read of Marius that in his fresher and more hardy youth he performed great deeds because he entered upon campaigns accompanied by courage and bravura, but in his old age lacking the heat in his blood and his vigor of spirit, he did not accomplish anything worthy of his old reputation as is seen in the Social War.[16] This courage was outstanding in Alexander the Great; he had nothing else of a great captain except for a marvelous greatness of spirit and of heart joined to an equal good fortune. Seleucus[17] in the final battle with King Demetrius, seeing his own soldiers fleeing, dismounted from his horse, took his helmet from his head so that he would be recognized and jumped in among the first line; with this action he revived their *virtù* and conquered. We read that Caesar sometimes pushing forward restrained and stopped the army which had turned to flee, so that more than once the standard-bearers kept their standards in hand. Among Christians princes and captains George Castriotes[18] deserves high praise who in a thousand encounters with the Turks was always the first in the

---

[14] Johann Casimir, while serving as administrator of the Palatinate from 1583–92, re-established Calvinism there.

[15] Proverbs 2:22.

[16] The Social War, 91–89 BCE, was fought between Rome and other cities of Italy.

[17] Seleucus I Nicator (359–281 BCE) founded the Seleucid kingdom.

[18] Also known as Skanderbeg (1403–68), an Albanian hero who converted from Islam to Christianity.

fight; it is estimated that in various battles he killed with his own hand two thousand Turks. But I do not say that the general, and much less so if he is the prince, ought to throw himself into the midst of dangers; his task is not to fight but to order, to govern, and to stand over the combatants. But he ought always to show spirit and heart and readiness, and in cases of necessity to confront dangers, in order to prevent flight or to enliven the soldiers who are tired, slow, or frightened, or for another similar necessity. And he ought to do this with the greatest care possible because the welfare of the army depends on his life.

5 Of Cheerfulness

Not of little importance is a certain cheerfulness and liveliness of countenance which keeps the soldiers cheerful and in good spirits which depends for the most part on the demeanor of their commander and, if they do not go gladly and fiercely into battle, they will not accomplish anything worthwhile. This is what happened to the Germans under the marquis of Vasto at the Battle of Cerisole.[19] In this regard among the Romans Papirius Cursor and Scipio Africanus excelled; Livy writes that there was never seen a captain more cheerful than Papirius in that memorable battle when he conquered the Samnites and Scipio when he defeated Hannibal and the Carthaginians in a feat of arms.[20]

6 Of the Ways to Indicate Certainty of Victory[21]

To the above-mentioned cheerfulness is joined a certain certainty of victory which keeps the soldiers cheerful and is indicated in several ways. On the day before the Battle of Cannae, before the clash of arms Hannibal withdrew to a hill elevated a little to see the Roman army; his friend Gisco, having seen the great number of men, because the Romans up to that time had never accumulated such a great force, remained nearly terrified, so that turning to Hannibal he said that the number of the enemy was astonishing. "But you do not understand," Hannibal replied, "a much greater wonder: that in so great a number of men as that you see and that seems to be wondered at by you, there is not one who is

---

[19] Alfonso d'Avalos, marquis of Vasto, commanded the imperial army when they were defeated by the French in 1544 at Cérésole in the Piedmont region of Italy.
[20] *History of Rome*, 10.40, 30.32.
[21] This chapter was included in the previous book starting with *RS* 1596.

called Gisco." With such words he caused those standing around to laugh because seeing their general joking at such a time and taking little account of the future battle, their heart and their daring grew wonderfully. In Africa when some men were brought before him who had been sent by the Carthaginians to spy on his army and their preparedness, Scipio, who according to the custom of war ought to have had them killed, had them led around to see everything in detail and then sent them back. By this act he increased the spirit of his own men and stirred fear in the enemy. Gracchus did something similar in Spain. When the Celtiberian legates asked him in what did he have so much confidence that he dared to attack them, he responded that it was in the good army that he had, and he had the military tribune arrange the units in order so that they saw them, and they compared their own with them. They were left astounded, and having reported what they had seen, they inspired such a fear in their own that they refrained from sending aid to the city that was under siege by the Romans.

7 Of Caution[22]

It will notably increase the spirit of the soldiers if the captain shares the opinion of an informed and cautious condottiere and is neither precipitous nor foolhardy and does not abuse the life and the blood of his own; for this it will help enough if he will be alert and industrious.

8 Of Alertness

Of great importance are alertness and quickness of mind in unforeseen circumstances which sometimes secure victory or avoid disaster, as the examples of Tullus, king of the Romans, of Datames, and of Gonzalo, the Great Captain, show. Tullus Hostilius[23] advanced with his troops along with the Albani, his allies who were led by Mettius Fuffetius, to attack the forces of Veii and Fideni. When they were on the point of an assault, the two-faced Mettius began slowly to distance himself from the Romans and to turn toward the mountains from where he would be able to see how the battle would turn out. The Romans who were next to him saw that their

---

[22] This chapter was deleted starting with *RS* 1596.
[23] Tullus Hostilius was a legendary king of Rome from 672–641 BCE; he defeated the troops of Veii and Fidene, cities not far from Rome.

flank was exposed by this movement, and, alarmed, they sent a messenger to tell the king. Recognizing the danger, he reacted to the threatening disaster with a quick order. He responded in a loud voice that they return to their location and not waver; it was at his order that the Albani had moved. This order raised in the soldiers of Fideni the suspicion that they had been betrayed by Mettius who aimed to encircle them, and so they retreated. So one word of a captain encouraged his own and stirred fear in the enemy. No less presence of mind did Datames,[24] the outstanding general of Caria, demonstrate; he rebelled against King Artaxerxes because the troops of Pisidia had murdered his son, and he marched against them. Mithrobarzanes, his father-in-law, who was captain of the cavalry and who doubted that things would go well for his son-in-law, fled from the enemy with the troops under him. Who would not be alarmed by this? But Datames, improvising, drew a great good from the evil. He spread it about that his father-in-law had moved at his order in order to deceive the enemy in this way, and he encouraged his own soldiers to follow and aid him. So Mithrobarzanes's troops, caught by the Pisidians on one side and by Datames, who turned up unexpectedly, on the other, were torn to pieces. No less worthy of being remembered in this place is the quickness of mind of Ferrante Gonzalo.[25] At the beginning of the battle with the duke of Namurs,[26] when he acquired the Kingdom of Naples for the Catholic King, he commanded the artillery to fire. He was told anxiously that the powder had been completely burned up either by treachery or by accident. Without losing a bit of his spirit because of this news, he said "I accept this augur of victory which we already celebrate happily with fire." With these words he revived the courage of his soldiers. When his troops were put to flight by the army of Mithridates, Sulla held them back and stopped them with these memorable words: "Go, comrades. I go here to die gloriously. Remember to respond when you are asked where you betrayed your captain, that it was here at Orchemenus."[27] These words were of such force that the Romans turned their faces and hurled the enemy back. In this last war between the Turks and Persians when his troops mutinied, openly protesting that they did not want to cross the

---

[24] Datames, an outstanding general, served as provincial governor of Cappadocia under the Persian king Artaxerxes; he eventually took part in a rebellion against the king and was assassinated in 362 BCE.

[25] The Great Captain.

[26] The battle took place in 1503 when the duke of Namurs led French forces.

[27] Orchomenus is in Boeotia in Greece. The battle referred to here was fought in 80 BCE.

River Canac, Mustafa, the Turkish general, quieted the sedition at first with good words as best he could but the following morning, mounted on his horse, he entered the river saying "Cursed be he who eats the bread of the Great Signor and does not come with me." And they immediately competed with each other to follow him.

9 Of Eloquence and Another Matter[28]

We have already spoken of eloquence elsewhere. It too will be a great instrument of a captain, to hearten frightened soldiers or stimulate the slack or to console the afflicted or to increase their spirit. Finally, eloquence is a general means to bring about nearly any good effect. Of no less importance is liberality and the other virtues which gain for the commander love and reputation which was discussed above. The Romans went to war gladly because of the confidence that they had of victory under the Papirii, the Manlii, the Scipios, and in the terror of the Cimbrian War they wanted no other captain than C. Marius because of the great concept that they had of his valor.

10 Which is Greater, Sea Power or Land Power

Now that we have increased and strengthened our troops and our forces, let us compare a little the one and the other: first sea power and land power and then cavalry and infantry.

Whether land forces are of greater importance than sea forces would not be worthy of debate if it were not said popularly that he who is master of the sea is also master on land, a thing that is manifestly contrary to reason and to experience: to reason, because land forces do not have need of sea power, but maritime forces do have need of land forces because it is the land that produces provisions, arms, and troops. Moreover, land forces are also good for the sea but sea forces not so for the land as experience demonstrates that no empire based on sea power has ever expanded much on land, not the Cretans, even though Aristotle says that their island was made by nature for command of the sea,[29] and in effect its people were the first to prosper with naval glory, nor the Lydians, the Pelasgians,[30] the Rhodians, the Phoenicians, the Egyptians, the

---

[28] This chapter was eliminated starting with *RS* 1596.   [29] *Politics*, 2.10 (1271b).
[30] Ancient name for the inhabitants of the Peloponnesus.

Milesians, even though they succeeded one another as masters of the sea. On the other hand, all those who have had a great empire on land have made themselves masters of the sea whenever they wanted to do so. So the Romans with their landed power created within a space of forty days a powerful fleet and more with which they finally seized the dominion of the sea from the Carthaginians. Caesar did not have any naval forces but when the need arose he created within two summers such a great force that he conquered the Veneti,[31] who were masters of it; he forced Great Britain to sue for peace and pay tribute, and then, having defeated Pompey, who possessed powerful land forces, he had no rival on the sea. Since the decline of the Roman Empire, the Vandals, the Saracens, and the Turks have been lords of the sea, barbarian peoples, born far from the sea, without knowledge of wind, without experience of naval matters; but with their land forces they finally occupied the ports and the islands. The Vandals who passed on from Spain into Africa under their King Genseric, attacked Sicily and Italy, and sacked Rome, the capital of the Empire, without any opposition. The Saracens, having seized Africa and Asia, easily took possession of the islands, harassed Constantinople, and ravaged large areas of our lands. At the same time the Turks with the great power that they had acquired on land became masters of the water so that their fleets now for more than a hundred years have sailed and sail without resistance through our waters as well as theirs. The Portuguese have had for their enterprise in India two excellent captains: Francisco de Almeida and Afonso de Albuquerque.[32] The two differed greatly in the way that they conducted war in those lands. Almeida did not want to commit himself to the conquest of cities and lands but intended solely to maintain control of the ocean with a powerful fleet and so to be master of trade and to force all the merchants who wanted to sail there and the princes who possessed ports, to pay them tribute. But Albuquerque thought that a storm would be able to sink the fleet or weaken it in such a way as to deprive it of its strength and reputation and that it was not possible to remain powerful on the sea without forces on land. So he occupied the kingdoms of Malacca and Ormuz and the famous city of Goa where he constructed an excellent arsenal, planted a colony of Portuguese, and fostered in every way the conversion of the infidels, so that

---

[31] The Veneti dwelt on the Atlantic coast of the southwest of France.

[32] Francisco de Almeida (*c.* 1450–1510) was the conqueror and first viceroy of the Indies; Afonso Albuquerque (1453–1513) was the conqueror of Goa, Malacca, and Ormuz, and is considered the hero of Portuguese expansion in the East.

it can be said that he laid the foundation of the dominion that nation possesses in India. If the city and environs of Goa had not supplied wood to construct the ships and the galleys and metal to cast the artillery and men to supply the fleets and arms to arm them and provisions to support them, it was not possible that the Portuguese would have remained such a long time amidst so many powerful enemies.

It is true that maritime forces greatly assist land forces, not because they add to their strength but because they give them mobility. A land empire the greater and more spacious it is, the slower and more unfit for movement it is. Troops are not able to assemble easily nor provisions to be transported nor munitions to be stored in one place. The horses grow weary from the length of the journey, the soldiers become sick because of the change in the air, the transport of the things necessary to sustain troops and to carry on the war is an infinite expense. This can be seen in the land campaigns of the Turks going forth from Constantinople to the borders of Hungary and Persia and then returning when in addition they lose the greater part of the summer plus so many soldiers due to hardship and misery, so that the gain does not correspond to the expense. Now armadas make campaigns easier because of the ease of transport; in little time they carry great armies to distant places along with all necessary provisions, and he who is powerful on the sea is able to harass the enemy spontaneously in many places and so keep him always immobilized and in suspense. So Cosimo de' Medici said one cannot speak of a prince of great power who has not joined naval forces to those on land.

11 Which is of Greater Importance, the Cavalry or the Infantry

Speaking absolutely, the infantry is of much greater importance because its value extends to many more effects than does the cavalry. Let us concede to the latter superiority in open country because truly he who in open spaces is superior in cavalry will ordinarily conquer. So Xanthippus shows; aware of the advantage that the Carthaginians had with elephants and horses, he conquered the Romans solely by transferring the war from mountainous areas to plains. And Hannibal's victories against the Romans did not for the most part take place otherwise than from the advantage that he had in cavalry in open country, so that Fabius Maximus, aware of this, never abandoned the hills and sites where the cavalry could do nothing. Nor should the victories of the Turk over the Christians be attributed to any other cause than the great number of horses with which he has always overcome in flat territory. Those who say that the strength of the Turkish military consists in the Janissaries greatly deceive themselves because before the Janissaries were created the Turks had mounted campaigns of much greater importance than they have made since: they took Bithynia, crossed the Straits, occupied Philippopolis[33] and Adrianople, routed the princes of Serbia and Bulgaria, twice conquered the Christian forces united under King Sigismund[34] without being ever conquered except by the great Tamburlaine.[35] After the foundation of the Janissaries they endured overwhelming routs by Ladislaus, king of Poland,[36] John Hunyadi,[37] George Castriotes, Husan Hassan, king of Persia,[38] by the Mamelukes, by Matthias Corvinus, king of Hungary,[39] by the last league of Christian princes, and by the present king of Persia. And there is nothing to the claim that the Janissaries have sometimes reversed the course of battles seemingly lost and snatched victory from the hand of their enemies because the Janissaries, encircling the person of the Grand Signior, moved fresh against the enemy already worn out by fighting and killing and so defeated them, something which a large company of cavalry, which advanced fresh, or any other sort of soldiers, would have done even better. As for the Janissaries, which normally number twelve to fifteen thousand, why should they be feared by a Christian prince who opposes them with an equal number of Germans or Swiss, Spaniards or Italians or Gascons hardened in the military? In what instance will the former yield to the latter? In strength of body or vigor of spirit? Christian infantry has never been inferior to the Turkish but we have been ordinarily defeated by the great advantage that they have had in cavalry which has cut

---

[33] The capital of Thrace, today Plovdiv in Bulgaria, seized by the Turks in the fourteenth century.

[34] Sigismund I (1368–1437), king of Hungary and Croatia from 1387, king of Germany from 1411, king of Bohemia from 1419, and Holy Roman Emperor from 1433.

[35] Tamerlaine or Timur (1336–1405), founder of the Timurid Empire, a late branch of the Mongol Empire.

[36] Without a doubt Botero refers to Ladislaus III, king of Poland from 1434–44, although he never won any victory (*BD*, 386, n. 2).

[37] 1400–56, a leading Hungarian military and political figure.

[38] Uzun Hasan (1423–78), a Turkmen chieftain who defended Trebizond against the Turks. He was emperor of a briefly existing empire combining parts of present day Iran, Iraq, Anatolia, Armenia, and Azerbaijan.

[39] 1458–90.

off the roads for us, obstructed our plans, hindered our provisions and reinforcements, surrounded us on every side, exhausted, defeated and killed us, at Varna,[40] Nicopolis,[41] Mohacs,[42] Eszeg,[43] on the Livenza,[44] and in other places. Also we have seen that Turkish arms that have conquered forces composed of the finest infantry have been routed and vigorously harassed by peoples strong in cavalry: by the Mamelukes, the Hungarians, the Poles, the Muscovites, and the Persians. The infantry then yields superiority to the cavalry in flat and open spaces, where this infantry is nevertheless of the greatest importance, but it comes first in all other aspects of battle in which in fact the cavalry is useless. First, the cavalry is completely in the hands of the infantry; fighting and skirmishing are common to the one and the other but more to the infantry because one is not able to employ the cavalry in many places such as hilly territory, woods, vineyards, and valleys, and it has little or no part in the siege or defense of cities. So we see that peoples that are strong in cavalry but without soldiers on foot may well have overcome the enemy in the field but they have not been able to hold territory of importance because once the enemy has recovered in the cities and fortified places they have not been able to besiege, to attack, or to storm them, as happened to the Parthians in the wars against Crassus and Mark Antony and to the Persians in ancient times when they fought against the Roman Empire, and in our times in the wars against the Turks because in this last war, not to speak of others, the Persian, because of his advantage in cavalry, has made a great slaughter of Turks in open country but because of a lack of infantry has not been able to seize or occupy cities of importance nor to drive the Turk out of cities that he has taken nor out of fortified places.

So we conclude that cavalry is superior to infantry in open country but that the infantry, which is also of the greatest importance even in open country, outweighs the cavalry in every other military situation.[45]

---

[40] Varna, in the east of Bulgaria, was the site of a battle between Murad II and Ladislaus Jagiello assisted by John Hunyadi on November 10, 1444.

[41] Site of a battle between Bayezid and Stephen Lazarevic of Serbia, September 25, 1396.

[42] The battle at Mohacs on the Danube between Suleiman and Louis II of Hungary took place on August 29, 1526.

[43] Eszeg was a fortress in Slavonia.

[44] The Livenza is a river in Friuli where many battles were fought but none where the Turks defeated the Christians (*BD*, p. 387, n. 4).

[45] Chap. 12 follows here starting in *RS* 1590; see Appendix C.

APPENDIX A

Of the Means to Calm Troubles Once they have Arisen[1]

But because no matter how much prudence you have, *necesse est ut eveniant scandala* (scandals necessarily come)[2] and disturbances spring up, it is necessary also to see how uprisings already under way can be pacified. Troubles arise then either of the people against the prince and his officials or of the nobility in rebellion or division into factions. First I confess that, as every illness of the human body cannot be healed, *tollere nodosam nescit medicina podagram, nec formidatis auxiliatur aquis* (medicine does not know how to heal every troublesome gout nor do the frightening waters help),[3] so with government order cannot be restored after every disorder.

Kingdoms and republics also have their incurable and sometimes deadly sicknesses. Italy, at another time divided into Guelphs and Ghibellines, testifies to this, which without remedy tore it to pieces and ruined it altogether.

But, to do what can somehow be done, we say that troubles and disturbances are such that the prince sees himself either to be superior and with the advantage or inferior in resources, and he should be considered

---

[1] This chapter was added in *RS* 1590 at the end of Book Five.
[2] Matthew 18:7.   [3] Ovid, *Letters from the Black Sea*, 1.3.23–24.

inferior even when he thinks himself to be equal. In the former case it is fitting to use force and find a remedy at the beginning and cut out the root as quickly as possible, and I will say also, with the silence and secrecy that is possible so that the ringleaders will be removed before anything else is known of it.

But if the prince sees himself in danger, it is necessary to think about conquering by yielding and by the wise allowance to give vent to the furor because ordinarily uprisings of the multitude have no leader with authority so that it happens that they quickly cool down and lose their strength because of disunion. But the prince ought not to leave the place of the tumult or distance himself from it in some way as did Henry III, king of France, during the troubles in Paris,[4] because the absence of the prince diminishes the respect for him, inspires the leaders, and gives enthusiasm to the mob; the revolutions in Flanders show this. Bajazet II, at the time of the rebellion of his son, Selim I, although his guard composed of Janissaries inclined to the son, did not take to flight but with the majesty of his presence and the gravity of his words acted in such a way that the Janissaries were ashamed to abandon him, let alone to betray him. The Emperor Charles V, when he heard of the rebellion of the citizens of Ghent, traveled from Spain to Flanders as soon as he could and with the authority of his presence quieted the troubles, punished the rebels, and with the help of a good citadel, secured that indomitable city. The Romans ordinarily used two ways to pacify uprisings: the first was to seize the leaders from the midst of the mob, the other to divert the mob from domestic troubles to foreign wars, a practice also of Pericles in Athens, because just as the doctors calm the peccant and disturbed humors of the human body by sending them away and diverting them elsewhere by way of cauterizing and blood-letting, so the wise prince placates the angry people by leading them into a war against their enemies or with other means to restrain them from their evil intention and to direct them elsewhere. The crowd is, as Horace says, *bellua multorum capitum* (a beast with many heads),[5] so that when it rages it is necessary to take hold of it by one head or by another and manipulate it with dexterity, making use of the hand or the stick or the reins or the halter. And here it will help to have at hand a supply of benefits and a variety of ideas with which

---

[4] This alludes to the Day of the Barricades in Paris on May 12, 1588, when Henry III fled the city at the arrival of the duke of Guise who received an enthusiastic reception from the people.

[5] *Epistles*, 1.1.76.

to delight them or to inspire fear, suspicion, and hope in them before restraining them and leading them back to obedience. It will help to have the assistance of persons who are loved and appreciated by the rebels and are endowed with a lively intelligence and eloquence. Agrippa[6] pacified the Roman people with the memorable tale of the human body and its members. But no less excellent was the clever invention of Calavius by which he rendered the people of Capua capable of reason, which is commemorated by Livy.[7] That people was so infuriated with the senators that they wanted them all dead. Calavius did not oppose their furor; instead, having first informed the senators of his intent, he assembled them all in one place and then, addressing the people, he showed that he was in agreement with them; then he said, "because you have determined to kill all the senators, it is first necessary to choose from among you the persons most suitable to replace them." And beginning with the most hated senator, he said, "We will put to death such a man." Then the whole people shouting approved his judgment. "But let us see," said Calavius, "whom we will put in his place." Then the shopkeepers and manual laborers pushed forward, first one and then the other, for this position, unwilling to yield to another so that as the competition increased so did the tumult, and they quarreled with one another. The same happened with the nomination of the second and of other senators. The end result was that not wanting one of them to be preferred over another, they quickly agreed to allow the senators not only to live but to retain their offices.

In Florence when the city was in flames and in danger of ruin, Francesco Soderini[8] who was the archbishop came forward in his pontifical robes and with the clergy behind him and with the majesty of religion made each person return home.[9] In many places the intervention of preachers and the efforts of men considered to be saints or of singular virtue have been useful.

If they cannot all be pacified together, it will help to make use of all suitable means to divide them. When none of the above-mentioned means is effective, well before taking up arms it is better to concede to

---

[6] Marcus Vipsanius Agrippa (63–12 BCE) was a Roman general, statesman, and architect and a close associate of Emperor Augustus.

[7] *History of Rome*, 2.32.8–12. Pacuvius Calavius was the chief magistrate of Capua during the Second Punic War.

[8] Francesco Soderini (1453–1524) became a cardinal in 1503; he held a number of bishoprics but was never archbishop of Florence.

[9] It is not clear to what event this applies, perhaps to the siege of Florence in 1529–30; Soderini had then been dead for several years (*BD*, 231, n. 2).

them what they demand, in whole or in part, because, since the two foundations of empire and government are love and reputation, if by yielding you lose some reputation, yet you preserve love; this you ought to apply much more easily with natural subjects than with acquired ones. And if you are able also, always aid your reputation by using those means that make it appear that you desire that which you cannot prevent and that you give lovingly that which is taken from your hand by active force, as do the merchants who sometimes not having the wind to carry them to trade where they had planned, travel to do their business wherever the wind leads them. There was a count in Flanders, whose name I do not remember, against whom the mob of Ghent rose up, each one of them wearing a white hood as a sign of their rebellion, and in a mad rage turned the land upside down. The count worked hard to pacify them and make them take off their hoods, but with little success. Why was it necessary to make such an effort in so small a matter? Instead he should have put on a white hood himself and so remained the leader of his people.

But such a concession ought to be understood as applying to things not to persons; it seems to me to be very harsh that the prince is reduced to the point of giving over his minister into the hands of an angry multitude as did Amurath, king of the Turks, some years ago.[10] In such an act there occur such indignities that he ought to have preferred that his minister be taken by force rather than to hand him over in one way or another, that is, provided he has been a faithful minister and was without fault and it was not possible to hide him or to have him flee or in some other way to get him out of danger.

An excellent method is to pretend, when this is possible, not to know of a disorder which cannot be remedied without a greater disorder, as Charles V did wisely in the case of the duke of Infantado.[11] But, if a scandal arises from among the barons, this can happen in two ways; either they plot against the prince or they break up into factions. If they plot against the prince, it is necessary to make use of the same remedies as was said of the multitude, and it will be much easier to create disunity among the barons than among the multitude because it is much easier to win over some from many than to win over many out of an infinite multitude. The

[10] This alludes to the assassination in 1579 of Mehmed Pacha Sokullo, grand-vizier of Suleiman (then Selim II), and finally of Amurath III (*BD*, 232, n. 2).

[11] This alludes to a conflict between the duke of Infantado and an official of Charles V. The emperor preferred not to proceed rigorously against an affront to the official in order to avoid a rising of the grandees of Spain (*BD*, 232, n. 3).

life of Louis XI, king of France, who was one of the most astute princes there ever was, can serve as an example and a mirror for him who finds himself in distress or danger from sedition or plots. But if they turn the kingdom upside down because of their private differences with the result that they form parties, here greater circumspection is necessary because the controversy will then be over a private or a public matter. If a private matter, then it will be necessary to compel them to remit it to judges who will decide the case or to arbitrators who will settle the matter without showing favoritism to one side or the other so as not to alienate one of the parties as did King Francis I in the suit between Madame Louise, his mother, and Charles, duke of Bourbon, who rebelled because the king favored his mother.[12] The anger borne against princes and their states follows in great part from favors granted without any basis in justice. But if agreement cannot be reached in a case because evidence is lacking or because it would cause greater trouble than the controversy itself, as in the case of the enmity between Henry, duke of Guise,[13] and Gaspard de Coligny, Admiral of France, who was accused of having had Francis, father of Henry,[14] murdered, then the prince with his authority ought to impose silence and banish the heads of each party from the court to countries far from each other, or in some similar ways.

But if the difference has a public aspect, which is often used to hide private passions, then if he is not able to cover it over or root it out, the king ought to make himself leader of the better part. And he deceives himself if he thinks to protect himself from imminent dangers to the state and from similar rivalries or factions by providing a counterweight to the parties, raising up in turn the weaker and pushing down the stronger. This method was tried in France where, with this tactic, the above-mentioned factions maintained themselves and grew in such a way that with the passage of time the kingdom remained divided into two parts, each with such a following and power that nothing remained to the king but the name.

---

[12] Louise of Savoy claimed the fiefs of the Bourbons after the death of Suzanne of Bourbon in 1521. As a result of the favoritism shown by Francis I to his mother, Charles of Bourbon went over to Emperor Charles V and served as one of his generals (*BD*, 132, n. 2 and 233, n. 1).

[13] Henry I of Guise was suspected of having ordered the assassination of Coligny at the time of the St. Bartholomew's Day Massacre in 1572.

[14] Francis of Lorraine, duke of Guise, was killed by a Huguenot noble in 1563, and Coligny, leader of the Protestant party, was accused of having ordered the murder.

I conclude this part by saying that the uprisings and civil wars that are not ended in their beginnings are not ordinarily ended except by the ruin of one of the parties, as is seen throughout Roman history and in events in France and in Flanders, or with the division of the state. The reason is that the evil that in its beginning is as it were a stream that one can cross on foot becomes as it progresses a formidable force. Anger turns into hatred, and an uprising into rebellion and treason. And if one party has a notable advantage, it will lay down its arms only with the ruin of the enemy. If neither side has a significant advantage, they will end the war out of fatigue, and each will remain with its area. So the sum of human prudence in matters of state consists in two words: *principiis obsta* (resist beginnings), because ordinarily, *modicis rebus primii motus consedere. Omne malum nascens facile opprimitur; inveteratum fit robustius* (the beginnings consist of little things; every evil is easily suppressed aborning, once established it becomes stronger).[15] No one begins to disturb the republic with a great offense, but he undermines the foundation of great things by neglecting little things.

[15] The second phrase comes from Cicero, *Fifth Philippic*, 31; the first is an interpolation (*BD*, 234, n. 3).

In the Accumulation of Wealth One Ought Not to Continue *ad Infinitum*

If every human action has a predetermined end, the accumulation of treasure ought not to proceed *ad infinitum*, but rather conform to the other resources of the state; otherwise the excess has something of the monstrous because it lacks proportion with the other members and has something of the unfit and out of place and will always serve as bait and then as booty to enemies. Now the end of the resources of a prince is the preservation and expansion of the state. It is preserved by defense and expanded by offense but for neither defense nor offense is infinite treasure required but that which is proportionate to the rest of your power. Not for defense because if the scale and length of a war would not exhaust your treasury, they would consume your people and country if your other resources were not proportionate to your treasure. Perseus, king of Macedonia, Sardanapalus, king of Assyria, and Darius, king of Persia, were ruined with treasuries that were full; Ptolemy, king of Cyprus,[1] had seven million at the time when he received the news that the Romans, for this reason, had seized his kingdom. Despairing at not being able to defend himself because the rest of his resources did not correspond to his wealth, he killed himself. Pompey himself during the war that Caesar

---

[1] 80–58 BCE.

waged against the republic left a full treasury for his enemies. Hulagu the Tartar[2] after taking Baghdad left the caliph to die of hunger among the heaps of riches that he had avidly accumulated, and Muhammad II had Stephen, prince of Bosnia, shot, because he preferred to ruin himself by saving the treasure that he had amassed rather than to spend it on arms.[3] Finally, I do not find any notable example of a state being lost because it lacked money but because the prudence and valor of the captains, the number and discipline of the soldiers, the quantity of munitions and provisions, and the other resources on land and sea were clearly not equal to the accumulated gold. And it ordinarily happens that he who accumulates treasures, in order to avoid expenses, neglects every other means to maintain his grandeur and reputation; he does not pay his soldiers, does not employ men of reputation and skill, does not resupply munitions, does not repair the walls of dilapidated fortresses, does not dig ditches, and does not construct warships. Finally, all his thoughts are directed to acquiring money while everything else is abandoned. But what use are the treasures of Croesus or Midas to a prince who has been attacked by sea but does not have in his state or among his allies wood to construct galleys and ships, nor craftsmen, nor sailors, nor oarsmen, nor tools, nor other necessary things? And if attacked by land does not have a supply of horses or artillery, nor captains, nor soldiers to oppose the enemy in the field, nor provisions, nor munitions, nor men adequate to protect his cities and fortresses? Money is said to be the sinews of war because it coordinates your forces and locates them where they are needed. But if you have no forces, of what use will it be? He who has nothing to spend is as poor as he who has nothing to buy. But if infinite treasure is not sought for defense, it is much less necessary for offensive operations and for attempted conquests; a campaign, for which you have to spend without measure of your own funds, is not a campaign of acquisition but of damage and loss because all those enterprises ought to be considered foolish which are not able to maintain and sustain themselves; so we read that the Carthaginians abandoned some undertakings, even acquisitions already made. And the Romans having lost in various shipwrecks in the Second Punic War more than seven hundred large ships with a huge number of soldiers, abandoned the sea, more out of necessity than skill.[4] The

---

[2] Hulagu Khan, grandson of Genghis Khan, took possession of Baghdad on February 10, 1258.
[3] Mehmed II (1432–81), called "the Conqueror," conquered Bosnia in 1463.
[4] This should refer to the First rather than the Second Punic War (*BD*, 278, n. 1).

Chinese showed much greater prudence because when they ruled nearly all the islands of the Eastern Ocean[5] and the greater part of India, realizing that such a task consumed infinite riches, arms, soldiers, materials, they determined to abandon it and to withdraw to their own country, and they issued a law that prohibited sailing in those lands and making offensive war there. The Emperor Hadrian abandoned that part of Britain that lies beyond the River Tweed, today called Scotland, which had been conquered by Julius Agricola,[6] just as he abandoned the provinces beyond the River Tigris which had been subjugated by Trajan.

Since an immense treasure is not necessary either to defend your state or to conquer another, it is necessary to limit it in proportion to your other resources. How?, someone will say. It is a difficult thing and not very well-advised to say precisely the quantity or the sum which the one assembling treasure ought not to surpass because this depends on the circumstances of individual states, whether they are open or enclosed, with many or few ports, abundant or barren lands, with much commerce as Flanders or with little as Poland, bordering on powerful enemies or princes nearly equal to them. But if someone requires that I provide some rule in this matter, I would say that the accumulation [of treasure] does no harm so long as it does not disrupt normal commerce and exchange because up to this point one can set aside something for future needs without disadvantages for the subjects. But the ruler who withdraws so much [treasure] that it deprives merchants of the means to carry on commerce and artisans to exercise their profession and to exchange what the earth produces and human industry creates, strikes at the roots of his state and weakens it in such a way as to make it useless for his service. So as the stomach which does not digest and distribute food further but only causes the exhaustion and corruption of the other members [of the body] as well as of itself, so the prince who devours and keeps for himself the wealth of his subjects without distributing it proportionately and sharing it according to their needs, consumes and ruins his subjects as well as himself.

But in order to know more exactly how much he can set aside without doing notable damage to his people, it is necessary that the prince know in detail the amount of money that leaves his state for the goods

---

[5] Botero refers here to all the maritime space encompassed by the north of the Indian Ocean, the South China Sea, and the East China Sea (*BD*, 278, n. 2).

[6] The Roman general Gnaeus Julius Agricola (40–93 CE) completed the conquest of Britain. Hadrian began the construction of Hadrian's Wall to shut out the barbarians in 122 CE.

that are imported and the sum that is made or enters for the goods that are exported, and to see to it that the amount which he sets aside is not greater than that by which the income surpasses the outgoing payments. But when the income is less than the outgoing payments the prince ought not aim to increase his treasure because he will not be able to do so and if he tries to do so, he will ruin his state; it will be better to make every effort to make his subjects more industrious, in agriculture as well as in crafts and commerce, of which I have spoken elsewhere. It is said that the king of China has more than one hundred million in gold as income which, although to some this seems incredible, I consider to be most true on the supposition that that be true that is written about the size of his empire, the fertility of the land, the mineral deposits, the innumerable multitude of artisans and merchants, the convenience of the paved streets throughout the whole realm, the presence of navigable rivers, the number, size, and density of the cities, the subtlety of the intelligence and the industry of the people which does not allow one hand's breadth of land to be lost nor one ounce of material, no matter how poor it is, to which they do not give some artificial form if only, as Giovanni di Barros and others write, to propel their carts with sails.[7] To this is added the inestimable expenses of the king; because, supposing that there is in China altogether a thousand million scudi and that there is taken in each year another thirty or forty for the goods that are exported and are dug from the mines without losing one dram of gold or silver, it would not be a great matter that the king has annually an income of one hundred million on the condition that he does not spend each year seventy or more because, as water rises as much as it falls, it happens easily that the prince who spends much also takes in enough for himself because he draws a profit from that which he spends. It is impossible to draw a profit over a long period from a state that does not acquire from outside while not spending a great deal. In effect, let us suppose that in a state such as this, there are ten million scudi and that the prince has a revenue of one million and that he does not spend more than one hundred thousand. Then it will happen that in a dozen years or more his subjects will lose everything and the prince will no longer be able, I will not say to clip but even to fleece them.

---

[7] João de Barros, *Terceira decada da Asia* (Lisbon, 1563), 1.2, chap. 7; see also Giovanni Pietro Maffei, *Historiarum Indicarum libri XVI* (Florence, 1588), 6, 113c (*BD*, 280, n. 4).

APPENDIX C

Against Whom the Prince Ought to Deploy his Military Forces[1]

Military forces ought to be employed for defense of our own or for the acquisition of another's. The defense of one's own is so just that there is need of no other proof than to consider the weapons of animals, horns, teeth, claws, and kicks, all given to them by nature for the conservation of their being; and so roses are armed with thorns, ears of corn with bristles, chestnuts with shells. Finally, nature is so solicitous in this that princes have no need to be instructed in its art. But they ought to take care not to exceed limits in such a way that defense becomes offense every time that they are presented with an easy opportunity. In this the Romans behaved in an excellent fashion because, if their enemies remained unconquered, they never denied them a fair peace, which ought to be the goal of every war, nor should it be denied except to those from whom one could not hope for it except by their destruction or who had committed a deed that ought to be punished by their extermination as an example to others. As Sallust said of the Romans, *Duabus his artibus, audacia in bello, ubi pax evenerat, aequitate, seque rempublicam curabunt* (These two virtues,

---

[1] Starting with *RS* 1590 this chapter was added at the end of Book Ten and at the end of the whole work. It corresponds to the last chapter of *The Prince* where Machiavelli summons the Medici ruler of Florence to take up arms and lead a coalition to drive the foreigner out of Italy.

boldness in time of war and fairness in time of peace, permitted them to provide for their needs and for those of the republic).[2] And so just is defensive war that offensive war can have no other justice than that which it receives from defensive war, nor is it possible to have any instance in which offensive war is licit except in defense.

How then, someone will say, can I expand my state? By defending the public good. Now the public good is of two sorts, spiritual and temporal. The temporal is civil and political peace, the spiritual is religion and the union of the church of God. The one and the other are opposed and disturbed by two sorts of enemies, heretics and infidels; the former are internal, the latter external, and so the former are more dangerous than the latter because the infidel intends primarily to attack the temporal good and as a result of this, the spiritual good. But the heretic aims chiefly at the spiritual good and following upon its ruin, the temporal good. But because war is the ultimate remedy which ought to be employed against the heretic, it is not so universally licit for all to wage war against heretics as it is against infidels. But every prince ought with all his power keep this pestilence at a distance. He who openly seeks to withdraw men from obedience to the church of God will seek to withdraw them much more easily from your rule and obedience. And it is not to be wondered that God permits so many revolutions of states against their princes because these princes care little for the disobedience of their peoples toward His Majesty. Yet there are not lacking today men, no less impious than foolish, who give princes to understand that heresies have nothing to do with politics. And although there is no heretical prince who will for reason of state allow the exercise of the Catholic religion in his domain, there are not lacking princes who make profession of being good Christians who freely permit heresies in their kingdoms; this demonstrates how true is that saying of the Lord that the children of darkness show more prudence in their affairs than do the children of light.[3]

But he who wants to wage war cannot excuse himself by saying that he has no public enemy against whom he can show his courage, an enemy who always thinks of nothing less than the oppression of Christendom and who has such great military forces that to resist him, let alone to overcome him, would bring much greater glory than could be acquired by taking up arms among Christians. We have the Turk at the door, we have him on our flanks, and do we seek reasons for war more just or more

---

[2] Sallust, *Conspiracy of Catiline*, 9.3.   [3] Luke 16:8.

honorable? Cato when he wanted to show the Romans the danger that
hung over them from their enemies, made them look at some fresh figs
recently brought from Carthage.[4] How much nearer is Valona[5] to Italy
than Carthage was to Rome? M. Varro wanted to unite Epirus to Italy
with a bridge. Perhaps some will say that the enemy is near but with
few troops? The Romans feared the Carthaginians whom they had often
conquered and subjugated, and do we disdain the Turk who has taken
from us so many fortresses, so many cities, so many kingdoms, and two
empires? Who dominates Africa, who rules Asia, who holds more countries in Europe than do all the states of the Catholic princes? Who because
of our discord has grown in such a way on land, already for three hundred
years, that he maintains mastery there and has no rival on the sea? An
enemy who in time of peace is better armed than we are in time of war?
An enemy whose treasures are inexhaustible, his armies innumerable, his
supplies endless? Who on the day of battle covers the plains with his cavalry and in the assault on cities piles up mountains of earth and makes
a ladder on the walls of the fortresses with the mass of his own men?
An enemy finally who up until now has not lost anything of importance
that he has once acquired. Fernando de Toledo, duke of Alba, who had
taken part in so many wars and won more victories than any other man
of his times, nevertheless used to say that he had done nothing because
it had not been granted him to see himself before an army of Turks.
Truly I do not know with what judgment reason of state[6] would show
itself to be more an enemy of Christians than of Turks or other infidels.
Machiavelli exclaims impiously against the church, and against the infidels he does not open his mouth, and the armies of Christian princes are
so intent on ruining one another as though they had no other enemies
in the world. The emperors Comnenus, Alexius, Kalojan, and Manuel[7]
followed similar rules in order not to allow the Christian princes of the
west to expand in the lands taken from them by the Turks; they opposed
with all their power the campaigns of Gottfried, the Emperor Conrad,
and others against those barbarians. What happened as a result of this?
The barbarians first chased ours out of Asia and then they brought the
Greeks under their feet. Behold, the fruit of modern politics! The lords
of Venice, attacked from every side in the days of Julius II by nearly as

---

[4] Pliny, *Natural History*, 15.18.   [5] Today Vlora in Albania.
[6] In *RS* 1590 and *RS* 1596 there is added here, "if something so irrational, not to say bestial,
merits the name of reason."
[7] Alexis I (r. 1081–1118), John II (r. 1118–43), and Manuel I Comnenus (r. 1143–80).

many rulers as there were in Christendom,[8] consistently refused the aid offered them by Bajazet II, king of the Turks, so that God did not abandon them, indeed he enabled them nearly miraculously to recover the rule over Lombardy that they had lost.

[8] The League of Cambrai in 1508–09 included France, Spain, and the Holy Roman Empire.

Of Reputation

BOOK ONE

1 What is Reputation

I recall that some years ago when talking with the famous poet Torquato Tasso about reputation, among the other things regarding this matter that he wisely remarked and said was that just as the vine-dresser waters often and trims the useless and superfluous branches so that the vines may produce more and better grapes, so he who wishes to acquire reputation must banish from his life and his actions all that is improper or unworthy of a person of high estate. Hence he concluded that reputation requires frequent pruning. This derivation seemed to me, while respecting the authority of such a great man, more subtle than true because, first, reputation exists not in the person who is said to possess a reputation but in the one who considers that another has a reputation,[2] and secondly, that it is born not of a lack or a defect but of excellence and of great worth. So I think that to repute is nothing other than to rethink or to

---

[1] These three chapters are taken from Botero's *Additions to the Reason of State* (*Aggiunte alle Ragione di stato*) first published with *RS* 1598. The text used here is taken from *Della ragion di stato di Giovanni Botero, con tre libri delle Cause della grandezza delle città, due Aggiunte e un Discorso della popolazione di Roma*, ed. Luigi Firpo (Turin, 1948), "Della Reputazione," Book 1, chaps. 1–4 (pp. 413–24).

[2] "la riputazione non è nel riputato ma nel riputante."

reconsider a matter more profoundly, and that a man of reputation is one whose *virtù* cannot be easily understood or comprehended and merits to be frequently considered and esteemed; this is what reputation is.

Many things have something I do not know what similar to reputation, such as credit, authority, esteem, wonder, fame, but they all are quite different from it. Reputation is not the same as credit although it overlaps with it to a degree; credit applies to private persons, reputation to public ones. It differs from authority because this is in the captain with respect to the soldiers; reputation, on the other hand, is in the soldiers with respect to the captain, so that we say "to have authority" and "to be in reputation."[3] Authority is toward inferiors and to those nearby, reputation extends also to foreigners and to those at a distance. Yet there is sometimes little difference, as when Tacitus speaking of Corbulo[4] said *Multa auctoritate, quae viro militari pro facundia erat* (with much authority which in a professional soldier took the place of eloquence),[5] or when Sextus Victor[6] said of Antoninus Pius, *Orbem terrae nullo bello per quatuor et viginti annos sola auctoritate rexit* (By his authority alone without any war he governed the whole world for twenty-four years).[7] This is perhaps the same as esteem but with the addition of "great," so that the Latins had no other way with which they could designate a man of reputation then to say *Virum magnae existimationis* (a man of great honor).[8] Yet esteem is in a superior with respect to an inferior; one does not say that the servant esteems his master but, on the contrary, that the master esteems the servant. But reputation is in the inferior with respect to the superior. Wonder has some similarity to reputation but it is not the same. Wonder extends also more to things speculative and natural than to those human and practical but reputation includes only practical things. Wonder arises because we do not understand the effect, so that eclipses of the moon and the sun, the comet and other such things appear marvelous to one who does not understand the reason for them. Reputation emerges not because we do not know the reason for its effect but because we do not easily understand its greatness. It appears that fame agrees to a degree with reputation as when Tiberius felt with his hand *publicum sibi odium*

---

[3] "essere in reputazione."
[4] Corbulo (7–67 CE) was a Roman general, brother-in-law of Emperor Caligula.
[5] *Annals*, 15.26.
[6] Sextus Aurelius Victor (320–90 CE) was a historian and politician of imperial Rome.
[7] *A Collection about the Emperors*, "Antoninus Pius"; he governed Rome from 138–61 CE.
[8] Perhaps a reference to Cicero, *On the Republic*, 3.17.

magisque fama quam vi stare res suas (the public hatred of him and the fact that his power was based more on reputation than on force).[9] But it is not the same because fame extends also to evil things, contrary to reputation.

2 What is the Origin of Reputation

We assign reputation only to those whom we have considered to have by their excellence and greatness surpassed the ordinary limits of human virtue[10] and have in themselves I do not know what of the heavenly and the divine. Reputation ought to be considered the child and the fruit of an excellent virtue[11] and of all perfection. A small good that does not extend beyond the confines of mediocrity is well suited to elicit love but not reputation, because, being easily understood by the intellect, it suddenly moves the will or the appetite which takes pleasure in it, embraces and loves it, but a preeminent *virtù* takes hold of and seizes the intellect so much in consideration of it that the will and love can have only a small part in it. So Aristotle teaches that we love the equal and the lesser, we reverence the greater, and we honor and beatify heroes and personages who by the loftiness of their *virtù* and perfection have passed beyond the ordinary limits of human nature.[12] So those *virtues* add to reputation which have the quality of the lofty and the admirable and elevate the prince above the earth and carry him beyond the number of common men. *Tentanda via est, qua me quoque possum tollere humo, victorque virum volitare per ora* (It is necessary that I take a path that permits me to lift myself above the earth and to fly victorious beyond the limits).[13]

Now a man only exalts himself through subtlety of intellect and vigor of spirit, and because the reputation of a prince is located in the opinion and the concept that the people have of him, the matters with which he ought to concern himself in order to acquire such great good ought to be those in which the people have an interest. And these are peace and war because with the arts of peace he keeps his subjects quiet and with those of war he keeps enemies at a distance.

Such civil ways secured the fame of divinity among the ancients for Orpheus, Amphion, Rhadamanthus, and Minoe.[14] No less did men raise

---

[9] See Tacitus, *Annals*, 6.30.   [10] *valore*.   [11] *virtù*.
[12] See Aristotle, *Politics*, 7.13 (1332).   [13] See Vergil, *Georgics*, 3.8–9.
[14] See Horace, *Art of Poetry*, 391–96. They were figures of Greek mythology. Orpheus was the chief of poets and musicians. Amphion, founder of the city of Thebes, symbolized the

themselves up with victories and triumphs. *Res gerere et captos osten-dere civibus hostes attingit solium Jovis et coelestia tentat* (To lead military enterprises and to display enemy prisoners to fellow citizens is the glory that reaches heaven and touches the throne of Jupiter).[15] When the same Horace wished to praise Caesar Augustus fully, he rendered him excellent in both the one and the other, *Cum tot sustineas tanta negotia solus, res itali-cas armis tuteris, moribus ornes, legibus emendes* (From the moment that you alone undertook such important negotiations, defended Italy with arms, adorned her with customs, corrected her with laws).[16] While conceding to the Greeks the knowledge of how to plead cases and to fashion with marvelous delicacy statues of marble and metal and to note and describe the movements of heaven and the stars, Vergil did not wish to claim for Roman greatness anything else but civil and military prudence. *Tu regere imperio populos, Romane, memento; hae tibi erunt artes, pacique imponere morem, parcere subjectis, et debellare superbos* (You, O Roman, govern the peoples as sovereign; these are your arts, to impose terms of peace, to pardon the conquered, and to put down the proud).[17] Among the Jews there have been two kings of incomparable reputation, one for the art of war, David, and the other for the art of peace, Solomon. And in Rome two personages acquired eminent names, one for valor of arms, that is, Pompey called the Great, and the other for civil prudence, Quintus Fabius Rullus, called the Greatest.[18]

Nor should anyone wonder that the Romans honored the latter with a greater title than the former because as we have said elsewhere, it is much more difficult to preserve than to extend rule. So as Heracles, ambassador of Antiochus, said of the Romans, *Parari singula acquirendo facilius potuerunt, quam universa teneri* (It was easier for them to have acquired provinces one by one than to maintain them all).[19] Pyrrhus, king of Epirus, excellent in the waging of war and the craft of arms, because he did not know how to keep what he had acquired, was accounted a gambler who played the dice well but did not know how to make use of his winnings. And in war itself it is more praiseworthy to conquer with counsel than with the sword because in the former manner of waging war the enemy is overcome along with the complete preservation of one's own

superiority of intelligence over brute force. Rhadamanthus and Minos were, according to Greek mythology, models of just judges in this and the future life.
[15] See Horace, *Epistles*, 1.17.33–34.   [16] Ibid., 2.1.1–3.   [17] *Aeneid*, 6.851–53.
[18] Quintus Fabius Rullus served as consul five times in the later fourth century BCE.
[19] Livy, *History of Rome*, 37.35.

army, whereas in the latter *la vittoria sanguinosa spesso suol fare il capitan men degno* (the bloody victory often is accustomed to make the captain less worthy),[20] so that having learned that Alexander the Great after having acquired so great a state said that he did not know what he ought to do, Caesar Augustus wondered why he did not consider it a much greater work to govern what he had acquired than to have acquired it.

Now states just as they are ruined by the stupidity or the cruelty or the lust or the ineptitude of princes, so they are preserved and expanded by the wisdom and justice, the temperance and fortitude of the same; and these virtues produce the effects of greater reputation and wonder with the multitude the more elevated and eminent they are. Prudence is common to peace and to war, justice (where I include religion) and temperance belong more to peace, courage more to war than to peace.

3 Of the Importance of Reputation

It is necessary that every principality is supported by one of three foundations, that is, by love or by fear or by reputation, of which the first two are simple qualities and the third a composite of the one and the other. Of these love is by its nature without a doubt stronger and more suited to keep the people more devoted and subjected because it is of all our affections the most powerful and of the greatest strength; in addition it is the first and the principal one and that which gives vigor and movement to all. So Plutarch compares it to a dictator in whose presence every other magistrate yields.[21] So one would not be able to improve on that rule which was based completely on the affection of the subjects. But on the other hand there is no form of government more uncertain and false, not because of a defect in this love but because of the imperfection of the subjects because it is too difficult for a prince to conduct himself with such measure and circumspection with his subjects that for a long period he fully satisfies and contents them. Our spirits are by nature insatiable and difficult to please. *Or mi diletta e piace quel che piu mi dispiacque* (Now that delights and pleases me that displeases me more).[22] So we see that princes who are elected to great applause and with a marvelous celebration are then soon abandoned or dead; the whole history of the Roman emperors is full of them. Just as prime matter is not long content with

---

[20] Ariosto, *Orlando furioso*, 15.1.3–4.   [21] See Plutarch, *Amatorius*, 21.14–15 (768a).
[22] Petrarch, *Canzoniere*, 2, Sonnet 22.

one form,[23] so our spirits from hour to hour seek some novelty in everything but principally in the manner of government. The multitude is by nature prone to grumbling and with difficulty remains satisfied, and the present government usually appears always to be hard and stern, and yet *ferenda regum ingenia*, says Tacitus, *neque usui crebras mutationes* (it is necessary to bear up under the temper of sovereigns, lest there be frequent changes).[24] It is impossible then that so many thousands of men agree and concur in the love of one, and not less impossible that one always operates in a way that pleases all. A good look, a favor, a grace that is made to one rather than to another is apt to render bitter every previous kindness and to cancel out the memory of every past benefit, to place hate where love once lodged.

For these and for other reasons many princes, not trusting the moods of their subjects, have departed from the way of love and based their rule on fear as in something stronger and more secure because love is in the power of the subject but fear depends upon him who makes himself feared, and the ways to make oneself lovable are not as secure and universal as those that make one feared. And if this is true for subjects, it is much more true for strangers who have no other bond with you except that of proximity and of fear of your forces. But it is necessary that these carry themselves in such a way that fear is greater than hate; hence when Cato the Utican asked his teacher how Sulla, whose many cruelties were seen, lasted so long, he responded, because he is more feared than hated. Reputation is composed of love and fear, which is better than the one or the other because it contains that which is good and useful in both, that is, it takes from love the union of the subjects with the prince and from fear the submission because the former unifies and the latter subjects.

But someone will ask me which has the greater part in reputation, love or fear. Fear without a doubt, because just as respect and reverence so also reputation is for the eminence of *virtù* from which proceeds species of fear rather than of love. This can be easily understood by this: love is a passion that conciliates spirits, fear draws them back; the former unites, the latter draws them apart; the former makes equal, the latter makes unequal. Now it is clear that in reputation there appear many more features and effects of fear than of love because it has greater strength to pull back, to separate, and to render unequal. The same thing can be easily

---

[23] Here the author alludes to the Aristotelian doctrine of matter and form.

[24] *Annals*, 12.11.

understood from this: there is nothing more contrary to reputation than disdain, so that Dio Cassius writes that having perceived that because of his old age he had become contemptible and had so lost all reputation, Emperor Nerva adopted Trajan and set him up as emperor.[25] Ovid was also of this opinion then when having vaguely said that after the ancient chaos things remained confused for a long time, without the distinction of a majority and a minority, so that the gods of lower rank often sat themselves near Jupiter and Saturn, he added that finally honor and reverence assigned to each his grade and his appropriate seat. From this was born Majesty next to which were seated Respect and Fear. *Hinc nata Maiestas, quae mundum temperat omnem, quaque die artu est edita, magna fuit. ... Consedere simul Pudor et Metus. Omne videres Numen ad hanc cultus composuisse suos* (From this was born Majesty, which governs the whole world and was grand from the day that it came to light ... Next to it were seated Shame and Fear. Then you would have been able to see all the divinities imitate it with their proper attitudes.)[26] Moreover, to be feared is of great importance for reputation because one can maintain it without love. So Livy wrote that even if Camillus had assigned the spoils of the city of Veio[27] to the treasurers, to the anger of the soldiers, *severitate imperii victi, eandem virtutem oderant et mirabant* (overcome by the severity of their commander, they hated and admired his rigor).[28]

Now one can know how great reputation is from this: that dead men by their shadow have performed deeds of living men. As we read of El Cid,[29] a personage of great valor at arms, his soldiers after his death placing his likeness on a horse, by his presence alone conquered a great army of Moors who were approaching the city of Valencia. Baldrino Panicaglia[30] had such a great reputation among the soldiers that even after his death they were governed by him as they carried his embalmed body with them and they pitched his tent as when he was alive, and with certain auguries probed for his opinion and were governed by them. The Turks took to flight at the sight of the troops of George Skanderbeg who was already dead since they believed that he was still alive and guided them, and then that by carrying his relics with them they acquired strength and shared in his courage.

---

[25] *Roman History*, 63.3.   [26] Cf. *Fasti*, 5.25–26, 29–30.
[27] An important Etruscan city.   [28] *History of Rome*, 5.26.
[29] Ruy Diaz de Vivar (*c.* 1040–99), the Spanish national hero.
[30] I have not been able to identify him.

4 Grades and Types of Reputation

Reputation is divided by some into three grades since it is, they say, either less, or as great or greater than that to which it is attributed. About this we say first that if reputation is an effect (as was demonstrated above) of outstanding *virtù*, to be a prince with a reputation that is less than is appropriate is not a benefit but a defect not so much of reputation as of the *virtù* of which it derives. As for the rest, reputation is of three types, of which one is natural, the second artificial, and the third we will call adventitious. Natural is that which is as the lamp of the light; so it proceeds from the eminence of *virtù*, and as the midday shadow is enough to be equal to its cause. Artificial is that which by the industry or the artifice of the prince surpasses the limits of that which is reputed; such was the fame of the riches of Alfonso II of Ferrara.[31] Adventitious is that which without the prince's action is attributed to him by the false opinion of another. Now true reputation is that which we have called natural; it is content to be equal to the thing reputed, that is, it results as a quasi reflection of his outstanding *virtù*. The other two types are as it were alchemy, which not consisting of solid principles, last briefly in comparison, more briefly as in a refiner's dish, and are accustomed to produce sometimes laughter and disdain, sometimes danger and damage. Without adducing ancient examples, Carmagnola and Paolo Vitelli show this a little before our time.[32] These two captains, who were thought to be of much greater value than in fact they were, fell prey to the opinion that it was due to treason that they had not wanted to carry out that which in fact they had been unable to accomplish because of the difficulty of the enterprise. So Carmagnola was decapitated by the Venetians for not having taken Cremona and Vitelli by the Florentines for not having taken Pisa by storm. And before them when Alcibiades lost a part of the fleet, the Athenians blamed this not on misfortune but on his wickedness, and he was banned by them. On the other hand, that other was, says Tacitus, *maximis provinciis per quatuor et viginti annos impositus, nullam ob eximiam artem, sed quos par negotiis neque supra erat* (placed at the head of the most important provinces for twenty-four years, he had nothing of exceptional merit, but was adequate to the business and nothing more).[33]

---

[31] Reigned 1559–97.

[32] Carmagnola (*c.* 1382–1432) and Paolo Vitelli (1461–99) were Italian condottieri.

[33] *Annals*, 6.39. The allusion is to Gaius Poppaeus Sabinus, a Roman politician who served as consul in 9 CE and as governor of Moesia from 12–35.

But I do not deny that as with bankers it always helps to have greater credit than capital, so with a prince it is useful and a benefit to be held in greater esteem than his quality justifies. But this is called opinion rather than reputation. Two things belong to reputation regarding what we are now considering: one is to conceal one's weaknesses, the other is to reveal one's greatness without ostentation; and if it is not unsuitable that it surpass the limits of the truth, it is expected that it remain within the limits of verisimilitude. But if reputation derives from *virtù*, what is to be said of military strength and treasure? Do not these also give rise to reputation? I say that reputation depends properly upon the wisdom and valor of the prince; the other things produce the effect of that which we are discussing not in themselves but with respect to the *virtù* and the loftiness of the intelligence and spirit of him whose instruments they ought to be. What reputation did the treasure left to him by Tiberius ever bring to Caligula if he was held to be a beast? What did the greatness of the Roman Empire bring to Claudio if he was considered an idiot? Just as neither a miser because of his riches nor a coward because of his strength, so neither will a prince who lacks prudence and valor enjoy reputation because of his treasure or because of his army.

Index

This index does not include topics and concepts that are listed in the extensive Table of Contents.

Index

Index

CAMBRIDGE TEXTS IN THE
HISTORY OF POLITICAL THOUGHT